THE PROFESSIONAL GUIDE

DYNAMICS OF TOUR GUIDING

KATHLEEN LINGLE POND

JOHN WILEY & SONS, INC.
New York • Chichester • Weinheim • Brisbane • Singapore • Toronto

Copyright © 1993 by Kathleen Lingle Pond. All rights reserved
Published by John Wiley & Sons, Inc.
Published simultaneously in Canada

This publication is designed to provide accurate and authoritative information in regard to the
subject matter covered. It is sold with the understanding that the publisher is not engaged in
rendering professional services. If professional advice or other expert assistance is required,
the services of a competent professional person should be sought.

Library of Congress Cataloging-in-Publication Data:

Pond, Kathleen Lingle.
    The professional guide / Kathleen Lingle Pond.
        p.   cm.
    Includes bibliographical references and index.
    ISBN 0-471-28386-X
    1. Tour guides (Persons)—Vocational guidance.   I. Title.
    G154.7.P66   1993
    338.4'791023'73—dc20   92-9817
Printed in the United States of America

10   9   8   7   6

For Vern,
and
for every proud, impassioned guide

Contents

Preface

These are invigorating times for tour guides around the world. As the twenty-first century draws near, travel and tourism is emerging as the world's largest and most dynamic industry. Tour guides, long the orphans of the industry, are now entering the spotlight. The industry, the media, government officials, and the general public are beginning to see that a tour guide's role extends well beyond welcoming and informing visitors. Indeed, the tour guide is entrusted with the purest of public relations missions: to encapsulate the essence of a place; to be a window onto a site, city, region, or country; and even to create a mirror for visitors, enabling them to better understand their link to the history and culture of their hosts.

More important than the recognition that tour guides have begun to receive is that guides are now demanding more of themselves. Over the past few years, several guide guilds and associations have emerged worldwide, galvanizing the profession and exploring such long-ignored issues as education, certification, and business practices, among many others. Colleges, universities, and proprietary schools are beginning to offer certificate and degree programs for guides. The guiding profession appears to be in its ascendancy as it seeks to create and adhere to higher standards.

And yet, the profession has a long way to go in responding to its challenges. If one were to observe a random sampling of guided tours, the results would be both impressive and appalling. Hiring a guide today is not unlike throwing craps, and the odds are nearly equal for getting a competent, personable guide. From city to city, the qualifications, regulations, educational programs, pay rates, and virtually all other standards vary greatly. Throughout most of the United States, anyone with the gumption to call himself a guide may, in fact, practice as one. And yet, the public—and even travel industry professionals—often has no idea where or how to hire a competent tour guide, as many guides are woefully unskilled at marketing themselves.

The purpose of *The Professional Guide* is to provide guides, both practicing and prospective, with a better understanding of their role as interpreters of their regions, as well as guidelines to create a viable full- or part-time career. I have attempted to cull relevant wisdom from the fields of education, interpretation, marketing, museum studies, business, psychology, and, of course, travel and tourism, and to present it in a palatable and useful fashion. By drawing on the experiences and advice of guides in many areas, it is my hope that this book will benefit all guides.

The Professional Guide is the first textbook designed for the instruction of a wide variety of tour guides, to be used in a variety of ways: as the basis for a complete course to be taught in colleges, universities, and proprietary schools; as needed in segments, for use in seminars or specialized courses; or as a reference for experienced guides.

Curiously, guides in the United States have never had the benefit (or burden) of a commonly accepted course of study, or even a commonly accepted philosophy or set of professional guidelines or standards. As a booming traveling public demands more of the travel industry in general, and of guides in particular, guides themselves are seeking instruction and growth. *The Professional Guide* attempts to respond to that search.

A professional guide is in varying degrees a business person—often freelance, sometimes employee; a travel industry representative; a public relations representative for his or her site, city, region, and country—as well as an educator, an entertainer, and a public speaker, among other roles. Thus I have endeavored to sift through the legions of literature within those disparate areas and present it to guides in a practical form. I have drawn much from the field of interpretation—which is, in fact, guiding in semantical dress that is thus far foreign to most professional guides in the commercial sector.

I have attempted to present guiding theory and a framework for practice without focusing too closely on academic detail. The average potential tour guide in a classroom—or even the seasoned guide on the street—might wonder what interpretation, Carl Rogers, neurolinguistic programming, or de Tocqueville have to do with giving a tour of Los Angeles. I would argue that these topics—and many other seemingly tangential sources—can offer immeasurable opportunities and rewards for both the guide and the traveler. While I do not presume that the theories and techniques offered here will be embraced by all within the field, it is my hope that they inspire thoughtful, enthusiastic dialogue and further exploration, both inside and outside the classroom.

Although my emphasis is on the experience of the tour guide in North America, my associations with guides worldwide indicate that guides everywhere will find this book useful. And while the primary audience for *The Professional Guide* is the guide in the commercial sector, others in related fields or positions will surely benefit from this book. Tour managers, who travel with groups and manage all aspects of a tour, may wish to polish their interpretive skills or supplement their incomes by guiding in their own towns or regions. Interpreters in the public sector may wish to venture into the private sector or, at the very least, gain a broader knowledge of it. Docents, the volunteer guides in museums, private homes, and parks (who, ironically, are often the best-trained and most knowledgeable interpreters) might want or need to transform their avocation into a vocation. Others within the tourism field will, I hope, be inclined to learn more about this vital component of their industry, in order to better serve travelers. And finally, experts in virtually all fields might wish to convey their knowledge and passion to a public increasingly eager for journeys of all kinds.

The public perception of American guides compared with their international colleagues suffers for a variety of reasons. At the top of the list is the lack of educational standards for guides in the United States. Although many guides have degrees in history, art history, museum studies, and so forth, guiding requires few qualifications and little or no training in its practice (for example, communication and marketing skills), resulting in a wide range of quality. Further, seasonal employment rarely carries the connotations of other professional careers; such has been the case with guiding. More often than not guides are freelancers, with few job benefits and meager wages, and until recently there have been few opportunities for steady employment or advancement. Thus, the public's perception of guiding suffers. At the end of an intensive five-day tour of the Washington, D.C., area, a high school student from Chicago approached his guide and said, "You seem to be very intelligent and well-educated. Why are you a tour guide?" Guides throughout the United States are routinely asked, "Do you get paid to do this?" or "Is this your *real* job?"

And yet all guides are struck by the tremendous opportunity they have—on a daily basis—to affect people profoundly, and even to alter their perceptions or eliminate prejudices. Good tour guides capture the essence of a place and ignite an interest or new understanding about their region and its culture. And travelers respond to effective guides with extreme gratitude and appreciation.

With this luxury comes responsibility. It behooves all guides to learn as much as possible about their region and the world, and to make the extra effort to sort facts from juicy legends, to travel and explore other sites and regions, to read about and listen to those from other cultures and eras, so that they might better understand visitor perspectives. Most European countries and many developing countries have long required college-level instruction for guides, embodying these elements. Such educational opportunities have only recently become available in the United States.

Change does not occur without struggle, however. While many guides are eager to embrace new educational programs and adopt higher standards, others are loathe to accept change and the work inherent in it. Surely, many veteran guides will regard the years prior to 1990 as the halcyon days of guiding, characterized by the ability to create one's own rules, a freedom from required education or training, little or no government or industry regulation, and no discussion of such uncomfortable subjects as liability and renewable certification. But it is clear that more educational programs and stronger guidelines are needed if the guiding profession in the United States will move forward and withstand the scrutiny of an increasingly global society.

While I seek to increase professionalism within and draw more recognition to the guiding profession, I hasten to add that a tour guide is but one of many key players within the hospitality industry. Guides are called to serve their visitors and their regions. The best guide understands that he or she is not the star of the show but is merely a facilitator, a spark for nudging visitors to venture beyond the cocoon of a motorcoach and a cozy hotel room and discover the rewards of a region and its people for themselves. To have meaning, the visitor's journey must delve deeper than the guide can lead, so that he or she becomes part of the tapestry of the place. In this way, the most enduring, most important role of the guide is that of conduit.

Virtually every guide would agree that the pursuit of a guiding career—full-time, part-time, or en route to another career—is indescribably rewarding. Vigdis Finnbogadottir, President of Iceland, began her impressive career in public service as a tour guide. While serving as Honorary Chairperson of the 1988 Global Conference, "Tourism: A Vital Force for Peace," in Vancouver, British Columbia, she said, "While I was campaigning to become president of my country, I felt so grateful that I was once a tour guide. Because of that experience, I understood my country so intimately."

Anyone who interprets their site, city, or region for visitors comes finally to regard guiding as both a privilege and a responsibility. I feel similarly about the writing of this book, and it is in the same spirit that I offer it—the first of its kind for the instruction of guides. Understanding fully the evolving nature of the guiding profession (and that we are now in its Stone Age) it is my hope that this book provide guidance, inspiration, and a foundation for guides and those who wish to become guides.

A few words about the language: Throughout the text, I have used the terms "guide" and "interpreter" interchangeably. They have become for me synonyms, although I am well aware that they reach very different audiences, and among those audiences may have contrasting connotations and definitions. Also, owing to the limitations of the English language, I reluctantly surrendered to the traditional but sexist use of the pronoun "he," rather than clutter the text with the "he/she" construction or contort sentences so that singular pronouns never appear. On subsequent re-readings of the text it occurred to me that perhaps that particular limitation of English was, for this book, a fortuituous advantage. Guiding has too long been regarded as a woman's dalliance; perhaps the "he"'s and "his"'s floating throughout the book might serve to imbue readers—female *and* male—with the relatively new concept that guiding is appropriate for both genders.

ACKNOWLEDGMENTS

Everyone should be so fortunate as to have one or more colleagues who are also true friends—always willing to listen, share ideas, and provide vital feedback. For me those individuals are Janice Holliday and Marcella Wells. I am deeply grateful for their wisdom, generosity, and support. My life is enriched—as is this book—because of them.

I would also like to thank Doris Pond, Valene Smith, and Catherine Shilts for reviewing the manuscript, and David Edgell, Jeff McHugh, Michael Burke, and Lucy Beard for reviewing specific chapters.

I thank Donald Hawkins for encouraging me to undertake this book. I also extend thanks to my editor, Pam Scott Chirls, and her assistant, Julie Markoff, for their encouragement and patience, which was tested to the extreme, and special thanks also to my copyeditor, Joy Aquilino.

I would also like to thank the friends and associates who influence my work: Lou D'Amore, Gabe Cherem, David Edgell, Howard Reichbart, and my students at Northern Virginia Community College and elsewhere.

Whether they realize it or not, those who enter the guiding field owe thanks, as I do, to Edd Farrell and Michael Marshall, founders of the Professional Guides Association of America (PGAA). Their vision and diligence in creating an association has provided a forum for education and nurturing, industry networking, and planning.

I would also like to thank my cherished friends and Washington, D.C., colleagues, Peggy Wood, Deborah Androus, Pam Leigh, Kamal Al-Faqih, Tim Flowers, John Stein, Chris Salyer, Sheldon Caplan, Robert Gunn and others in the guild of professional tour guides of Washington for the years of learning and laughter that have made guiding an adventure and a passion.

I am also grateful for the support of my family, especially my in-laws, Dana and Doris Pond, who generously provided me with this writer's dream: a secluded cabin amidst their beautiful forest. Without that time and private space, this work might still be unfinished.

And finally, my deepest gratitude goes to my husband Vern, who has listened, cheered me on, and made this possible—and who makes it all worthwhile.

Foreword

International tourism is an industry with a long and interesting, if little-known, history that spans many centuries. The 1992 completion of this landmark book, *The Professional Guide,* on the 500th anniversary of Columbus' voyage to the New World, prefaces a new chapter in tourism chronology: International Tourism in North America.

The arrival of significant numbers of foreign visitors (or inbound tourism) to the United States and Canada is of recent origin, and a brief historical perspective is merited. For several centuries, residents of Europe, Asia and Africa regarded North America as a wondrous if somewhat mysterious place to which friends and families departed. Some of these migrants disappeared into the continental vastness, but many individuals sent back letters describing opportunities in this new land and urged relatives to join them. Some even enclosed passage money. However, the long sea journey, the size of the continent, and the relatively expensive hotels combined to preclude all but the wealthy (or very adventurous) from coming to America simply to tour.

Modern tourism began immediately after World War II, thanks to the development of commercial propeller aircraft. By the early 1950s, DC6-Bs were island-hopping across the Atlantic, offering reasonably reliable commercial service as well as affinity charters for an expanding university student market. In that decade, Europeans and Asians were still primarily involved in postwar economic reconstruction, and a North American vacation was out-of-reach. By contrast, many Americans had profited from wartime employment in defense industries and had discretionary income to take advantage of this new transportation mode. Millions began to journey to Europe every year, including college students who could easily and safely hitchhike within Europe, and sleep in youth hostels or even barns. *Europe on $5 a Day* was a popular and realistic travel guide for independent travel. Other Americans traveled on motorcoach tours—then a new idea in travel—and learned to rely on their knowledgeable tour managers (or couriers or escorts). Most Americans traveling abroad accepted these guides as a matter of course, and gave no thought to the fact that our nation had not initiated the appropriate curricula and certification programs that produced these trained professionals. The advent of jet aircraft in the 1960s increased the flow of traffic to Europe and Asia, but still America remained a land of dreams, too expensive for the average overseas visitor.

The expanding economy of the 1980s brought the first rush of international visitors to the United States (and Canada), but both government and the travel industry were slow to recognize the social and economic significance of this inbound tourism. Thus, until the 1990s, the United States and Canada remained the only two major nations without a program of tourist guide training and certification.

In the absence of American and Canadian tour managers and guides, the international visitor is deprived of the opportunity to learn about the United States and Canada through contacts with host guides. Most American and Canadian towns lack trained step-on guides able to provide concise and interesting information about the local community. Beyond this, tour managers and guides should also be an important new avenue for employment on this continent.

Thus, *The Professional Guide* is a pioneering work that establishes the essential requirements for professional tour personnel. Even more importantly, the book captures the essence of the social and psychological attributes needed for guides to succeed in this highly personal host–guest industry. Travel agents are often labeled "dealers in dreams" because their ability to package the travel product is basic to client enjoyment. However, it is the tour manager, and the local sightseeing guide, whose one-to-one presence and personal warmth, combined with expertise, literally transforms a paper itinerary into living reality. Qualified tour managers and guides are the best asset a travel company can have, and their importance to the visitor is unquestioned. Professional guides truly *are* the "dream-makers"!

Kathleen Lingle Pond and Van Nostrand Reinhold are to be commended for their foresight in developing this important American contribution to international tourism.

Valene L. Smith
Professor of Anthropology
California State University, Chico

I. An Evolving Profession

1 *The Tour Guide: A Historical Overview*

"History balances the frustration of 'how far we have to go' with the satisfaction of 'how far we have come.' It teaches us tolerance for the human shortcomings and imperfections which are not uniquely of our generation, but of all time."

—Lewis F. Powell, Jr.

THE EARLIEST GUIDES

Guiding surely ranks among the world's oldest professions. Humans have roamed the earth since they emerged, and the earliest historical accounts refer to those who lead the way—"pathfinders," "bear leaders," "proxemos," and "cicerones"—all antecedents of today's guides.

The earliest excursions were not undertaken for pleasure's sake but out of necessity, since survival—not recreation—was the primary goal. The first travelers moved about to gather food and escape harsh climates, and so the first guides simply offered geographic direction. Eventually enterprising men traveled for the trade of spices, gold, silver, and other valuables, and the accounts of their travels frequently refer to the need for safety escorts to guard against thieves. It is no wonder that the word *travel* is derived from the Old French *travaillier,* meaning "to labor or toil."

Once their most basic needs for food, shelter, and safety were satisfied, humans began to travel in order to understand their place in the world, to represent and protect their territories, to align themselves with others, out of sheer curiosity and for pleasure. As one might guess, travel for these somewhat loftier reasons was at first highly undemocratic, the privilege of the wealthy.

Specific references to guides abound in the annals of history, from the Roman Empire through the Middle Ages, throughout the Renaissance and into the modern age. And guides have always garnered mixed reviews. In ancient history, as now, accounts of the decorum of guides were often less than favorable. Guides have been variously described throughout history as nuisances, opportunists, charlatans, and zealots, "having the inability to stop, once [they] launched on [their] patter." Indeed, in a detailed discussion of travel and guides in the ancient empires, one historian could not resist leaping twenty centuries from ancient

Rome to remark, "from all accounts, local guides have not improved very much in the course of two thousand years" (Casson 1974).

More favorable antecedents of present-day guides did exist, however. The most notable of these were the guides of the Grand Tour (from the fourteenth through the eighteenth centuries), known as *cicerones,* named for the learned Roman orator, Cicero. Cicerones were among the most esteemed guides in European society, entrusted with representing their region and its history and educating privileged young men of the British aristocracy.

Perhaps the ambiguous references to the role and image of guides throughout history are what prompted Dr. Erik Cohen, researcher and professor at The Hebrew University of Jerusalem, to assert that today's guides descend from two models in history: the pathfinder and the mentor. The pathfinder is the "geographical guide who leads the way through an environment in which his followers lack orientation, or through a socially defined territory to which they have no access" (Cohen 1985). According to Cohen, these guides had no specialized training and existed throughout the Greco-Roman era and again during the age of the Grand Tour. Today, pathfinders serve special-interest travelers in remote locations; for example, by acting as mountain and fishing guides.

The mentor role, according to Cohen, is much more complex and heterogeneous and thus more difficult to trace historically. These guides, who served as personal tutors or spiritual advisors, played an important role during the Grand Tour era and are prevalent characters in classical literature; Cohen cites Virgil and Beatrice in Dante's *Divine Comedy,* the Interpreter in Bunyan's *Pilgrim's Progress,* and Mephisto in Goethe's *Faust* as examples. He also suggests that the pathfinder and mentor correspond to today's positions of tour manager (who accompanies groups on long excursions) and tour guide, respectively. While interesting, Cohen's exploration of these roles may be too dichotomous. More recently, virtually all tour guides and tour managers have been called upon to usually play several roles, including both pathfinder and mentor among them.

THE ANCIENT EMPIRES

The era of the great empires—3000 B.C. to A.D. 500—spawned travel as we know it today in the Western world. That the ancient Persians, Assyrians, and Egyptians traveled in an organized fashion is certain. In fact, it is said that the Seven Wonders of the World were created with sightseeing in mind. Although travel during most of this era was slow and dangerous, countless voyagers persevered by both land and sea.

During the Greek Empire tourism saw its first major developments. Although the Greeks built few roads, travel by sea flourished. This facilitated the widespread use of Greek language and currency. Shows, feasts, and festivals—

among them the Olympic Games, which began in 776 B.C.—proliferated, offering even greater purpose and pleasure in travel.

As tourism flourished, so apparently did the number of guides. "In setting forth to see a site," according to one account, "the ancient visitor's first problem was the same that so often confronts his counterpart today—to run the gauntlet of local guides lying in wait for him, the 'leaders around' (*periegetai*) or 'explainers' (*exegetai*), as guides were also called in Greek", (Casson 1974). "Proxemos," guides whose function was to assist fellow citizens traveling abroad, may correspond to today's tour managers.

The popular Greek satirist Lucian (A.D. 120–180) offered several spoofs on the travel boom and on guides in particular, notably one in which a group of voyagers, on a visit to the Underworld, went to Purgatory, where "guides showed us around, and for each victim, filled in the biographical data and reasons for punishment" (Casson 1974). In another satire a character prays: "Zeus, protect me from your guides at Olympia, and you, Athena, from yours at Athens" (Casson 1974).

Perhaps the finest accounts of travel in the ancient empires were those of Herodotus, whom Cicero called the first historian and whom many regard as the first travel writer. Herodotus traveled widely and faithfully recorded in rich narrative much of what he saw and learned. The accounts of Herodotus yield a foundation for our knowledge about a significant portion of the Western world between 550 and 479 B.C. His vast wanderings included Southwest Asia, where he was born, most of Greece, Egypt, Libya, Syria, Babylonia, north to beyond the Danube, and east beyond the Black Sea. Herodotus's *History* contains many references to guides, many of them disparaging. He was particularly critical and suspicious of guides who had a propensity for reciting, with great authority, dates, dialogues, and other specifics about people who had lived hundreds of years earlier. Casson and other historians concede, however, that guides and their work were both useful and "even essential. . . . At a site such as Olympia, where there was a . . . forest of statues . . . the accumulation of hundreds of years of dedications . . . a tourist was helpless without a guide" (Casson 1974).

Travel surged in ancient Rome. The well-known earlier achievements of Greece, combined with Rome's legendary paved roads and great economic success, allowed even middle-class citizens to travel in a way never before known. In fact, Feifer (1985) called Imperial Rome "the first culture genuinely to produce mass tourism, in both the letter and the spirit of the term." In the second century A.D., he notes, Rome was at its peak. Greece—for its fabled mythology, its monuments (as impressive then as today), and its Olympic games and other festivals—was the most popular destination of the Romans.

Throughout the reign of Rome sightseeing proliferated in both Rome and Greece. Ilium, the fabled country of Homer, had a thriving tourist business, featuring guides in great numbers to point out "every significant place or feature mentioned in the *Iliad*. . . . They showed the strip of beach where the Greek ships had been pulled up, the plain where the battles had taken place, [and] the site of the Trojan War," which they regarded as the pièce de résistance (Casson 1974).

Eventually Rome fell victim to its own success: so large, it was unwieldy to manage and control; so powerful, it produced internal forces which eventually undermined it. The impact of Rome's decline was felt throughout the Western world.

THE MIDDLE AGES

The period of time between the fall of Rome and the Renaissance, known as the Middle Ages (approximately A.D. 500–1500), is perhaps erroneously portrayed as a time when little happened. The fall of Rome led to the decay of roads, trade, and the economy in general, and a waning of desire for travel and in travel development, particularly during the early Middle Ages (also known as the Dark Ages). However, although roads and communications systems declined along with Rome's political structure, the Roman Catholic Church prevailed as the basis for social unity and power.

The longest and most prevalent type of journey at this time was the religious pilgrimage, a holiday primarily of the upper and middle classes to such places as Winchester, Walsingham, or Canterbury. Encounters with thieves and rogues of all sorts along the way were not uncommon, and those who made pilgrimages were often appropriately fearful. Not surprisingly, references to guides during this era highlight their roles as pathfinders, protectors, safety escorts, and even bribers to assure safe passage.

One account suggests that a guide was paid a large fee "because he not only led the way but also guaranteed safe-conduct, i.e., ensured proper behavior on the part of his brethren." The large sum "amounted to half the cost of a camel," and such a fee indicated—to this historian, at least—that this was "not just any country bumpkin, but a skilled professional" (Casson 1974, 317–318).

THE RENAISSANCE AND THE GRAND TOUR

The image of tour guides reached new heights—and depths—during the Renaissance. Accompanied by "traveling tutors," young men of the upper classes journeyed from Britain on the Grand Tour, a prescribed, celebrated route from England through France, Germany, Austria, and Switzerland, winding their way toward the final destination, Italy. The Grand Tourist was expected "to return from his travels with a broadened mind as well as a good command of foreign languages, a new self-reliance and self-possession as well as a highly developed taste and grace of manner" (Mead 1914). Since these journeys were taken for educational and cultural reasons, the individuals or groups were usually assigned to one personal tutor, also called a *bear leader, antiquarii,* or, most frequently, a *cicerone.* It was this person who would remain with the traveler and his entourage throughout the journey. The cicerone was intended to be articulate, multilingual, and well-versed in many subjects, including history, literature, architecture, and current affairs. Many of the tutors and guides of the Grand Tour era were distinguished clergy, students, schoolmasters, writers, and historians. Some went on to become quite successful, among them Swiss historian Paul Henri Mallet, author Robert Weed, poet laureate William Whitehead, and philosopher Thomas Hobbes.

Competition for the best cicerones was keen, for it was understood that "how frequently a parent's expectations were realised depended to a large extent upon the boy's travelling tutor" (Mead 1914). In the words of a contemporary expert on education, Vicesimus Knox, the ideal tutor was "a grave, respectable man of mature age." In addition to his duties as pedagogue and guide, the cicerone would "watch over the morals and religion of his pupil," both of which, unless great care were taken, were sure to be "shaken from the basis and levelled with before the end of the peregrination" (Mead 1914).

Indeed, these journeys offered many temptations for the Grand Tourists and their entourages, who were greeted everywhere by eager valets, ruffians, wigmakers, and salesmen of every variety, including many selling guiding services. Safety was as much an issue for these travelers as it was for travelers during the Middle Ages, so guides who could also provide protection from robbers and rogues were in demand. For this reason, Grand Tour travelers of the seventeenth to nineteenth centuries often hired a *vetturino,* a driver of the Italian four-wheel carriage (called a *veturra*). "Rich tourists were frequently exploited by these one-man operators," Casson writes, "but often the *vetturino* was able to 'fix' things with highway robbers and others to ensure safe conduct" (Casson 1974).

Many references were made during the Renaissance to British and European royalty and upper class individuals hiring guides. British writer and philosopher Francis Bacon in 1597 remarked on the need for a personal guide/courier when traveling, especially one who was a linguist and who knew the "right" people to meet and the proper things to see. Likewise, Charles II reportedly visited Stonehenge "secretly" in 1644 with a guide (Cross 1991).

But the cicerone's image was not pristine. As with guides everywhere, cicerones were met with mixed reviews. Once again, the surge of tourists inspired many to become guides, and available and assertive guides in the streets were too ubiquitous for comfort. "Everywhere guides awaited the traveller. Between 1606 and 1659 Hans Hoch, a member of the Papal Swiss Guard, showed some 1,300 visitors around the sights of Rome. . . . Hardly had the traveller passed the town gates and the tollbooth . . . reached his inn and changed out of his dusty travelling clothes, when he was at once accosted by eager would-be guides," writes Lochsberg (1979).

In 1701, Heinrich von Hysen noted, "These antiquarii or ciceroni, as they are called, never failed to turn up and to press their good offices" (Lochsberg 1979). In *The Grand Tour of the 18th Century,* William Mead puts it this way: "The multiplication of tourists called into existence a swarm of local guides whose competence left much to be desired. . . . With undaunted confidence [they] fastened themselves upon the tourist, offering to explain everything worth seeing in the city. Against these cormorants travelers were repeatedly warned. Most of these so-called guides were, indeed, impudent charlatans." Another historian calls them "incompetent place seekers who deserved the derision with which they were treated" (Mead 1914). The chief complaint about guides throughout history seems to be the aggressive manner in which they attempted to gain business. Gradually, the well-worn path to and through Italy could be traversed by the middle classes. And, in spite of occasional fallow periods, travel on the continent has more or less flourished ever since.

The first "package tours" were likely those available during the medieval period, from Venice to the Holy Land, when a trip's cost would include passage, meals and wine, accommodations, donkey rides, and bribe money for protection. The latter amenity was perhaps the most critical. According to some accounts, group travel was essential because traveling alone was simply too dangerous (Coltman 1989).

THE MODERN AGE

Throughout the seventeenth and eighteenth centuries, travelers to and within the New World were explorers more than pleasure excursionists. Indeed, the first travelers were ordinary, often indigent, explorers traveling to find a new way of life. Inhabitants of the New World were well aware even into the nineteenth century that their continent did not hold the holiday allure of the Old World. Few New-World travelers or guides are known to have existed during this period.

Owing to the vast distances and the limitations of time, money, and transportation, pleasure travel to and from the New World was a dalliance of privileged and curious Europeans. The three best-known European writers who visited the New World in the nineteenth century—Charles Dickens, Frances Trollope and Alexis de Tocqueville—traveled widely and wrote comprehensive accounts of their travels, but rarely mentioned guides. Even if guides were available to them, it is likely that these inveterate travelers, whose objective it was to explore and probe the country in great depth and then write about it, would not have been as eager to hire a guide as would others. Such has always been and will continue to be the case—that many independent travelers prefer not to hire guides.

It would seem that Mark Twain would also fall into this category. Twain traveled vast distances and tirelessly recorded his adventures, often writing with great disdain about his guides. In a well-known passage in *The Innocents*

Abroad, he portrays his European guides as humorless, self-absorbed "necessary nuisances," and describes (with apparent amusement) his efforts at harassing guides.

"Many a man has wished in his heart that he could do without his guide; but knowing he could not, has wished he could get some amusement out of him as a remuneration for the affliction of his society." Twain was happy to report that he and his traveling companions "accomplished this latter matter, and if our experience can be made useful to others they are welcome to it." The following is but one of several examples of successful harassment, as recorded in *The Innocents Abroad:*

We have taken it out of this guide. He has marched us through miles of pictures and sculpture in the vast corridors of the Vatican, and through miles of pictures and sculpture in twenty other palaces; he has shown us the great picture in the Sistine Chapel, and frescoes enough to fresco the heavens—pretty much all done by Michelangelo. So with him we have played that game which has vanquished so many guides for us— imbecility and idiotic questions. These creatures never suspect—they have no idea of a sarcasm.

He shows us a figure and says: "Statoo brunzo." (Bronze statue).
We look at it indifferently and the doctor asks: "By Michelangelo?"
"No—not know who."
Then he shows us the ancient Roman Forum. The doctor asks: "Michelangelo?"
A stare from the guide. "No—thousan' year before he is born."
Then an Egyptian obelisk. Again: "Michelangelo?"
"Oh, mondieu, genteelmen! Zis two thousan' year before he is born!"
Relief for overtasked eyes and brain from study and sightseeing is necessary or we shall become idiotic sure enough. Therefore this guide must continue to suffer. If he does not enjoy it, so much the worse for him. We do (Twain 1869).

For all of Twain's acerbic criticism of his tour and guides, one year later, on hearing of a similar excursion departing, he wrote: "I am moved to confess that day by day the mass of my memories of the excursion have grown more and more pleasant," and that "nothing would gratify me more than to be a passenger" (Twain 1869).

Bret Harte, who otherwise praised Twain, noted, "With all his independence, Mark Twain seems to have followed his guide and guide books with a simple, unconscious fidelity. He was quite content to see only that which everybody else sees, even if he was not content to see it with the same eyes" (Twain 1980).

Guides in the United States: The Gettysburg Battlefield Guides

Among the first well-documented tour guides in the United States were those who emerged immediately after the Battle of Gettysburg to escort the deluge of friends and relatives who came there to see or identify the wounded and dead.

"The horror of Gettysburg did not end with the battle," the Gettysburg National Park records indicate, for as soon as it was over, families and friends who could not locate their loved ones poured in to the town to visit hospitals and morgues and search the battlefield. Gettysburg residents escorted these grief-stricken visitors and offered them their version of what had happened. When the Commonwealth of Pennsylvania provided a cemetery for those who had fallen in battle, the numbers of visitors to Gettysburg increased dramatically.

Initially, visitors arrived by train in the center of town, several miles from the battlefield. According to National Park Service records, "In these early days, many local citizens drove hacks over the battlefield and served as a combination driver/guide. Race Horse Alley, half a block from the railroad, was the site of numerous livery stables. People disembarking from the excursion trains often boarded huge wagons filled with seats for a day-long tour of the battlefield" (U.S. Department of Interior 1989). Apparently, a guide's success was more dependent on his entrepreneurial skills and access to horses and carriages than on his knowledge of the battle.

When the Gettysburg National Military Park was authorized by an Act of Congress on February 11, 1885, the War Department inherited a system that had gradually grown into a tradition in the thirty-two years since the battle took place. At that time, however, there were about a dozen individuals who were making a substantial part of their living by guiding visitors through the battlefield for a fee. By 1915, with the availability of the personal automobile, the number of travelers increased sharply, guiding became quite lucrative, and the number of guides had grown to more than 100. "Anyone could conduct a tour and almost anyone did" (National Park Service 1983).

War Department records from this time indicate numerous complaints from visitors about the guide service. "Irresponsible guides were charging such fees as the traffic would bear, and were telling accounts of the battle as suited their fancy. During 1915, an unusual number of complaints and several incidents forced the War Department to undertake regulation of the guides" (U.S. Department of Interior 1989). A War Department regulation was enacted stating that after October 17, 1915, only guides licensed by the department would be allowed to conduct visitors through the battlefield for a fee. Regulations covering fees, solicitation, conduct, length of tours, and even personal cleanliness were established. Also, guides were required to take an examination to prove that they were adequately informed about the battle to act as guides.

The first examination for Gettysburg Battlefield Guides was given on September 2, 1915. Ninety-one of the ninety-five taking the test completed it successfully, and based upon their scores, were rated as first-, second-, or third-class guides. Almost all of these guides attended classes and were given the opportunity to take a new examination to earn a higher classification.

The purpose of the licensing procedure was to protect both the public and those people who were eminently qualified to be guides by refusing to license those who were obviously unfit and by revoking the licenses of those who did not comply with the regulations. According to War Department records, "regulations were upheld by the courts when unlicensed guides were arrested for conducting tours over the battlefield after October 17, 1915" (U.S. Department of Interior 1989). By all accounts, licensing improved the quality of the guides after 1915, and there is no doubt that it immeasurably improved their morale and status.

In 1933, when Gettysburg National Military Park was transferred to the Department of the Interior, the National Park Service inherited the guide service. The present force includes approximately seventy guides, who are self-employed but managed and administered by a National Park Service supervisor. To ensure that an adequate force of guides exists to serve the visiting public, written and oral examinations are periodically administered by the Park Service and new guides are hired as needed. Today the Gettysburg Licensed Battlefield Guides enjoy a reputation as knowledgeable professionals, which most agree is directly attributable to the training, evaluation, and recognition they receive.

The evolution of the Gettysburg Battlefield Guides—from overzealous and opportunistic to trained and respected—reflects in microcosm the role that training, evaluation, and regulation can play in advancing guiding to a professional status. Far from the shameful disservice guides offered to visitors in the nineteenth century, guides in Gettysburg today are nurtured by a system that carefully trains and evaluates them. As a result, visitors, guides, the town, and the site of the battle itself benefit. This story, as recounted in the National Park Service's Gettysburg annals, clearly illustrates the reasons, methods, and benefits of guide training and development.

Interpretation and the National Park Service   The Gettysburg Licensed Battlefield Guides are actually an anomaly within the National Park Service. As independent contractors, their status differs from other interpreters in the park system. As noted above, however, the National Park Service absorbed the Battlefield Guides into their system. By that time "interpretation" had long been incorporated into the Park Service philosophy. From the lessons learned at Gettysburg and elsewhere, guides with the National Park Service have developed their techniques for effective interpretation, and, for that reason, enjoy an enviable reputation worldwide.

Although Yellowstone National Park was established in 1872, the National Park Service did not become a bureau of the Department of the Interior until 1916. Stephen T. Mather, the first director of the National Park Service, is largely credited with pulling the Service together. Mather, a Chicago industrialist who made a fortune on Twenty Mule Team Borax, perceived that a national park system would hold "the highest potentialities of national pride, national contentment, and national health." Frustrated by what he felt was poor organization and missed opportunities to advance the Park Service cause, Mather wrote a letter of complaint to Secretary of the Interior Franklin K. Lane, an old college friend. When Lane responded, "If you don't like it, come and run the parks yourself," Mather accepted. This post offered Mather a fulfilling way to express his idealism, his love of his country, and his love of nature (Rosenow and Pulsipher 1979).

Mather visited Lake Tahoe and was impressed with Dr. Charles Goethe's popular nature trails and naturalist lectures based on outdoor learning methods Goethe had observed in Switzerland. The approach involved a well-informed naturalist who explained natural phenomena and their interrelationships to interested tourists. Mather persuaded Goethe to move to Yellowstone, the first national park to establish his program there. Successful at Yellowstone, Mather eventually transported this type of programming to other major parks. In this way interpretation, now one of the hallmarks of the park system, was born.

The Guide in Europe

The business of group pleasure travel as we know it today began in 1841 when Thomas Cook advertised an excursion train tour to a temperance meeting in England. Within a few years he was conducting tours to Paris and in 1856 led the first of many of his Grand Tours of Europe. As the tour guide/tour manager of these excursions, Cook has been called the patron saint of modern tour guides. To this day his namesake agency is one of the world's best-known travel agencies and a large employer of tour managers and tour guides.

The more recent development of the guiding profession and guide training throughout Europe is similar to that which occurred with the guides in Gettysburg. No evidence exists of organized guide services or training for guides prior to the twentieth century other than Thomas Cook's company training.

England was one of the first countries to regulate and train guides. In the 1920s many travelers visited Britain and opportunistic guides emerged from far and near. The wide range of quality and the guides' often competitive, aggressive approach toward visitors and each other prompted the London County Council and the Regent Street Polytechnic to run a training course for guides in 1936 to 1939. England's growing concern for guides and training was similar to that of other European countries in the prewar days.

World War II spawned a dramatic surge in transportation and communications, which irrevocably changed the nature of tourism. Travel became quicker, easier, and more widely available to the middle classes. The number of tourism organizations grew rapidly and tourism began to be recognized as a unified industry. As a result, the decades since World War II have been marked by a steady growth of tourism as a course of study in colleges and universities worldwide.

European guides have long been widely regarded as having the most advanced training and the highest guiding standards in the world. (The only exception is Israel, which may have the world's best-trained, most highly respected, and best-paid guides.) Much of the development occurred immediately after the war, when travelers, especially Americans, poured into Europe. To cite one example, in 1946 the British Travel Association (formerly The Travel Association of Great Britain and Ireland, established in 1929) reorganized and proposed a body of trained guides in London and other major cities. The London County Council reestablished its guide training program at Regent Street Polytechnic in 1949, and the Tourist Authority established (by 1951) an official status for "Approved Guides"; that is, accredited guides with a badge and certificate. Although modified today, the badge and certificate remains a prevailing source of recognition and pride among guides in Britain.

Guide training and regulation in most European countries mirrors the progress demonstrated in England, and since the 1950s has served as a model for the rest of the world where, until recently, few advancements in professional status have been achieved.

MUSEUMS AND DOCENTS

Any review of the development of guides and guide training would be remiss if it ignored the impressive strides made in the museum world. Museum guides, usually referred to as docents, are consistently among the most effective and best-trained site-specific guides. Ironically, despite their extensive training and sterling reputation, docents are, in most cases, volunteers. Thus, many of the most effective, "professional" interpreters are unpaid.

Although museums have been in existence for many centuries, the first museum boom occurred worldwide during the second half of the nineteenth century, throughout the Far East, Europe, Asia, India, and North and South America. In the early years of the twentieth century museums became more concerned with preserving and interpreting their collections for the general public, and offered the first organized training in museum studies. The well-known Ecole du Louvre emerged in the 1920s to train curators for the French museums, and in 1930 the Museums Association of Britain awarded their first diplomas in museum training. Courses in these programs stressed art history, natural history, or the primary focus of the particular museum's collection.

Since World War II, education and mass communication have become primary goals of museum curators, and training for museum docents in even the smallest local museums surpass most present guide training programs in the private sector. Today, much of the museum world has adopted and contributed to the tenets of interpretation.

TOWARD A RESPECTED PROFESSION

Every esteemed profession—medicine, law, and education, among others—can trace its growth in a manner similar to that described here. Where once anyone could claim to be a doctor or nurse, and people were often at the mercy of untrained charlatans, today these professionals' earned and valued designations signify academic achievements and experience, and patients are assured of at least a basic standard of care.

History illustrates the value most visitors place upon travel and effective interpretation, and those working within the field of professional guiding today are encouraged that the efforts thus far have been worthwhile. Yet, in spite of an acute understanding of the need for standardization and training, and the dramatic efforts being made in the field toward those goals, much must still be done to advance guiding as a respected profession. More than three decades ago geographer and anthropologist Dr. Valene Smith wrote "Needed: Geographically-Trained Tourist Guides (1961)," in which she exposed the dire need for and the value of guides trained in geography. In the article, she described her extensive world survey of tourism, in which she found that some countries of the world—most notably Japan and the former Soviet Union—do have extensive educational requirements for guides and guides who greatly enhance those countries' images. And yet, Smith noted, "as a nation, we [the United States] are poorly prepared to receive tourists and to accord them the educational services we ourselves receive in their homelands." Smith strongly advised geographic training for guides conducted by professional geographers in colleges and universities throughout the country. "Such a program would enhance our educational status in the eyes of the rest of the world," she said. Although "Geography for Travel" courses have since been implemented in travel and tourism programs, in the 1990s few guides receive geographic instruction.

Perhaps one day the travel industry, the guiding profession, and guides themselves will demand higher educational standards of guides. Then and only then could the role of the guide reflect the standard and stature of the cicerone of the early Grand Tour era.

SUMMARY

Tour guides have always had a place—albeit at times on the lowest rung—in society. History indicates that people, from Herodotus to Twain to today's traveler, dislike uninformed and overzealous guides. And yet the same travelers (even Twain!) acknowledged that competent guides were necessary and desirable. History has shown that training, evaluation, and regulation of guides yields great rewards not only for travelers and guides, but for sites, cities, and whole societies as well.

2   *Profiles of Today's Tour Guides*

"In blue blazer and natty scarf (one typical vision), you stroll through life with well-mannered groups of sensitive adults as they view the storied sites of antiquity. . . . Just think: you are traveling for free, and getting paid, to boot! . . . The reality can be jarringly different."
— Arthur Frommer, New World of Travel 1990

To be a tour guide is to live the dream of many. A recent survey noted in *Time* magazine revealed that "tour guide" ranked second only to "owning one's own business" as the most commonly named "fantasy job" of women in the United States (D'Arcy Masius Benton and Bolles Poll 1987). And why not? The prospect of having a job which pays one to vacation with people from all over the world is, for many people, irresistible.

And yet, the work of the tour guide is vastly misunderstood. To begin with, most people are surprised to learn what a tour guide really does and, for example, that travel itself is not always inherent in a guide's work. By international definition, a tour guide—one who conducts tours of a site, city, or region—interprets a particular place and often, therefore, does not travel. However, due to the vast regions in the United States and Canada, tour guides in these countries often travel longer distances than their counterparts in other parts of the world. (The travel industry's term for one who travels with groups is *tour manager,* a term little known outside the industry.)

Even within the travel industry confusion abounds. Guides have been aptly called the orphans of the travel industry, somewhat hidden as they are within the trade. Unlike most other players in the tourism business—such as travel agents, tour operators, meeting planners, and airline employees—tour guides operate independently, as freelancers, almost always from their homes. Many of them work for several agencies or organizations in small blocks of time for each. The seasonal and part-time nature of the work in most regions imposes limitations on the amount of work and income available through guiding, and few guides can make a reasonable living exclusively through guiding. Consequently, most guides do not bear the typical expenses of running a small business, such as incorporating, advertising, and renting separate offices and equipment. This in turn further limits their visibility, stature, and income. Often guides are retired, work a second job, or fill other freelance positions, such as writing, consulting, or teaching. Typically guides acquire work through a combination of nurturing their own small networks and serendipity. All of these factors contribute to the undefined and "hidden" status of guides.

The enigmatic nature of freelance guides was apparent to the founders of the Professional Guides Association of America (PGAA), whose greatest obstacle in starting the association was locating guides. Elaine Curl, one of the PGAA's founders and owner of the Convention Store, in Washington, D.C., says, "It's crazy. Guides are one of the most vital links in the whole operation, and we who employ them can never find them! Yet whenever I meet guides, I hear them complain about not being able to get enough work to make a living. Something's not making sense here." When the founders of the PGAA persevered and found guides and tour managers, their inevitable response was gratitude. Member guides agree that an association that represents them is necessary. Still, locating these freelancers and organizing such a diverse, independent collection of people remains a challenging process.

If most travel professionals are unfamiliar with guides, the lack of knowledge in the industry runs both ways. Even guides who work directly with and for tour operators or travel agencies are often surprisingly unfamiliar with the industry as a whole, the manner in which it operates, and the many players in it. In addition, a lack of cohesiveness and cooperation exists between the government and the travel industry in many countries (particularly in the United States), which disenfranchises not only guides and other travel professionals but visitors as well. In the growing movement toward organizing and professionally accrediting positions within the travel industry, it is vital that guides develop a deeper understanding of their field, so that they may be recognized and their work examined and supported. Before delving more deeply into a discussion about the various types of guides, a few words about the terminology are necessary.

DEFINITIONS

Definitions and descriptions for guides overlap considerably and vary from region to region, country to country, between the public and private sectors, and even within the travel industry. Some terms are recognized and used by only a small segment of the population. It may also be germane to note here that the term "tour guide" has a pejorative connotation to many including the traveling public, as well as those who call themselves interpreters and docents. One reason is that, for many, the word "tour" itself connotes typical, static sightseeing, which Arthur Frommer assails as "vapid." And, as noted in the previous chapter, many feel that tour guides historically have earned reputations as nuisances. For that reason many avoid the use of the word "tour," and even "guide." Some New York City guides have adopted the term "urban historian."

Perhaps it is also necessary to point out that the term "tour guide," while specifically defined within the industry, has been used so widely and over such a long period of time that it has acquired an imprecise meaning to the public that would encompass the tour manager, museum docent, and park naturalist. Thus, docents or interpreters might label themselves as such to others in the industry but might simply call themselves guides when talking to the general public. Says one Colonial Williamsburg interpreter, "I get so tired of telling people, 'No, not a foreign language interpreter; a historical interpreter.' So most of the time I tell people I'm a tour guide. That they always understand."

And yet, within their professional spheres, these similar but distinct categories of guides often have an attachment to their own labels, possess considerable professional pride, and are surprisingly unfamiliar with the work and worlds of the others. For example, the broadest terms *guide* and *interpreter* are, to some, virtually synonymous and encompass all guiding professionals. Yet they represent "guiding" worlds that function separately, view their roles differently, and have such different connotations that to use them interchangeably is confusing and often even offensive to some.

The disparities among guide definitions were readily apparent at the first national convention of the PGAA in February 1989. Although the PGAA's primary goal was to assemble and unite guides, tour managers, docents, and all related individuals, these tasks seemed formidable and, to some, undesirable. Not only did guides hold fast to their own labels, but many had decidedly unfavorable views about the others. Several tour managers, for example, resented ever being called guides and saw their role as so different as to be a separate profession. For some tour managers, their image of tour guides, (whom they call "step-on guides" or simply "step-ons") mirrors the same negative image many nontrade people have of guides: loquacious, dogmatic, joyless lecturers, who expound endlessly, and often without regard for their audiences' interests. Tour managers also expressed views that guides are often provincial and have little regard for the rest of the world, and many perceived guides as lacking in the social skills that are required of tour managers (and in which they take great pride).

On the other hand, some tour guides express a similar distaste for tour managers. While viewing tour managers' travel experiences and close ties with the public as enviable, guides sometimes look smugly upon the tour manager as one who makes a living by simply coasting along, merely skimming the surface. With less specific knowledge required of an area's geography, history or culture, tour managers accompany groups, assuring that passengers have hotel rooms, meals, and flights home. These are tasks that many guides perceive as insubstantial, and therefore the role of manager as not as important or professional as their own.

A growing number of people alternate between guiding and tour managing and see them as quite similar, however. Catherine Shilts, president of PGAA, says, "As a professional who strives to have extensive knowledge regarding the areas we pass through and convey that information to many passengers, I consider myself a tour guide who also manages the necessary details." She continues, "More and more tour operators today are demanding that their tour managers also be excellent guides, as the two roles become inseparable once on the road."

Interpreters, yet another category of guides, did not even enter the PGAA picture until the second convention in 1990; even then, only one interpreter was present. Still, the dialogue between interpreters and guides is just beginning and is somewhat limited. There are several reasons for this. For one, many interpreters work in the public sector, which traditionally has not interacted with or been regarded as part of the travel industry. Some tour guides regard interpreters as too academically oriented, often failing to realize the relevance of theory to field work.

Those who call themselves interpreters are already well-represented professionally within the field of interpretation. Since 1957, when Freeman Tilden defined and explored interpretation in his classic book, *Interpreting Our Heritage,* a vast amount of research and literature has proliferated in the field. The National Association for Interpretation (NAI) offers a variety of publications and has active regional chapters throughout the United States. The NAI also publishes a professional trade journal and hosts an annual convention to help provide a network for practitioners and to promote relevant research. Considering the impressive work already done in the field of interpretation, it is no wonder that many practitioners embrace the term "interpreter" rather than "guide," for which there is no similar accepted body of knowledge or course of study.

Today, the PGAA and NAI openly communicate with and address the concerns of all guides and interpreters. There now exists a growing body of people with a foot in each camp who recognize the benefits to be gained from merging the academic and professional merits of the one field with the commercial applications of the other.

Perhaps the clearest way to illustrate the perceptions about and labels for the wide variety of guides is to look at a typical package tour. For example, passengers on a tour from Great Britain to the east coast of the United States would likely meet several representatives of the private and public sector, all of whom might be regarded as guides: the guide who accompanies them from England and remains with them throughout the tour, the guide who gives a tour of New York City, the guide in the Metropolitan Museum of Art, the guide in Independence Hall, and the guide in Colonial Williamsburg. All could be called tour guides and, in fact, usually are by the general public. Yet all have specific names and roles, different backgrounds, and even differ philosophically in their opinions about what they do. Most of these individuals, in fact, would not normally refer to themselves as guides.

Indeed, the guide accompanying the group throughout the tour is called a *tour manager.* It is a *tour guide* who leads visitors on a tour of New York. A *docent* guides visitors through the Metropolitan Museum of Art. A *park ranger* might speak to visitors in Independence Hall. And, in Colonial Williamsburg, an *interpreter* would lead a group on a walking tour. Of all the individuals mentioned above, only the guide in New York City would call himself a *tour guide,* and he is also known within the field as a *city guide, local guide,* or *step-on guide.*

Throughout Europe and most of the world, the term "tourist guide" rather than "tour guide" is used. Proponents of this term argue, rather convincingly, that the guide is interpreting for the tourist rather than for the tour, and thus is more appropriately a tourist guide. Some U.S. guides, especially those who are in more frequent contact with their international colleagues, have even suggested a formal change in the terminology, but to date the label "tour guide" prevails in North America.

The role of the European tourist guide corresponds to that of the tour guide. Generally, however, tourist guides in Europe are much more rigorously trained and more highly regarded. Many are trained to conduct tours in all regions of their country. Some conduct tours in other countries, although this is a highly controversial matter in many countries, and some countries are seeking to make such "unqualified persons" illegal.

Clearly, attempting a thorough overview of terminology is critical, even if difficult. The following discussion elaborates on the most commonly used terms: *tour guide, interpreter,* and *tour manager.* Also included are descriptions of the *heritage interpreter, escort interpreter, driver-guide, adventure guide, docent,* and others.[1]

TOUR GUIDES

A tour guide, in its purest industry definition, is "one who conducts a tour," or one with "a broad-based knowledge of a particular area whose primary duty is to inform." Synonyms for tour guide used within the industry include *tourist guide* (commonly used throughout Europe and in many other parts of the world), *local guide, city guide,* and—arguably the guide's least favorite—*step-on guide* (which is often shortened to the even more unfortunate *step-on*). Outside the industry, the term tour guide is widely used to describe the various professionals who are in any way engaged in guiding people, including tour managers, docents, and interpreters.

Isolating only one job description for tour guides is difficult, inasmuch as guides perform a variety of functions in virtually every kind of place one can

---

[1]I prefer the terms *guide* and *interpreter* (as opposed to *step-on*) and *tour manager* (as opposed to *escort, tour escort,* or *tour leader*). In addition, I prefer to use them interchangeably and do so, but for the sake of the discussion that follows I have attempted to consider all types of guides within the contexts that they would place themselves. The many industry labels referred to throughout the text are defined in the Glossary.

visit. Some guides are self-employed and create and market their own tours; others are employed by the travel industry and conduct predesigned tours; still others are employed by corporations or through local, state, provincial, or national governments.

The scope of a guide's terrain and expertise also varies considerably, from tours of a specific piece of art, to a room, to a large metropolitan area, to a region of hundreds of miles. A tour guide's terrain is usually determined by geography or history. In some parts of the United States, it is common for tour guides to have expertise in the culture and history of a broad region. For example, most seasoned Boston tour guides become fluent in the geography and history of Lexington and Concord because of the close proximity and historical links of those two cities to Boston. Many New Orleans guides, especially those who are themselves Cajun, routinely venture into the nearby Cajun parishes and are intimately familiar with their history and lore. Many guides conduct tours in the broad regions of the southwest United States and the large provinces of Canada.

The tour guide is regarded by many as primarily an educator, as contrasted with the tour manager, whose role has more administrative and social aspects. In many cases, a tour guide joins a long tour only during the time when it visits his or her site, city, or region. This might mean that a guide is with a group for only a few hours. In some regions, however, it is common for guides to remain with a group for several days, in which case the guide often assumes a dual role as guide and tour manager. Clearly there are no fixed rules about a guide's role.

The types of guides discussed below include urban guides, government guides, driver-guides, business or industry guides, adventure guides, and tour managers.

Urban Guides

Cities throughout the world have always produced inhabitants who delight in telling their region's story. Although a few large agencies employ their most popular guides full-time, most urban guides are freelancers who contract their work on a tour-by-tour basis.

Qualifications, job descriptions, working conditions, and all other aspects of the tour guide's work vary considerably. In many cities (even those in which tourism is a major industry) there are virtually no qualifications or acknowledged standards for guides. Such is the case in most cities throughout North America. By contrast, in Israel, throughout Europe, and in many other countries, educational and professional standards are high. (See Chapter 6, "Education," and Appendixes B and C.) It should come as no surprise that working conditions for guides—including salaries, benefits, and status—are generally more favorable in places where the qualifications are more stringent.

In most cities or regions in the United States, virtually anyone (even one who has arrived in town only a month earlier) can be a guide. There are, however, several cities—including New York, New Orleans, and Washington, D.C.—that require guides to have licenses.

To obtain a "Class A" license in Washington, D.C., a guide must have lived in the metropolitan area for at least two years. ("Class B" licenses are issued to those who live outside the area.) Prospective guides must pass a basic physical examination and submit fingerprints and three business and three personal recommendations before taking a 100-question examination covering the history, government, architecture, building locations, and other aspects of the city. Licenses are renewed annually by passing a doctor's examination and submitting a passport-size photograph and a $28 fee. The process in New York City is similar, except that guides renew licenses every two years at a cost of $60.00.

In some cities, training or certification programs offered by businesses or associations have become so highly regarded by guides and hiring agencies that they serve as tacit regulation. One example is the San Francisco Tour Guide Guild's certification. Only experienced guides can apply. Qualified guides take a written test of 125 questions about San Francisco and the entire Bay Area. With a passing grade, guides are then given an oral examination in which they appear before the certification chairperson and several colleagues and respond to simulated scenarios and a variety of questions.

New Orleans, Charleston, and Savannah also require testing and licenses for guides. Surprisingly enough, however, many other large cities, including Los Angeles, Houston, Chicago, and Philadelphia, have no regulation of or requirements for guides as of this writing.

Canada is making great strides in supporting its travel industry and the guiding professions. Unlike the United States, Canada assertively attempts to unite government and industry through Tourism Canada, which oversees tourism development. In addition, the Alberta Tourism Education Council is working toward a provincewide (possibly to become a nationwide) certification process for all "service professionals," including waiters, concierges, maîtres d'hôtel, and eventually, tour guides. Other organizations actively working toward elevating standards among Canadian guides are the Pacific Rim Institute of Tourism (PRIT), and the Canadian Tour Guide Association of British Columbia, headquartered in Vancouver.

Guides who contract to the travel industry can do so in a number of ways. Some work for tour operators (see Chapter 3, "Tourism"). As "step-on" guides, this scenario involves literally stepping onto a motorcoach and conducting a small segment of a tour that is supervised by a tour manager. In such a case, the guide works under the direction of the tour manager for that brief tour.

Some urban guides work for tour operators, travel agencies, and ground operators in the combined tour guide/tour manager role. In this case, a guide is assigned to a group for the entire time it is in a region. Like the tour manager, the guide meets the group at their point of arrival in the city, assists in coordinating all attractions, meals, and hotel check-ins, and remains with the group until it departs. Throughout the tour, the guide is also expected to give extensive commentary on the region. This dual tour guide/manager role is quite common in regions dense with museums, historic buildings, and other visitor attractions. The dual role is also very common with veteran guides who, over time, have broadened their areas of expertise and prefer the closer interaction with people that tour managing offers. The combined role is also appealing to some tour managers, who, over years of exposure to a region, become so knowledgeable about it that they can effectively assume the role of guide. In such cases, guides are bound to adhere to all local regulations. (For example, since both Washington, D.C., and New York City require licenses for guides, anyone wishing to conduct tours in both places must obtain and keep current two local licenses. A growing number of guides maintain more than one license.)

Tour operators and travelers often welcome the dual tour manager/guide role, as such manager/guides—particularly the most colorful and insightful— offer continuity and familiarity. In addition, combining these roles is more cost effective.

Guides and tour managers themselves have mixed feelings about combining the roles. Some welcome it for the variety and the broader opportunities it offers them. Others, who prefer not to perform both functions, feel that combining the roles devalues both. Under such circumstances, both guides and managers stand to lose assignments and income. In a profession which seeks to adopt and enforce higher standards, tour guides are concerned that tour managers who conduct tours in their cities not only take away potential work, but might also misrepresent the city. Tour managers, on the other hand, express concern that many guides lack the qualities, skills, and knowledge they feel are necessary to manage a tour.

Cities which host conventions also provide work for tour guides, as tours are usually an integral part of a convention schedule. Such tours are normally planned by destination management companies (DMCs), who maintain rosters of available freelance guides. In an increasingly competitive business, DMCs attempt to offer visiting organizations innovative, unusual tours and events, and then hire—either as independent contractors or part-time employees—those guides who they feel can best represent their company and conduct an effective tour. A small number of these DMCs offer benefits, higher pay, or even full-time status to their favorite guides. Otherwise, in a freelance market, they are always competing with other companies for the best guides in the area.

Many tour guides alternate between extended tours for tour operators and the brief (one-day or half-day) tours for destination management companies. Most guides appreciate the variety this brings to their work as well as the year-round income it provides, for conventions can and do occur throughout the year. Most tour business, on the other hand, is highly seasonal.

Other opportunities for city guides exist with incentive firms, public relations firms, corporations, real estate agencies, colleges and universities, foundations, and individuals, among others. (Finding and marketing to these various outlets as well as issues such as liability and financial considerations are covered more fully in Chapter 12, "The Business of Guiding.")

Urban Guides Beyond "the Industry" As travel surges in popularity and telecommunications create a more homogenous global village, travelers are more frequently searching for that which is unique to a place, and experiences that delve deeper into the heritage, personalities, neighborhoods, and lifestyles of a region. Increasingly, travelers seek tours that spring from, involve, and benefit local people rather than simply capitalize on them. A growing number of individuals and organizations are emerging to respond to this trend. Although they offer some of the most enriching travel experiences known, many of these organizations are not considered part of the travel industry and, thus, are not always readily available to the mainstream traveler. Such organizations include museums, historical societies, colleges and universities, proprietary schools, churches, clubs and associations, special interest groups, and countless others. The participants in such tours are varied, and include members of the organizations, interested locals, and even tourists. Guides in these cases are usually experts in their fields (architects, historians, dancers, storytellers, archivists, artists, artisans, or naturalists) and many of them rank among the most effective interpreters available. Such guides are found not only in large metropolitan areas, but in smaller, less-visited towns, where their audiences are local people eager to better understand and celebrate their own heritage.

Fortunately, many of these experiences are becoming more widely known and available to tourists. This trend is one of the most gratifying aspects of tourism, as it not only entertains and educates but promotes community pride and goodwill. Programs like these, borne out of the communities themselves, are particularly rewarding when they put visitors in touch with locals, as these experiences can link people of different cultures in a natural, meaningful, and memorable way.

Countless programs could be included in this category, including those conducted by the Smithsonian Resident Associates in Washington, D.C., and in large and small museums throughout North America; New York City's Open Center, the nationally syndicated Learning Annex, and other companies specializing in short courses and local tours; and many others, too numerous to mention here.

Many of the best examples of these locally inspired experiences are walking tours, which are increasingly popular among both locals and travelers. New York City boasts a long, proud tradition of lively walking tours, reaching back to the turn of the century when Mayor John Huston Finley, the quintessential walker, escorted well-known, informal walking tours. The Museum of the City of New York, the "granddaddy" of organized walking tours there, began offering tours three decades ago when Henry Hope Reed, once president of Classical

America and active in the arts, returned from Paris with the concept. Themes for New York walking tours are both varied and unusual, and include tours of cast iron buildings, literary tours, crime tours, tours of Millionaire's Row and of "Mark Twain's New York."

Scores of independent guides carve out a living by combining guiding, writing, lecturing, and consulting. Lou Singer, one of the best-known and most successful guides, calls himself "the only one-man international conglomerate in the world. I could literally take you on any street of New York," he says, "and we could spend half a day there talking about its architecture, its well-known personalities and lore." Another of the city's most respected guides, Gerard Wolfe, author of *New York: A Guide to the Metropolis,* taught courses at New York University's School of Continuing Education and offered a variety of walking tours. Now at the University of Wisconsin, Wolfe is eager to point out that Milwaukee (as well as "virtually every city") also has interesting walking tours. In Milwaukee, for example, tours are offered through the university, museums, and several commercial establishments. Los Angeles, San Francisco, Seattle, Miami, Baltimore, and many other cities now offer a wide variety of walking tours.

In many regions and particularly in cities, some guides become so popular and their work so highly regarded that they themselves become part of a region's

Figure 2.1
Deborah Androus, Washington, D.C. guide, conducts a tour for a student group. (*Photo by Grant Doyle.*)

lore. Such is the case with Philadelphia author, historian, guide and bon vivant John Francis Marion. Dubbed the "Happy Historian," Marion is well known for his books and tours and is recognized by everyone. Says one Philadelphian, "Quite simply, he's a legend."

Government Guides

State, local, and national governments employ guides to show their most important historic, cultural, political, and scenic facilities to visitors. At the national level, many prominent landmarks offer guided tours. In the Parliament Buildings in Ottawa, and in Washington, D.C., at the U.S. Capitol, the Supreme Court, the Library of Congress, and the Department of State, guides regularly conduct tours for a steady stream of visitors. The Capitol, the most frequently visited of these, has thirty-three full-time guides. Since the Diplomatic Reception Rooms at the Department of State have limited visitation, a small number of guides there are employed part-time. At the Pentagon, military personnel (noted for their tradition of conducting their entire one-mile tour while walking backward) give regular tours by appointment.

In Washington, D.C., the federal government awards concession rights to Tourmobile, Inc., to conduct tours in federal park areas. Tourmobile conducts tours daily in the heart of the city, (stopping at the U.S. Capitol, museums on the National Mall, the White House, and monuments and memorials) as well as regional excursions to Mt. Vernon and Arlington Cemetery. Tourmobile provides extensive training for its guides and employs them year-round, hiring additional temporary guides for the busier summer months.

While some state capitol buildings employ guides full-time, others have volunteer or part-time guides, or utilize other full-time employees (such as historians or librarians) to conduct tours when the need arises. Capitol buildings that are particularly historic and more frequently visited, such as the Annapolis State House (which served briefly as the U.S. Capitol), are more likely to offer steady employment.

The Virginia State House in Richmond offers one of the finest examples of consistent, impassioned interpretation. There, eleven paid, part-time "capitol hostesses" are supervised by a full-time supervisor who trains the guides and oversees the program. Although new guides are given a wealth of information to study, Charlotte Troxell, the current supervisor, says, "we have no spiel. It has to be fresh and spontaneous. Although we provide them with a lot of information, each guide is encouraged to present her own version, letting her own personality shine through."

Cities and towns throughout North America with unusual or historic government buildings employ full- or part-time guides, depending upon the need. Philadelphia, for example, has several guides employed through a city program entitled "Hospitality Philadelphia Style." Guides in this program conduct tours of the venerable City Hall. Toronto's CN Tower, Baltimore's National Aquarium, Chicago's Sears Tower, and countless other municipal buildings employ tour guides throughout the year. The United Nations also employs professional, multilingual guides from all over the world who work year-round.

Driver-Guides

As their name implies, driver-guides conduct tours while driving motorcoaches, vans, or cars. Although this dual role is quite common throughout the world, it is met with mixed reviews and is illegal in some areas. In Austria and Cyprus, driver-guiding in motorcoaches is not allowed; yet Israel, a country that upholds extremely high standards for guides, licenses driver-guides. Throughout the United States and Canada, while traditions and regulations for driver-guiding vary, no cities prohibit it.

Opponents of the driver-guide concept argue that driving a vehicle with passengers is already a formidable responsibility without adding to it the distraction of interpreting a region and interacting with passengers. Further, opponents add that although the roles of both driver and guide are important, they are different and to combine them is an insult to both. This combination can also be a disservice to visitors. For similar reasons, even some drivers are opposed to the expectation that they give tours. Some say that the likelihood of one individual excelling in both roles simultaneously is not strong. And finally, since parking is often limited for large passenger vehicles, the driver-guide is restricted to that which he can explain to passengers from major thoroughfares. This often prevents passengers from gaining valuable interpretation of parks, alleys, building interiors, and many other inaccessible places. Tour guides often oppose the driver-guide concept for the above reasons as well as the fact that driver-guides can take work away from guides.

In contrast, many driver-guides and their employers feel differently. They contend that neither the safety of passengers nor the interpretation is compromised by a skilled driver-guide. More and more coaches are equipped with free-standing microphones, allowing drivers to drive and speak easily. The most important public buildings usually have guided tours, so visitors receive the same level of interpretation as do those who have a separate guide. And those who hire them claim that they hold their driver-guides to the same standards of knowledge and guiding skills required of tour guides.

Indeed, many of the most popular and effective interpreters in any region are driver-guides. After thirty years as a Washington, D.C., Metrobus driver, Earl McBride (affectionately called "Big Mac") is one of the city's finest and most cherished interpreters. His intimate understanding of the city, its history, and its people, ranks favorably with that of nearly any city historian. And his charisma, infectious enthusiasm, and love for people make him inspirational and truly memorable. McBride is just one example of innumerable fine driver-guides in cities and towns throughout the world.

Business or Industry Guides

Many corporations, large and small, hire guides to conduct tours of their facilities to educate visitors, promote their business or industry, and maintain (or uplift) the image of their organization. These guides are trained by the organization to speak, often quite technically, about a variety of topics to a wide array of visitors, from colleagues to casual visitors. Some of these guides are, to an extent, company spokespersons, called upon to convey the company philosophy or mission, and, for that reason, may have training in presentation skills or sales techniques.

Tours of automobile or airplane manufacturing plants, for example, serve to educate the public as well as create an image about the business conducted there. Wineries often combine tours of their facilities with an introduction to how wine is made, followed by wine tastings, which they hope will further educate and inspire visitors to purchase their wine. In this case, the guide is, in part, a salesperson. A guide who gives tours of a nuclear power plant might be hired to educate the public as well as uphold an image of a business that cares about the public. In this case the underlying mission of the guided tour might be to persuade the public about the safety and benefits of nuclear power. This image-building opportunity makes the guide's work an important public relations tool, and such a guide must be extremely knowledgeable about the technicalities of the operation. The effective guide must also be poised and diplomatic in responding to controversial or difficult questions.

Adventure Guides

The dynamic, burgeoning field of adventure travel demands a growing number of guides with diverse and special skills. Included in this category are mountaineering guides, bicycle guides, fishing guides, white-water rafting guides, and so on. Work as an adventure guide generally evolves from a serious devotion to a sport or activity. Increasing popularity of these guiding opportunities has created a certain competition in the field and has heightened concern about safety and liability. This concern has spawned many intensive training courses for guides. Perhaps the finest example of these is CRET, the esteemed official mountain guide training school in Charmoinez, France, which offers rigorous training in mountaineering skills, first aid, client relations, and much more.

At present there are approximately 2,000 certified fishing guides in the Rocky Mountain region of the United States. These guides are trained in extensive (and often expensive) programs, up to two weeks long. The Western Rivers Professional Guide School offers an intensive twelve-day program, including sessions such as "Clients and the Fishing Guide" (taught by a psychologist), "The Professional Fishing Guide," "Recreation Liabilities," "First Aid," and "Your Role as a Captain," as well as the more predictable lectures on nature, fly casting, and technique. Guides who successfully complete these programs serve one-year apprenticeships before they are able to operate independently as certified professional guides. Other similar professionally run fishing-guide schools, and a growing number of schools and courses for other types of adventure guides, are operated throughout the country.

Tour Managers

Arthur Frommer called it "a dream job, the fantasy career. . . . Just think: you are traveling for free, and getting paid, to boot!" The reality, he goes on to say, "can be jarringly different." Still, most tour managers[2] wouldn't trade their jobs to do anything else, and competition for tour managing is keen.

A tour manager is, as the name implies, one who manages a tour; that is, one who, as an on-site representative of the tour operator, is responsible for the smooth operation of a group tour. He or she assures that travelers get what they pay for: that the itinerary is followed, that all have satisfactory hotel rooms and meals, and that local sightseeing and promised events are fulfilled.

The amount of in-depth commentary a tour manager provides varies with the individual. The traditional industry standard held that tour guides joined groups in major cities and sites, and tour managers provided light commentary when no guide was available. As noted earlier, however, many tour managers today are so experienced and knowledgeable that they adequately function as both tour manager and guide. In fact, in North America, with keen competition among tour managers and a more sophisticated traveling public, tour managers are expected to provide much more than light commentary. Chris Salyer, general manager of the Washington, D.C., office of USA Hosts says, "These days people are disappointed when they don't get European-style concierge service and university-level expertise, because they've experienced it elsewhere. It's keeping all of us on our toes."

Although the tour guide, not the tour manager, is the focus of this book, their similarities and overlapping roles make it essential that they understand each other and can work together. This is especially true today in light of the field's growth in popularity and status. More people are attempting to remain in the field and make a living in it.

---

[2]Synonyms for the position of tour manager are "tour escort," "tour director," "trip director," and "courier," the latter used more widely in Europe.

INTERPRETERS

Although the word "interpreter" has many accepted meanings (among them "translator of foreign languages" and "one who communicates by sign language"), the interpreter referred to in this text is one who practices the art of explanation or, as defined by the National Association for Interpretation, "the art of revealing meanings and relationships in natural, cultural, recreational and historical resources."

Since interpretation emerged in the National Park Service and has been widely adopted by the public sector, many people assume that interpreters are strictly public-sector guides. This is a misleading perception, however, since many interpreters exist as guides in foundations, corporations, and other realms of the private sector. To many, the distinction between guide and interpreter is minor.

Gabriel Cherem, one of the leading researchers and educators in the field of interpretation, cites these two general characteristics of an interpreter:

1. He is based on-site and offers firsthand experiences with that site or with subject matter and real objects found at that site. Occasionally, . . . he leaves his on-site base of operations and travels to surrounding communities to offer off-site interpretive programs as well.

2. He serves voluntary, non-captive visitors who are in a leisure frame of mind and who anticipate an enjoyable experience (Cherem 1977).

Although the discussion thus far has treated guides and interpreters synonymously, these two characteristics serve to distinguish them somewhat. Guides, in fact, are very likely to leave a site and travel within surrounding communities. And although most passengers on a tour are there voluntarily for leisure and enjoyment, they are often to a greater degree captive, bound to motorcoaches, hotels, and the schedule of a tour.

It is important to note the significance of Cherem's work in uniting guides and interpreters. Two decades ago, Cherem called guides and interpreters "awakening giants," responsible for making sites "come to life," and proposed that they unite to create a greater level of professionalism. In his seminal paper, "Professional Interpretor:[3] Agent for an Awakening Giant," he wrote:

Today, hundreds of people in dozens of fields interpret their sites for visitors. In the future, as explorations of new frontiers continue, there will be hundreds more. To unify

---

[3]Cherem proposed the "interpretor" spelling of the word to distinguish it from the foreign language interpreter or translator. Although at least one other leader in interpretation adopted it, "interpreter" has remained more commonly used in the field.

a dozen diverse fields of public contact under the superheading "interpretor," we must seek out interpretor relatives in many formerly unrelated fields.

The time has come for all individuals performing the interpretive function to be called "interpretors," regardless of their public or private base of operation, and regardless of the site or of the subject matter they are interpreting at that site. This general unification will not only be a boon to hundreds of visitor publics, it will also create a network for the healthy interplay of ideas and viewpoints between various types of interpretors. This should lead to a far greater level of efficiency and professionalism in interpretive programs" (Cherem 1977).

Cherem further proposed a system of classification which incorporates virtually all guides and interpreters (see Table 2.1). Beyond this, he outlines the variety of "fact bases" and backgrounds required of these interpreters. (These and other theories of Cherem's are discussed more fully in Chapter 5, "Interpretation," and Chapter 6, "Education.")

Numerous individuals have devoted their careers to experimentation in and the scrutiny, study, and practice of interpretation. Having been defined and established nearly eight decades ago, the field of interpretation has evolved into a respected field which offers practitioners at all levels a vast amount of literature, an active and supportive professional association and network, and undergraduate and postgraduate programs at scores of colleges and universities around the world. For this reason many individuals and institutions have embraced the field of interpretation, adopted its terminology and principles, and benefited from the field. These include private homes, museums, and sites all over the world, small and large, from a New Zealand garden to the Colonial Williamsburg Foundation.

In contrast to interpreters, most tour guides have had little professional or academic support, and no generally accepted courses of study or educational standards. Many commercial tour guides are unfamiliar with the ideas embraced by the field of interpretation, and many would argue that theory or academic work has little value for them. Other professional guides are becoming more aware of interpretation and believe that they have much to gain by tuning in to the field.

Department of State Escort Interpreters

In addition to guides who conduct tours of the Diplomatic Reception Rooms in Washington, D.C., the Department of State also hires a limited number of "escort interpreters" to accompany foreign visitors officially invited by the government. These individuals are generally well-educated linguists who travel with the visitor throughout the country, usually for one month, to translate for them. A small number of English-language escort interpreters are also hired. The role of the escort interpreter is similar to that of the tour manager in the private

Table 2.1
Traditional and Emerging Types of Interpretors

As Defined by Site

Title	*Site*
1. Park Interpretor	National, state, metro, and local natural and historical parks
2. Public Lands Interpretor	National, state, metro, and local forests, range lands, wildlife refuges, fish hatcheries, reservoirs, and other public lands
3. Historical Site Interpretor (Alderson and Low, 1976; Scanlon, 1974)	National, state, metro, and local historical sites
4. Museum Intrepretor (Carr, 1972, 1975; Edwards, 1968; Sore, 1977)	Historical, archaeological, natural history, science, and art museums
5. Zoo Intrepretor (Conway, 1968; Truett, 1977)	The zoological park
6. Arboretum Interpretor	The arboretum or botanical garden
7. Theme Park Interpretor (Morgan, 1974)	Disney World, Six Flags, Sea World, etc.
8. Tourist Site or Resort Interpretor (Mehrabian, 1976; Utah State University, 1972–77)	A particular tourist site, region, or resort
9. Farm Interpretor (Bush, 1977; Dickerman, 1977; Mich. Dept. of Agriculture, 1977)	Vacation or showplace farms and ranches, outdoor markets, grocery stores
10. Industrial Interpretor (Ashbaugh, 1974)	Private industrial operations, including automobile assembly plants, breweries, canneries, wood processing plants, nuclear power plants, mining company lands, oil drilling operations
11. Urban Interpretor	A particular city, including all its man-made and natural components
12. Governmental or Legal Interpretor	State and national legislatures, supreme courts, executive branch offices, local law enforcement agencies
13. Transportation Corridor Interpretor (Badaracco, 1971; Capelle and Perfrement, 1977; Nelson, 1974)	Based in a vehicle and interpreting the corridor environment and region through which the vehicle (airplane, train, bus, monorail, ship, and so on) passes

As Defined by the Subject Matter Interpreted at the Site

Title	*Fact Base*
1. Interpretive Naturalist	Natural history, ecology, environmental issues
2. Resource Management Interpretor (Vitas, 1975)	Forest, range, wildlife, fisheries, and watershed management
3. Recreational Interpretor (Zink, 1974)	Fishing, camping, boating and other outdoor recreational activities
4. Historical Interpretor (Macauley, 1975)	History (local, regional, national and world)
5. Archaeological Interpretor (Zurel, 1975)	Archaeology, pre-history
6. Cultural Interpretor	Anthropology, ethnic or religious groups
7. Sky Interpretor (Chamberlain, 1976; Chamberlain, 1977)	Astronomy, constellations, weather
8. Energy Interpretor (Stephenson, 1976)	Energy production, use, and conservation
9. Marine Interpretor (Sharpe, 1976a)	Oceanography, the sea or large bodies of fresh water; shoreline, above water and underwater phenomena
10. Agricultural Interpretor	Food growth and processing

Note: Because of the evolving nature of the field, interpretors are classified here both by site and by subject matters they may interpret at the site. References given in this table may not refer to the word "interpretor" directly, but they represent fertile ground for the giant, and point the way for further exploration by interpretors.

Cherem, Gabriel Jerome. 1977. The Professional Interpretor: Agent For an Awakening Giant. *Journal of Interpretation*: August.

sector, as the escort interpreter's primary duty is to assure that the visitors receive the accommodations, transportation, meals, and events they are promised.

The standard for language proficiency is extremely high, in general much higher than that of even the most prominent tour operators. Escort interpreters are expected to have excellent health and stamina, a broad educational background, and be very familiar with the "American scene." Although specific requirements of escort interpreters are vague, the process by which one becomes an escort interpreter is decidedly more time-consuming, rigorous, and daunting than is that within the private sector. After completing a detailed application, candidates are notified by letter whether they are being considered. Following notification, an interview of approximately one hour, usually with no fewer than three interviewers for each candidate, is scheduled. The prospective interpreter is asked specific and sometimes difficult questions not only about the United States and its history, geography, government, and current events, but also about topics concerning any of the regions from which the government hosts visitors. For applicants wishing to interpret in multiple languages, the interview is conducted, of course, in those languages. Many a prospective guide has emerged from these brutal interviews with new-found doubts about his ability to bear up well under stress.

By contrast, interviewers for guides and tour managers in the private sector have traditionally sought affable, sensitive individuals with a sense of humor and diplomacy, and interviews which focus on these qualities tend to be less intimidating. In recent years, however, as the guiding industry has become more sophisticated, with higher standards and keen competition, the interviews conducted for commercial firms are also becoming more challenging.

DOCENTS: VOLUNTEER GUIDES

Perhaps it is no coincidence that some of the best trained and most effective guides are volunteers, most commonly called docents. In many countries, especially in the United States, docents are found in almost every city and town at visitor centers, museums, historic houses, churches, and any places people commonly visit.

One might assume that anyone wishing to become a docent could do so quite easily, by virtue of volunteering his or her time. However, most museums and many private homes are highly selective regarding the docents they will train, since training and administering docent programs is time-consuming and expensive. For example, the quality of art education for docents at the National Gallery of Art and other specialized museums far surpasses that of many university programs. Lectures might feature curators, artists, and well-known experts in a field. Such programs are often the greatest attraction for docents.

Most museums consider docent training an ongoing process and offer educational programs throughout the year. The most prestigious museums offer courses of several months' duration and typically require that prospective docents attend these for one or more years before giving their first solo tour. (By contrast, most tour operators in the United States require no training for guides, since little is available at present.)

In exchange for their fine educational programs, most museums and historic homes require a commitment in both the number of hours or days per month a docent will work and in the number of years he or she is willing to commit. Often they prefer knowing that a guide in whom they have invested time and money will stay for at least two years.

While competition still prevails at the most prestigious museums and many highly qualified would-be docents are rejected the situation has changed much in recent years. With more and more women (traditionally the majority of docents) needing to earn income, many curators are reporting that the pool of qualified people able or willing to volunteer their time is rapidly diminishing. Museums are responding with increasingly generous benefits for docents, such as museum store discounts, parties, and access to special events.

SUMMARY

There are as many types of guides as there are places to visit. As leisure time and tourism increases, more opportunities for specialized guides will arise. The guiding fields are expanding and changing rapidly, presenting both a great challenge and an exciting opportunity for anyone considering the field of guiding.

II. The Industry and the Role of the Guide

3 *Tourism*

"International tourism in the twenty-first century will be a major vehicle for fulfilling people's aspirations for a higher quality of life . . . and, it is hoped, laying the groundwork for a peaceful society through global touristic contacts."

—David L. Edgell, Sr.,
International Tourism Policy

In the final years of the twentieth century, tourism, like guiding, is an "awakening giant" (Cherem 1977). "Awakening" is perhaps a more accurate label than "emerging" or "growing" because, indeed, tourism has long been an important though largely unrecognized economic and sociological force. More recently, tourism seems to be wresting itself from obscurity and emerging as a strong, unified industry.

And giant it is. According to the Travel Industry Association of America (TIA), tourism will surely rank as the largest global industry by the start of the twenty-first century (Cooke 1990). Worldwide, tourism is an ever-expanding $2 trillion industry. In the United States alone, tourism produces approximately $380 billion in gross income (USTTA 1991), making it the nation's third-largest retail industry. Currently, the tourism industry generates 5.8 million jobs in the United States alone (Cooke 1990). Moreover, travel and tourism is the leading export for the United States, producing a growing net trade surplus. This phenomenon is mirrored in all countries where tourism is a major force.

Tourism yields more than financial rewards. The desire to travel has inspired staggering advances in transportation, communications, and other technologies. And by bringing together individuals from around the world, tourism provides educational, cultural, and diplomatic rewards. Lou D'Amore, founder and director of the International Institute of Peace Through Tourism and promoter of the concept of tourism as a force for peace, states that

Tourism, properly designed and developed, has the potential to help bridge the psychological and cultural distances that separate people of diverse races, colors, religions and stages of social and economic development. Through tourism, we can come rather to an appreciation of the rich human, cultural and ecological diversity that our world mo-

saic offers; to evolve a mutual trust and respect for one another and the dignity of all life on earth (D'Amore 1988).

Clearly, tourism holds great promise for the future.

TOURISM DEVELOPMENT

Despite its undeniable impact and potential, tourism is curiously devoid of political and economic support relative to its contributions. Although few industries yield more financial rewards, tourism, until recently, has received little government support for research and development and scarce attention in colleges and universities as a legitimate course of study. Nowhere is this more evident than in the United States, where tourism is one of the greatest contributors, in terms of dollars, jobs, industry achievements, and number of travelers. And yet, tourism in the United States has among the weakest national posturing in the world. Unlike many smaller, developing countries, for example, the United States has no cabinet-level position devoted to tourism issues. Considering government's important role in enabling tourism to thrive—through policy, funding, public relations, and research—many involved with tourism believe that such a lack of political and governmental support is damaging to the industry and to citizens.

Fortunately, the situation is changing. In the United States, the National Tourism Policy Act of 1981 created the United States Travel and Tourism Administration (USTTA). The formation of this agency, headed by an Undersecretary of Commerce for Travel and Tourism, has set the stage for a stronger government profile in tourism policy. Budgets for the promotion of tourism on the state level have increased dramatically over the past decade. Associations such as the TIAA lend powerful support to the realization of tourism growth. In recent years, tourism has come to be regarded as an important course of study in colleges and universities around the world, infusing the industry with knowledgeable professionals committed to tourism as a serious career.

Tourism as an Industry

Due in part to its vastness and its strength of influence in so many industries, tourism has been paradoxically undervalued and largely unrecognized as a single industry. By contrast, airlines, one of the largest components of tourism, are distinct entities and are, therefore, easier to categorize as a single industry. As such, airlines are well represented by corporations and associations, lobbyists and government organizations who promote and protect their interests. The same is true of the hotel and restaurant industries and other distinct sectors of tourism.

Another reason tourism is not widely regarded as a single industry is that any complete representation of tourism must include the public sector, or government, as a major component. Traditionally, government and industry are considered disparate entities, and treating them jointly as an industry creates confusion to some.

In light of these factors, which have long kept tourism in relative obscurity, Chuck Gee (coauthor of *The Travel Industry*) and other tourism educators and leaders have questioned whether a travel "industry" truly exists. If so, does it matter whether tourism is regarded as one industry? And if so, why?

A large and growing number of researchers, educators, and practitioners in travel and tourism emphatically believe that strong growth in travel and tourism will depend upon the ability of the many facets of the industry to unite and work together. Such unity might yield a wide variety of benefits to all, such as favorably impacting legislation and policy affecting travel, increasing promotion to stimulate travel, elevating public awareness of the economic impact of travel, and raising the standards and image of the industry as a whole. According to Aubrey King, executive director of the TIA's Government Affairs Council,

Within our own industry, among its various segments, we must give far greater emphasis to educating each other about what we all have in common. We simply must do a better job of making sure everyone in this industry is familiar not only with those issues that may affect their particular segments—as vital as they may be—but also with broader issues which may—even in the short run—be just as damaging to their interests (King 1990).

Whether the industry makes an attempt to address these goals, statistics indicate that a surge in travel in virtually all nations is inevitable and that a great tide of travelers can be expected in the coming years. If its deficiencies and important issues are not confronted, the industry will miss great opportunities—economic, political, and cultural. Many argue that a disjointed industry will render individuals and organizations ill-prepared to compete and communicate effectively, which will in turn reflect unfavorably on the nation. Conversely, attention to these goals will enable all travel professionals—including guides—to thrive and become a source of national and industry pride.

Our global economy binds the travel industry internationally. The decisions and policies of one airline immediately impact others, and that impact is then felt by hundreds of industries and millions of travelers. Consequently, it is imperative that the industry unite not only on regional and national levels, but internationally as well. The result no doubt will be "win-win," as travel, at its best, is symbiotic, offering immeasurable rewards for both hosts and guests.

According to Gee, the question of whether a single, cohesive travel industry exists, "is becoming increasingly less academic and more real as common denominators are identified and links among travel-related businesses are established through communications and practice" (Gee et al 1989).

A new approach to tourism as a unified industry can strengthen and empower guides, both individually and as a profession. Thus, the need for guides to better understand the intricacies of the industry and their role in it cannot be overstated.

Defining and Classifying Tourism

As befits a relatively young field, many diverse definitions of tourism proliferate. Jan Van Harssel, in *Tourism: An Exploration,* defines tourism as "activities concerned with providing and marketing services and facilities for pleasure travel" (Van Harssel 1988). In *The Travel Industry,* Gee, Makens, and Choy define tourism as "the composite of organizations, both public and private, that are involved in the development, production, and marketing of products and services to serve the needs of the travelers" (Gee et al 1989). Dr. David Edgell, director of the Office of Policy and Planning for the U.S. Travel and Tourism Administration, believes that tourism "has strong links to cultural pursuits, foreign policy initiatives, economic development, and provides an opportunity to increase worldwide understanding, mutual goodwill, and peace. The tourism industry includes the buying, selling, and management of services and products (to tourists), which might range from buying hotel rooms to selling souvenirs or managing an airline" (Edgell 1990).

These three equally valid definitions have entirely different approaches: tourism can be viewed as "activities," as "the composite of organizations" involved in commerce, or as a composite of smaller industries. These and other definitions and perspectives further illustrate the complexity of tourism.

So vast is the tourism network that it is difficult to discuss tourism in a succinct manner. One helpful point of departure is to trace the development of tourism from its origins to the most recent achievements and events. In doing so, it becomes clear that tourism developments in this century—particularly over the past fifty years—parallel the great advances in transportation and communication. Figure 3.1 highlights a few of the major events since World War II that have altered the development of tourism. Refer to Chapter 1, "The Tour Guide: A Historical Overview," for a survey of historical developments in travel.

The period since World War I is often referred to as the modern era. Historically, travel flourishes during times of peace, and such has been the case during postwar periods in the twentieth century. Following World War I, steamship travel increased dramatically, as did the number of travelers to and from the United States. Both World Wars impacted tourism dramatically by accelerating technological development, most notably in air travel, and by facilitating the movement of people around the globe. After World War II, air travel became widely available and began to dominate all phases of travel, bringing both a technological and philosophical boon to tourism. This enabled a more widespread interaction of cultures than ever before.

Moreover, the postwar boom spawned optimism in the future of travel. Many of the most important trade associations emerged during this decade,

Figure 3.1
Highlights in travel and tourism development, post–World War II.

1947 International Union of Official Travel Organizations (IUOTO) formed.

1951 The Caribbean Tourism Association (CTA) is founded to encourage and assist Caribbean tourism development.

1958 The beginning of the Jet Age; the world's first airline, PanAm, offers jet service from New York to Paris.

1960 Dawn of the Cruise Era: Holland America, Norwegian Caribbean, and Italian lines are available to travel agents.

1961 President Kennedy signs a bill allocating money for an agency responsible for promoting overseas travel to the U.S.

1968 Boeing 747 (first jumbo-jet) introduced.

1970 Amtrak created to revitalize U.S. passenger rail transportation.

1974 IUOTO becomes the World Tourism Organization (WTO); the U.S. Senate authorizes the Senate Commerce Committee to undertake a National Tourism Policy Study "to develop legislation and other recommendations to make the federal role in tourism more effective and responsive to national interests."

1976 The Concorde is introduced by Air France and British Airways, cutting travel time between London and New York to $3\frac{1}{2}$ hours.

1978 President Carter signs the Airline Deregulation Act.

1980 Delegations of 107 countries meet to create the Manila Declaration, recognizing tourism as a vital force, enhancing the world socially, culturally, educationally, politically, and economically.

1981 For the first time, foreign visitors to the U.S. outnumber its own visitors to other countries.

1981 Congress passes the National Tourism Policy Act and creates the United States Travel and Tourism Administration (USTTA).

1984 The Trade and Tariff Act establishes the Service Industries Development Program, for the improvement of the international competitiveness of U.S. service industries.

1985 American arrivals (6 million) in Europe break all records.

---

including the International Union of Official Travel Organizations (IOUTO), which became the World Tourism Organization (WTO) in 1975; the Pacific Area Travel Association (PATA); and in the United States, the American Society of Travel Agents (ASTA), the National Association of Travel Organizations (NATO), and the Travel Research Association, now the Travel and Tourism Research Association (TTRA). These organizations provided market research and support for their members and set the stage for the cohesiveness now being realized in tourism.

Some have called the years from 1960 to 1973 the "golden years" of world tourism, marked as they were by an annual rate of increase of 5 percent. Such growth enabled virtually all sectors of tourism to mature. The oil shortages in 1974 and again in 1979 prompted surges in fuel prices which contributed to declines in the number of travelers and tourism revenues. These fluctuations in the market slowed annual tourism growth to its present level of about 2 percent.

According to David Edgell, the 1980s may come to be recorded as "the most important decade for formulating policies on tourism. The effects of such policies," he says, "will have far-reaching consequences for the many individuals, firms, and other organizations engaged directly or indirectly in tourism activities." Still, he concedes, "tourism policy in the United States is in its infancy and needs to be nurtured, understood, and supported" (Edgell 1990, 23).

One of the most obvious examples of the advances in tourism in the 1980s is the number and quality of college-level travel and tourism programs which proliferated in that decade. And certainly the 1980s can be regarded as a coalition building phase for the industry, a period in which the industry—through such organizations as the WTO and the TIAA—began to recognize the importance of uniting all segments of travel and tourism.

Although few expect the steady surges of the 1960s to return, virtually all forecasters predict that growth in the travel industry will continue into the twenty-first century. The 1990s promises an increase in the number of travelers and, optimists say, the quality of travel, or at least the options for a better quality of travel. Greater numbers of people throughout the world will have more time and income for travel. Technological advances in transportation and communication will make travel more efficient and will expose more people to other cultures, increasing the desire to travel. Many believe that the travel industry is becoming more responsible, creative, and service-oriented and that it will contribute immeasurably to the quality of life around the world.

As already noted, the travel and tourism industry is so vast and far-reaching that it is difficult to describe it simply. However, the industry can be broadly divided into five major components: transportation, accommodations, food and beverages, destinations or attractions, and services. Even so, these seemingly distinct components are difficult to categorize and describe, for they are, to a large degree, interdependent. The latter category, services, is especially complex, as it includes both public- and private-sector entities which perform a variety of functions, including research, marketing, visitor services, and operations. Guides, for example, work for and within all of these components, and yet most would place them within the services category, along with tour operators, travel agents, travel consultants, and motorcoach operators.

In *The Travel Industry* (1989), Gee, Makens, and Choy offer an instructive model to describe the manner in which components of the travel industry relate to each other and to the traveler. They divide the industry into three general categories, which they call the *linking concept,* which includes (1) those who are *direct providers* to the traveler (entities such as travel agencies and airlines, which most people regard as the travel industry); (2) those who provide *support services* to direct providers and indirectly to the traveler; and (3) those in *tourism development,* who offer goods and services which directly and indirectly affect travelers, support services, and direct providers. Gee, Makens, and Choy describe this category as more complex and broader in scope than production of everyday travel services and as instrumental in creating long-term results. "Highly skilled individuals within a professional field such as planning, real estate, or architecture but specializing in tourism projects are employed in developmental organizations," they write (Gee et al 1989). Guides could be regarded as both direct providers and support services, as they have direct contact with travelers and they work for tour operators or travel agents as a support service.

The Role of Government

The government's role in tourism varies dramatically throughout the world. In the context of the linking concept, government can play a role in all three categories—as direct provider, in support services, and in tourism development.

In most countries the national government plays a particularly prominent role in policy, regulation, and promotion. In some countries, especially those with socialist systems, governments have played a major role in all aspects of tourism. Until recently, in the former Soviet Union all aspects of inbound tourism—research, marketing, and operations—were administered by Intourist, a government-run organization. Thus, everyone in tourism, including airline pilots, researchers, hotel employees, and tour guides, was a government employee. This policy is changing rapidly and significantly in recent years as more competition is being permitted there.

Outside the former Soviet Union, most operations—hotels, restaurants, attractions, and services—are privately owned. In the United States and Canada,[1] national, state or provincial, and local governments share with the private sector the duties of promotion and policy to the extent that the distinction between the private and public sectors in tourism can be vague and bewildering. Yet there are many important government-owned attractions, accommodations, publications, and services, such as visitor information services and national park facilities. The diversity within the industry need not be problematic, though it challenges the abilities of many diverse organizations and individuals to work together, create beneficial policies, gather accurate data, and advance toward a more unified industry.

One example of the great differences in government involvement in tourism is evidenced by regulation of tour guides. In the United States, no national policies for guides exist with regard to licensing, certification, training, pay and benefits, or marketing or conducting tours. Several cities require licenses for guides, but none of these cities requires any training, and only New York City regularly enforces the licensing policy.

Throughout Europe, government's role in regulating guiding varies. Although England and Germany have excellent guides and training programs, their governments exercise little control over guide training. Many countries, including Scotland, Ireland, France, Greece, and Belgium have government-

---

[1]It is beyond the scope of this text to thoroughly or equitably cover the role of government in tourism development and operations. For a more thorough comparison of international tourism policy, consult *The Travel Industry,* by Chuck Gee, James C. Makens, and Dexter J. L. Choy (New York: Van Nostrand Reinhold, 1989).

controlled guide training, and the national governments in Ireland, France, Denmark, and Portugal authorize guiding operations. In some countries, guide regulations are rigorous and "unqualified persons" guiding groups of travelers could even face arrest.

One result of inconsistent policies is a lack of consensus about the value of a guide's role. This results in low morale and a lack of professional pride. By contrast, in a field such as medicine, which universally requires rigorous training, the very title of nurse or doctor garners some respect.

The most significant international organization devoted to the promotion and development of tourism is the WTO. With more than 100 member nations, the WTO serves as a clearinghouse for tourism research and information, monitors trends in the industry, conducts educational programs, and works for the elimination or reduction of barriers to travel. Its 1980 conference in the Philippines produced the landmark Manila Declaration, which recognized tourism's potential to enhance the world in many ways—political, social, cultural, educational and economic—and the WTO's commitment to that ideal. Many have said that this historic declaration marked the beginning of a new era of responsible tourism.

Despite great differences among countries in the role of government, almost all have at least one organization devoted to promoting and regulating travel activities. These organizations are known as National Tourism Organizations (NTOs). In some countries, NTOs occupy full ministry or cabinet-level positioning, while in others they are far less powerful, sometimes occupying a post within a seemingly unrelated department. Other NTOs are funded and managed by both the public and private sectors. Although their roles, specific mandates, and budgets vary considerably, they have several standard functions. The WTO has separated these functions into five categories: (1) general administration of travel and tourism, (2) planning and investment, (3) research and statistics, (4) vocational training, and (5) promotion (Hudman and Hawkins 1989). Their many goals include: the development of inbound tourism; positive promotion of their national image; the creation, protection, and development of tourism resources; the preservation of their nation's heritage; economic development; and the promotion of tourism amenities.

Although there are many agencies within the United States government that address tourism issues, the official NTO is the United States Travel and Tourism Administration (USTTA), a bureau of the Department of Commerce. Its principal missions are to implement broad tourism policy initiatives, to develop travel to the United States from abroad, to reduce the nation's travel deficit, and to promote a friendly understanding and appreciation of the United States abroad. Even after it was established in 1981, the USTTA was given languid support. In fact, the USTTA faced real danger of being abolished in the mid-1980s. More recently its identity and budget seem secure, bolstered by greater support from the industry and Congress.

Governments also influence tourism on the state and provincial levels. In the United States and Canada, states and provinces allocate funds for destination marketing organizations (DMOs), which promote and develop tourism. These include convention and visitors' bureaus, chambers of commerce, state and provincial tourism offices, and regional alliances. The Louisiana Travel Promotion Association (LTPA) is an extremely active statewide association for individuals and organizations in all aspects of travel. The LTPA administers the Louisiana Certified Travel Professional program (LCTP) and, in 1990, began an escort certification program for industry employees who lead familiarization tours.

Other examples of regional alliances include multicounty areas or river valley villages which, when marketed together, draw more visitors than if they attempted to market their regions alone. California's Wine Country and the Pennsylvania Dutch regions are examples of these. These organizations usually concentrate their efforts on marketing and promotion through advertising, visitor information services, and familiarization tours, and by working with tour operators and travel writers. Many of these organizations are quasi-public, as they are comprised of and funded by both the private and public sectors.

Associations

No treatment of the development of tourism would be complete without attention to the powerful role of associations. De Tocqueville (1835) observed that Americans "of all ages, all conditions, and all dispositions constantly form associations. . . . Wherever at the head of some new undertaking you see the government in France, or a man of rank in England, in the United States you will be sure to find an association."

One could say that in the United States, whenever government, private industry, or individuals are not responding to the needs of a group, an association emerges to become its advocate. In travel and tourism, as in many fields, associations have been responsible for promotion, communication, research, fundraising, policy formation, member education and certification, and innumerable benefits to the industry. Associations play a powerful role in uniting the industry and elevating its image.

- *The Travel Industry Association of America (TIA)* is one of the largest and most important associations in the tourism industry. Its mission is "to promote travel to and within the United States" and its membership includes public- and private-sector organizations engaged in all phases of travel. The TIA has two active affiliates: the Travel and Tourism Affairs Council, formed to represent the industry on legislative and regulatory issues; and the United States Travel Data Center, which conducts and disseminates statistical, economic, and scientific research concerning travel, the travel industry, and travel-related industries.
- *The National Tour Association (NTA)* is the leading advocate in North America for group tours. Its members are tour operators and wholesalers, tour suppliers

(such as hotels, restaurants, airlines, and attractions), destination marketing organizations, and educators. The NTA has a nonprofit educational arm, the National Tour Foundation, which oversees the Certified Tour Professional (CTP) designation.

- *The United States Tour Operators Association (USTOA)* is comprised of the major tour operators of the United States who operate tours throughout the world.

- *The American Society of Travel Agents (ASTA)* is one of the largest and most active associations in the industry. In addition to travel agents its membership includes airlines, hotels, bus companies, public-sector organizations, and educational institutions.

- *The Travel and Tourism Research Association (TTRA)* is devoted to quality research and education in tourism. The TTRA conducts regional and national conferences and publishes the *Annals of Tourism Research,* a scholarly journal.

- *The Professional Guides Association of America (PGAA),* described in Chapter 2, is comprised of tour guides, tour managers, tour operators, educators, and other public- and private-sector affiliates. Its purpose is to support and promote the common interests of guides and tour managers. The PGAA administers the Certified Professional Guide (CPG) designation.

- *The International Association of Tour Managers (IATM),* headquartered in Lon-

Figure 3.2
The annual PGAA convention brings together tour managers and guides of the United States for educational programs, certification, and marketing and networking opportunities. (*Photo by Sharon Murphy, Today Photography.*)

don, is an international association for the common interests of tour managers. IATM holds an annual convention and publishes an association journal.

The Group Tour Industry

The group tour industry has come a long way since 1841, when Thomas Cook operated his twenty-five-cent round-trip tour to a temperance convention in England. Although most travelers prefer to travel with their family and friends, millions of travelers prefer tours.

Guides are hired by individuals, corporations, associations, and others in both the private and public sectors, but the segment of tourism with whom most guides regularly interact is the group tour industry. As freelancers, guides might simultaneously work for as many as twenty tour operators, ground operators, or destination management organizations. Likewise, an experienced guide might meet as many as 100 or more groups over the course of a year. Even so, many guides are surprisingly unaware of the complexities of the tour and travel industry.

The NTA broadly defines a tour as "any prearranged journey to one or more destinations and back to the point of origin" (NTA 1990). As such, a tour can involve any number of people, places, and events. It can be structured or open, simple or complex, long or short. Such diversity is especially appropriate today, as a wide variety of tours are designed to meet an increasingly diverse public. Tours are conducted to virtually every region of the world so that participants can learn, for example, to paint, to identify birds or architectural styles, to explore their roots or heritage, to work on environmental problems, or even to rebuild ailing monuments. Some tours are closely timed and chaperoned; others provide no schedule or guide for travelers, only instructions for locating hotels and transportation.

As stated, most people prefer to travel individually or in small, informal groups with family or friends, and for some the mere mention of taking a tour prompts tinges of claustrophobia. The typical "If It's Tuesday, This Must be Belgium" tours, with forty or more senior citizens traveling en masse, closely behind tour managers and guides, with busy, rigidly scheduled, and largely passive sightseeing itineraries still do exist. In fact, there is a large market for them! However, such tours are now only one of many options.

Millions of people prefer group travel, and there are many reasons why people enjoy traveling in groups. Tours are becoming increasingly more interesting and popular as they answer the new desires and needs of an evolving traveling public. Significant changes in tours over the past decade include trends toward

1. Smaller groups, allowing more flexibility and time for individuals to focus on the region and its people.
2. Specialized or themed tours, such as literary, bird-watching or architectural tours, as opposed to more general sightseeing.

3. More limited geographical ranges, rather than "Europe in Two Weeks" or the "Rocky Mountain States in Ten Days."

4. More categories of affinity groups. Where senior citizens once accounted for the vast majority of group travelers, demographics show that many other categories are now candidates for group travel, including families, singles, corporations offering incentives, environmental or exploratory groups, and grandparents and their grandchildren.

5. Less structure, more options, and greater flexibility in tour itineraries.

In addition, modern trends alter the ways in which people travel, which in turn impacts tour characteristics. For example, the trend of *responsible tourism* has encouraged tour operators and guides to become more sensitive to local concerns and to incorporate more contact between tour members and local citizens and events. *Rural tourism* encourages tour operators to introduce travelers to unspoiled country settings. Great interest in *ecotourism* has spawned hundreds of expeditions to developing nations to promote local involvement in tourism planning while assuring the continuance of a sustainable economy. And *adventure travel* includes trips with a recreational or exploratory emphasis. Many travelers even opt for *working vacations,* which feature trips to remote areas around the globe in which participants clean up or rebuild natural and cultural sites.

Although the "typical tour" is less typical and may be less popular, this does not mean that tours per se are declining in importance. Indeed, the qualities that have always attracted people to tours remain appealing: economy, security, freedom from some of the strains of travel (such as carrying luggage, driving, navigating, or coordinating transportation), accessibility to certain exclusive places, companionship, and the educational opportunities for which tours are known. The tour industry is thriving as it responds to the needs and desires of travelers.

Types of Tours   There are six distinct types of guided tours: package tours, custom tours, convention tours, incentive tours, fixed departure tours, and familiarization (FAM) tours.

A *package tour* is a vacation plan arranged by tour operators or wholesalers which provides, for a set fee, all or most of the required services: transportation, accommodations, sightseeing, attractions, and entertainment. There are three major types of package tours: the independent tour, the hosted tour, and the escorted tour.

Independent tours are commonly categorized as either *foreign independent tours (FITs)* or *domestic independent tours (DITs)*. These are tours arranged by travel agents or tour operators and are tailored to meet the specific needs and desires of individuals. FITs and DITs typically include transportation to destinations, lodging arrangements, and transfers, but are otherwise unscheduled, allowing travelers to plan activities and choose restaurants as they travel. The *hosted tour,* also relatively unscheduled, features a host stationed in a designated location and available for assistance. Independent and hosted travelers may wish to avoid guides altogether, but many will take part in fixed departure guided tours or arrange for private tours once they arrive in a city.

Escorted tours are usually more structured and feature a tour manager throughout. Escorted tours often incorporate local guides (or step-on guides) at major cities or sites. In some cases, a tour guide will be hired for the duration of the tour to serve as both guide and tour manager. This latter arrangement occurs most frequently in urban areas, where a group might spend a full week or more, or in cases where a guide is particularly knowledgeable about the region and feels comfortable in both roles.

Custom tours are those designed to fit the specific needs of a particular market or affinity group. As one would expect, these tours are often based on a particular theme and require that a guide have in-depth knowledge about that subject. An example of a custom-designed tour might be a garden club's visit to Savannah and Charleston for a spring garden tour. Another example might be an eighth-grade American history class visiting Washington, D.C., as part of their school's curriculum. While package tours are often offered publicly, and generally attract previously unacquainted participants, custom tours tend to be exclusive, and those who participate in them are frequently well-acquainted.

Convention tours are excursions provided for persons attending meetings and conventions. Most cities which host conventions have ground operators, tour operators, or destination management organizations who plan these tours. Generally convention programs offer both brief (half-day) local tours and longer regional tours. Guides are often hired to conduct these tours and to meet convention-goers upon their arrival at airports (called "meet and greet" in the industry).

Incentive tours are trips offered as prizes, particularly to stimulate the productivity of employees or sales agents. They are usually loosely structured and offer an array of choices for the participants. They are planned by tour operators, ground operators, and, most often, incentive houses, which specialize in this field. Tours offered to incentive groups are similar in length and nature to those of convention groups, so similar opportunities exist for guides. Incentive business is highly desirable and competitive, however, and incentive houses are particularly vigilant about offering clients the highest level of customer service possible. They are especially selective in choosing local ground operators and guides (whom incentive houses often call *trip directors*), and tend to perceive guides as hosts rather than educators or leaders. For this reason they sometimes place more emphasis on a guide's appearance and personality than on his or her knowledge of or experience in a particular area. Chris Salyer, general manager of USA Hosts in Washington, D.C., works regularly with incentive houses. "They want warm, poised, professional people capable and willing to give concierge-level service—similar to what one finds in Europe," she says. "And frankly, they tell me they're not finding what they need in most U.S. destinations—which means we all lose business."

Fixed departure tours are regularly scheduled public tours. Although these tours can last up to several weeks, they are more often brief, usually two-day, one-day, or half-day excursions. Fixed departure tours are especially popular in urban areas, highly visited regions, and in areas where tourism is well developed. Fixed departure tours are widely available throughout Europe, even in small towns and villages. In the United States and Canada, where receptive tourism is not as well developed, fixed departure tours are usually only available in major cities.

Fixed departure tours are ideal for many travelers in that they provide the advantage of having local guided tours for "insiders" without the daily structure of package tours. Many fixed departure tours require no reservations, allowing even greater flexibility to travelers. For these reasons fixed departure tours are more popular than ever, and the trend promises to continue.

Ironically, however, conditions for guides in fixed departure tours are often difficult. Because the prices of fixed departure tours are competitively low, and because passenger counts are generally not known until the moment the tour departs, owners of these firms cannot absorb the risk of hiring guides who may not be needed. Thus, many operators of fixed departure tours hire driver-guides. Although the concept of driver-guides is somewhat controversial in the guiding community (as discussed in Chapter 2), the obvious savings and the traditionally low price of these tours ensure that the practice of employing driver-guides for local fixed departure tours is likely to continue.

In North America, the largest fixed departure company is Grey Line, a bus company that operates in most major cities. So ubiquitous and reliable is Grey Line that, for many, its name is synonymous with sightseeing and is a standard means of introducing oneself to a city.

In recent years, more fixed departure companies have emerged to compete with Grey Line. Among the most successful of these is Old Town Trolley Tours. Begun in 1986 in Florida, Old Town Trolley Tours operates tours in Washington, D.C., San Diego, Boston, Miami, and Key West. Tourmobile, Inc., a sightseeing concession contracted to the National Park Service, offers tours of specific, major sites in Washington, D.C. Old Town Trolley Tours and Tourmobile differ from companies like Grey Line in that they offer regular stops, allowing people to disembark at places of interest and later reboard coaches as they please. Old Town Trolley and many other newer companies employ both drivers and guides for their tours. Rob Layrle, Vice President of Hotard Coaches, Inc., which owns the New Orleans franchise of Grey Line, says, "We really like the idea of hiring guides, but we found it wasn't at all cost effective. We would have to price ourselves out of the market or lose our shirts, so driver-guides are the solution." (It should be noted that many driver-guides are quite knowledgeable and professional, and that many companies, such as Hotard, hold them to high standards and provide extensive training.)

More lucrative opportunities for guides exist with fixed departure tour agencies that do require reservations. In order to provide guides and yet reduce their financial risks, these companies require reservations by a specified date. If not enough passengers register to justify their costs, the agency cancels both the tour and the guide. In this way, they can offer the advantage of trained, professional guides, which many travelers appreciate. Such tours are becoming more common throughout North America in conjunction with other trends in travel. For example, as more people seek to travel independently and to more rural areas, fixed departure excursions from cities to outlying rural settings are more widely available. In some cases, rural regions are attracting so many new visitors that fixed departure tours are even viable there. Most travel trends indicate that fixed departure tours will provide increased opportunities for guides.

Familiarization (FAM) tours are usually complimentary or reduced-rate travel programs designed to acquaint travel agents, tour operators, travel writers, and other industry personnel with a specific destination or to stimulate the sale of travel. Sometimes guides and tour managers themselves participate in FAM tours to acquaint themselves with a region. Some corporations sponsor FAM tours for employees they have recently relocated to familiarize them with the areas. FAM tours are commonly sponsored by destination marketing organizations or jointly sponsored by a variety of suppliers, such as an airline in combination with a ground operator and hotel. Employees of the DMO or sponsoring organization frequently conduct the tour, hiring a guide to provide a brief overview of the region. In other cases, a guide will conduct the entire tour. Usually only experienced guides with a solid understanding of the industry are chosen to conduct FAM tours. The differences between conducting FAM tours and conducting tours for the general public are discussed more fully in Chapter 10, "The Nuts and Bolts of Conducting a Tour."

Tour Planning   Tour planning and marketing is complicated and becoming even more so as tours diversify and grow in popularity. Traditionally within the industry, scheduled package tours are designed by tour operators or tour wholesalers and sold to the public through travel agents.

The terms *tour operator* and *tour wholesaler* are often used interchangeably to designate agencies that design and pull together all aspects of a tour, including transportation, accommodations, meals, and activities. In truth they have an important distinction. The tour wholesaler sells tours exclusively to retailers (mainly travel agents), and delegates most of its operations to a network of suppliers. Often the corporate names of tour wholesalers are unknown to consumers (and guides). Tour operators, on the other hand, sell tours to travel agents and directly to the public. The largest and best-known tour operators, such as American Express and Thomas Cook, own retail agencies. Some tour operators, also called *ground operators* or *receptive operators,* are more involved in the daily operations of a tour. Tour operators may also create custom tours, whereby affinity groups such as clubs, schools, and associations have tours designed specifically for them. Tour operators increasingly by-pass travel agents and sell tours directly to individuals and affinity groups. Tour operators probably employ more guides than any other sector of the travel industry.

In recent years, many individuals and nonprofit organizations have begun to offer package tours. This is a practice of great concern to private sector tour operators, as they are often competing for the same travelers. Another related trend is that local organizations of all kinds—historical societies, special interest organizations, colleges, universities and continuing education programs, and senior citizens groups—are offering public tours within their local regions. These provide opportunities for guides, and, in more and more cases, guides are designing these tours.

The Guide's Role Guiding has aptly been called the hidden profession of the tourism industry. As freelancers, guides operate on the periphery of the tour business, usually interacting with only one or two planners or schedulers. Moreover, the seasonal nature of guiding guarantees guides employment only in their region's busy season. In some places, such as in Alaska, the busy season is a window of as few as ninety days in which to secure work. Such seasonality offers the guide little security, and guides must make a choice. Some guides, retirees and those who are not sole household supporters for example, are content with seasonal, part-time status. Others must be more resourceful to stay in the field and survive. Some have other freelance pursuits, such as writing, acting, and teaching, or work as tour managers, traveling abroad during their region's busy season. Some eventually open their own agencies and spend the off-season as other tour operators do, planning and marketing their tours. Still others are employed in other roles within the industry during their off-season. Some tour operators and destination management companies retain their best guides year-round, finding their expertise invaluable in the planning of tours and itineraries. This arrangement is often "win-win," as they are able to have exclusivity of a region's best guides and tour planners, and the guides are able to make a reasonable living.

SUMMARY

Tourism is one of the world's most dynamic industries, and promises to thrive well into the twenty-first century. Many believe tourism is not only growing but is evolving into a unified and more socially responsible industry, and that guides have an important—if presently obscure—role to play in it. In order for guides to become true partners in industry, however, a new level of communication and cooperation by guides and other industry professionals is essential.

4   *The Traveler*

"We are the first generation in human history to fly to other continents as easily as people once boarded a train to the next town . . . the first generation in human history for whom travel is not restricted to an affluent few, but is available to many."

—Arthur Frommer,
New World of Travel 1990

THE "TYPICAL" TOURIST

Few creatures bear more ridicule than the tourist. Tourists can create queues, slow traffic and food service, make noise, and crowd museums, galleries, and stores. Archetypal images of "typical tourists" pervade our media, our conversations, and our consciousness: they are insensitive nuisances, bearing too much luggage and too little tolerance, recklessly snatching pictures and souvenirs "so we can say we've been here." Typical tourists care more about maintaining their familiar routines, food, and domestic comforts than genuinely tuning in to discover new people and surroundings.

Who is the "typical tourist," so often derided by locals, media, and even travel industry personnel? Nearly everyone has been a traveler at some time, and most people are, in fact, quite proud of their travels. Yet none perceives himself as "typical," and in recent years "tourist" has acquired a pejorative connotation. Some would say that a tourist, as opposed to a traveler, is "one who takes tours," and to many, tours themselves are suspect. For some, the word "tour" evokes the image of masses of unadventurous, demanding people from somewhere else; "tourist," therefore, connotes an aggressive though ultimately passive traveler who requires the security of a group and wishes to drive by only the postcard images of a place.

In many regions, travelers of all kinds, no matter how gentle or sophisticated, are consistently treated with disdain by the local population. Since travel to most regions is generally seasonal, travelers seem to inundate a region during its ideal season—a time when many locals would just as soon have their homes to themselves. For example, residents of the Washington, D.C., area often complain that the perennial gridlock of motorcoaches, cars, and masses of tourists on foot during the Cherry Blossom season prevent them from enjoying this popular, short-lived phenomenon. Residents of some regions of Florida find that the winter season is "not what it used to be," with the tourists "taking over." Recently, a well-known urban publication featured five pages of photographs of unassuming "typical tourists," catching tired, disheveled families and overweight senior citizens unaware, crowding favorite museums, eating, reclining inelegantly on statuary, and otherwise marring the local landscape. The article was accompanied by equally demeaning prose, with such captions as "Visitors from Another Planet" and "It's Hot, They're Weird, They're Here"!

Those unsightly intruders, one can presume, are the "typical tourists"—throngs of outsiders invading our home region and favorite haunts. To counter the pejorative "tourist," tour packagers substitute countless euphemisms, such as "traveler," "guest," "adventurer," "explorer," "wanderer," "vagabond," and "shunpiker" (one who shuns turnpikes). Similarly, travel brochures replace "tour" with appellations such as "adventure," "journey," "escape," "trek," "exploration," "experience," and "study."

All too often, unfortunately, reports of insensitive travelers are woefully accurate. Since World War II, when large numbers of Americans began traveling internationally, the concept of the "ugly American"—a demanding and often insensitive tourist—emerged. Blessed with a relatively high standard of living, Americans have long been accused of insisting on their usual conveniences wherever they travel, even in places where the local people sustain a vastly lower standard of living and where providing deluxe accommodations creates great economic or environmental strain. Many travelers, not just Americans, exhibit a tendency to cling to the familiar, and most need to be nudged beyond their comfort zones to taste unfamiliar food and endure different climates, customs, and modes of behavior and thinking. Clearly, both travelers and travel professionals could benefit from a more informed view of travel and a deeper understanding of the positive interactions travelers can have with local populations.

It is well worth noting, however, that more enlightened attitudes toward travelers do exist throughout the world. Some would say that better service and heightened sensitivity toward travelers—evidenced by the growth of ecotourism, rural tourism, and the popularity of such organizations as the Center for Responsible Tourism—is a hallmark of the 1990s.

A warm welcome and superior service have traditionally been evident in many regions where tourism is a dominant industry. In Hawaii, front-line workers and managers in hotels, airports, restaurants, and virtually all attractions seem instinctively prone to cheerful hospitality. Europeans have a well-known tradition of exemplary service, particularly evident in hotels and restaurants. And in many developing countries, service personnel, acutely aware of the impact of tourism to their survival, are respectful of and responsive to travelers' needs. Thus, in many of these countries—Kenya, for example—to be a guide is to be recognized as an important member of society.

As caretaker of the nation's parklands, the United States National Park Service has long referred to travelers as "visitors," invoking an image of a welcomed guest. According to Dale Ditmanson, of the National Park's Mather Employee

Development Center, the use of the word "visitor" is deliberate and important. In the case of Americans visiting national parks, "using the term visitor implies that people come to visit a place they already own," he says. "And, as their hosts, that we're there to serve them, not simply make a buck from them."

In spite of the above-mentioned stereotypes, there is no "typical" tourist any more than there is a typical person. To be sure, attempts to count, classify, and describe travelers collectively are interesting and invaluable. Statistics serve the industry well by informing suppliers of demands, forecasting future trends, and otherwise educating the industry. But generalizations about travelers can be misleading and even dangerous. It is often easy to forget that large groups of people are, in fact, composed of individuals with unique life experiences, perceptions, needs, desires, and goals, and much to share with local people. Each has paid for his or her rite of passage to the visited region, and each deserves individual attention.

Travelers are the very reason tourism exists and flourishes, and disdain for travelers is appallingly misguided. Every time a local person treats a visitor poorly or derides him as an intrusion, he is, in effect, "biting the hand that feeds him." He is overlooking the fact that, directly or indirectly, he is usually benefiting from the traveler's presence. As noted previously, the power of tourism is mammoth, as it is travelers who drive the dynamic tourism industry. Directly or indirectly travelers hire, fire, and support guides and others in the industry. Despite the potential for tourism to affect a region negatively, travelers more often contribute immeasurably by providing jobs, tax dollars, and the very reason that many businesses exist. In addition, travel and tourism is, to a large extent, a "clean" industry, generating relatively little pollution. Beyond the direct economic impact of tourism are the staggering advances in transportation and telecommunications, as well as opportunities for education, diplomacy, and cross-cultural understanding.

It should go without saying that the public and the industry must not merely endure travelers but—since they literally determine whether or not tourism exists—honor them by going the extra mile to understand and accommodate their needs. Far from being objects of ridicule, travelers should be warmly welcomed everywhere. Certainly one of the vital tasks of the travel industry—and specifically that of guides—must be to dispel the common pejorative perception of the "typical tourist" as an unwelcome intrusion. Guides must learn to respect and appreciate travelers for what they are: the lifeline of tourism and an economic and diplomatic asset to their own region or country. In the coming years, with virtually every country on earth competing for tourists, the local perceptions of and treatment by locals will become increasingly important.

Who Is the Traveler?

In order to better understand travelers and their needs, the travel industry and government agencies use a wide variety of methods to analyze and describe travelers, demographically, psychologically, and sociologically. As travel becomes increasingly available to a wider variety of people throughout the world, the profile of travelers changes. Statistics show that greater numbers of people are traveling to and from a wider variety of places, for many different reasons, and with a wider variety of interests, expectations, and needs.

Just as guides embody many roles, including leader, educator, host, and conduit, so do travelers have a wide array of roles. They are students and teachers, guests and ambassadors, clients and consumers. Travelers can be categorized in many other ways. As a way of illustrating the behavior of travelers and their impact on a region, anthropologist Valene Smith described travelers within the following seven classifications (1977):

1. *Explorers* are participant-observers, such as anthropologists, who travel alone or in very small groups and mesh with the local population and accommodate their lifestyle. They do not require special tourist accommodations or attractions and therefore pose little or no threat to local populations.

2. *Elite travelers* can afford to spend much in order to have unusual travel experiences. Like explorers, they are few in number and therefore do not impose a significant strain on local regions. But unlike explorers, they demand some degree of comfort in amenities.

3. *Off-beat tourists* travel alone or in very small numbers and seek to avoid crowds, other tourists, and typical sightseeing. They adapt well to local lifestyles and amenities and pose few problems for locals.

4. *Unusual tourists* tend to demand more amenities, but, through tours, also seek unusual, adventurous, or primitive experiences.

5. *Incipient mass tourists* represent the steady influx of business and vacation travelers. They usually travel individually or in small groups and demand Western-style amenities.

6. *Mass tourists* are large groups of middle-class travelers who inundate popular sites everywhere and also demand Western-style amenities.

7. *Charter tourists* always arrive en masse, generating a large volume of business but often desiring impersonal, standardized services. Impact on the local region is great, and, in order to accommodate these large numbers, tour operators must offer name tags, buffet lines, and little one-to-one interaction with visitors and locals.

Smith notes that as the number of tourists increases, different expectations emerge, more facilities are required to handle them, and more stressful contacts between hosts and guests occur. Moreover, she and others suggest that mass and charter tourists are so concerned with having Western-style amenities that they place an undue strain on local economies, environments, and cultures to provide those services. Ultimately, this contributes to the eradication of a region's unique lifestyle. "When charter tourism appears," she says, "nationality is no longer locally significant, for the only economic base able to generate charter tourism is Western society, whose members are fast approaching cultural and economic homogeneity."

As guides depend upon and interact with mass and charter tourists, it is vital that they have an understanding of the impact of mass tourism on both travelers and locals. The issue of socially responsible tourism will certainly become more important and be more widely discussed over the next few decades, and guides will have greater responsibility and opportunity to make a difference in this area. This issue and the guide's role in it are discussed later in this chapter and in Chapter 13, "Professional Ethics and Etiquette."

Characteristics of Travelers

In the years following World War II and the dawn of the age of jet travel, Americans have traveled in far greater numbers than those of other nationalities. In recent decades the complexion and nature of travelers have changed dramatically, to include travelers of virtually all nations and especially large numbers from Japan, Germany, Canada, and Great Britain. The global economy has irrevocably opened up travel lines and brought people together.

Although generalizations about people must always be tempered with caution, statistics combined with observations of prevailing trends can provide helpful sociological descriptions of travelers. In 1988, The United States Travel Data Center at the Travel Industry Association of America (TIAA) published a detailed sociological analysis of travelers called *Discover America 2000: The Implications of America's Changing Demographics and Attitudes on the U.S. Travel Industry.* This study offers an extensive profile of the United States population, both present and future. The premise of this analysis is that travel behavior is determined by a number of factors, including economic and social environments and generational influences (defined as the common set of values and attitudes shared by those who come of age during a particular decade). In this analysis, the Untied States population was defined within seven "generational groups." Each group was described fully in terms of lifestyle, work, earning capability, and spending habits, now and in the year 2000, with implications for their travel habits. The seven generational groups featured in the TIAA analysis are: the Baby Boomlets, the Baby Busters, the Late Baby Boomers, the Early Baby Boomers, the World War II Babies, the Depression Babies, and the World War I Babies. Although this analysis focuses on the U.S. population, to some extent this characterization can be applied to other groups as well, particularly those in the Western world. These groups and their likely travel patterns are described below.

1. The *Baby Boomlet* group, the youngest of all the groups, consists of those born between 1977 and 1988. This generation will be young adults with limited financial resources through 2000. While they are not direct purchasers of travel in the 1990s, they are significant in several ways. As children of the Baby Boomers, they will travel with their families more than others of the same age have done previously. In the 1990s, travel packagers and marketers must indirectly cater to this group by offering more attractive and convenient options for family groups. In 2000 and beyond, they will likely be more favorably inclined to travel

than others, and they are also likely to be more discerning and more demanding travelers. Travelers in this category will be strongly affected by television, new technologies, and trends emerging in the 1990s.

2. *Baby Busters,* those born between 1965 and 1976, were largely influenced by the 1980s, a decade marked by great spending, materialism, supply-side economics, independent thinking, frequent travel, a vast array of lifestyle options tempered with a realization that "you can't have it all." These characteristics, combined with such societal trends as a shrinking labor force, might lead this group, as the year 2000 approaches, to travel frequently, especially for business and within family groups; to be more demanding and difficult to please; and to be more familiar and comfortable with international travelers and visitors.

3. *Late Baby Boomers,* born between 1955 and 1964, were primarily influenced by the 1970s, a decade that saw Watergate, the end of the Vietnam War, the "me" generation; a decade characterized by self-analysis and self-fulfillment, with a particular emphasis placed upon youth and teenage subculture and the rights of women and minorities. These people are widely regarded as acquisitive, with a "live for today" attitude. As travel is likely an integral part of life for many in this group, they are frequent and demanding travelers, and are likely to travel often for both business and pleasure, alone or with their families, into the next decade.

4. *Early Baby Boomers,* those born between 1946 and 1954, were largely influenced by the 1960s, a decade noted for rejection of traditional values, the women's movement, and the inception of a concern for physical fitness, the environment, and civil rights. Travel forecasters expect this group to have great impact on travel trends as they approach their middle and later years with more money and time than any generation before them.

5. *World War II Babies,* those born between 1935 and 1945, were influenced largely by the 1950s and are described as having a strong work ethic and high standards, but as less demanding than other groups. With ample discretionary time and money, as people in this group retire they are more likely than other groups to prefer group travel.

6. *Depression Babies,* those born between 1924 and 1934, were influenced largely by the 1940s and are described as more cost-conscious and conservative. Those who travel prefer trips with their families or tours offering comfort, convenience, and value.

7. *World War I Babies,* those born before 1924, were influenced by the 1930s. They are the most frugal of all travelers. Family and financial security are top priorities for these people, and the few trips they are likely to take involve other family activities or health or medical purposes.

Where and How Are People Traveling?

Not only are greater numbers of people traveling, but they are traveling to a wider variety of destinations. As always, people will continue to travel to places that appeal to them as significant, exciting, convenient, and cost-effective. Many countries are beginning to recognize the potential of tourism as an economic stimulus. It is becoming increasingly evident that these countries are actively seeking ways to lure travelers to their region. A few of the many rising stars in travel are the South American countries of Peru, Venezuela, and Ecuador; Latin America and the Caribbean countries; and the Eastern European countries.

In countries with traditionally high visitation rates—the United States, England, France, and the former Soviet Union, for example—visitors are choosing to venture deeper into more rural or previously untapped areas and are more willing (and even eager) to do without amenities in order to experience the authentic folklife of an area. To cite a few examples, wine and canal tours are flourishing in France, bicycle tours and home stays are popular in many countries, and trekking in remote areas of the world—especially Peru and parts of India, Nepal, and Tibet—has never been more popular.

In general, the industry is responding to the blossoming, diversifying market with a wide variety of travel services and products. Examples of such trends include personalized itineraries; tours to rural and remote locations; study vacations; more comfortable and cost-effective opportunities for solo travelers, international travelers, and women; more adventurous tours affording greater contact with local populations; and more emphasis on superior, customer-oriented service, multilingual interpretations, and culturally and environmentally sensitive travel experiences.

Why Do People Travel?

Beyond the information that opinion polls and statisticians convey about travelers, psychologists and sociologists offer vital insight on the nature, needs, and desires of travelers. It behooves those in the travel industry to understand why people travel and what these reasons mean to guides and others in the industry.

Maslow's well-known *hierarchy of needs* is often applied to human travel behavior. Maslow held that man's primary goal is—or should be—the integration of self, or self-actualization, but that his actions and motivations are determined by a hierarchy, or chronology, of needs. His hierarchy of needs is often illustrated as a pyramid. These needs range from the most basic physical needs of food, water, and shelter (at the base of the pyramid), to acceptance, love, self-esteem, and finally, self-actualization (at the pyramid's vertex). Once fundamental needs are satisfied, an individual becomes better able or driven to achieve the next highest level.

Early humans traveled primarily to satisfy their most basic needs; most travelers today have long since satisfied these needs. Affluent enough to travel, they are generally seeking education, relaxation, companionship, and adventure, elements that could satisfy the needs of acceptance and even self-actualization.

Maslow's hierarchy can also be applied to one's daily travels, and this application is relevant—even vital—to the guide's interaction with travelers. For example, guides must always be mindful of passengers' daily hierarchy of needs. Indeed, travelers will be indifferent to even the most exhilarating ventures if they are hungry, thirsty, cold, or overheated. This application of Maslow's theory is discussed further in Chapter 7, "Leadership and Social Skills."

Lloyd E. Hudman (1989) identified reasons why individuals are motivated to travel: health, curiosity, sports, pleasure, spiritual or religious reasons, professional and business reasons, to visit friends and relatives, to explore one's roots, and status. In Hudman's model, virtually all kinds of excursions and tours fall within one of these categories.

THE GROUP TRAVELER

Although many people prefer to travel alone or with small groups of family or friends, millions of individuals prefer group travel, and their numbers are ever increasing. The National Tour Association cites comfort, safety, education, economy, and companionship as the primary reasons people opt for group travel. Group travel often offers the easiest and often the only way to gain access to some places.

Only a decade ago the vast majority of group travelers were senior citizens. Not only did retirees have more available time and money than others, they were more likely to seek the safety, comfort, and companionship that group travel offers. As mentioned elsewhere, however, the profile of the group tour traveler is changing. In recent years, the travel industry has responded to the growing number of travelers by providing a virtually unlimited menu of travel experiences and tours. Consequently, group travelers today include families, extended family reunions, corporate travelers, association executives, association members, clubs and affinity groups of all kinds, school groups, university and alumni groups, people with disabilities, greater numbers of foreign and domestic independent travelers (FITs and DITs) joining groups, and business and incentive groups. These and other groups are discussed in Chapter 3, "Tourism".

Because groups provide the greatest opportunities for guides, some of the more popular kinds of groups are noted below, along with a description of their characteristics and the special challenges they pose for guides.

Student Groups

Student tours are quite popular in some regions, particularly in historic places or in places that lend themselves in some way to a school's curriculum. Virtually every state and provincial capital is a destination for regional school groups, as are cities with zoos, fine museums, historic homes, and other educational attractions.

Students in groups usually fall between the ages of 11 and 17. Specific occa-

Figure 4.1
At historic homes, such as Thomas Jefferson's Monticello in Charlottesville, Virginia, guides will often interpret for hundreds of people in one day. (*Photo by Vern Wayne Pond, with permission of the Thomas Jefferson Memorial Foundation.*)

sions for student group travel include senior class trips, safety patrol trips, and trips in conjunction with specific curricula topics. For example, in the United States, most eighth-grade students in public schools study American history, and trips to historic areas such as Boston, New York City, Washington, D.C., and Virginia are popular.

Particular challenges are inherent when working with students. Students usually travel with their teachers, who act as chaperones. It is essential for chaperones and guides to establish clear ground rules, and, unlike most adult groups, students require discipline. Many guides find it best to allow accompanying teachers to set the organizational and disciplinary tone for the tour; as chaperones, their primary duty is the students' safety. Moreover, teachers are more familiar with the curriculum, the school's regulations, and the learning levels of the students, all factors that establish the tone of a student tour. It is understood that the guide will primarily conduct the tour at the level of understanding of the students rather than the adults'.

Business Travelers

Business travelers include those who are visiting a region primarily to conduct business, such as sales, research, meetings, and conferences. For guides and those involved in tours and sightseeing planning, the important distinction to keep in mind for business travelers is that sightseeing is usually tangential to their trip. Business travelers are therefore more likely to be interested in a light overview rather than an in-depth tour. In fact, many business travelers are regular travelers and may already have visited a region, may be pressed for time, or are simply looking for assistance in seeing a city or region on their own. In the case of conventions, tours are generally brief and structured and are usually prearranged by meeting planners.

Incentive Travelers

Incentive travelers are business people who have won trips by competing with their colleagues for sales goals. These people visit an area primarily for pleasure. The field of incentive travel is highly competitive and specialized, and most incentive tours are contracted through incentive houses, which have particularly high standards of service.

Families

Demographers point out that family travel is on the rise, owing to the rising numbers of baby boomers and senior citizens with children and grandchildren. As both of these groups have money and are devoting more leisure time to travel, catering to families is becoming a trend within the industry.

Hosting tours for families provides an interesting challenge as interpretations must appeal to two, and sometimes three, generations. In tours with parents and infants or toddlers, interpretations should be directed toward the adults, with consideration for their need to care for their children while moving around. Once children reach the age of four and older, however, parents will be grateful to the guide who directs commentary toward the children and who interacts with them, asking them questions, getting them to talk about what they know and what they want to know about the area. Although it may seem awkward for some guides to speak on the level of a ten-year-old while adults are present and participating, parents themselves are usually more comfortable with this arrangement, as they are accustomed to viewing places through the eyes of their children. Many guides talk primarily with children, adding occasional comments and clarification for adults.

Senior Citizens

Recently the American Association of Retired Persons (AARP) held a workshop for tour managers entitled "Working with the Senior Citizens." In one exercise participants were asked to name characteristics of the older traveler. A voluminous stream of responses ensued, some favorable, some unfavorable, some contradictory. The responses included: demanding, slow, patient, impatient, forthright, repetitive, punctual, and so forth. Participants quickly saw that, despite their belief that they could stereotype senior citizens, the characteristics of older people simply reflect those of human nature as a whole. Contrary to some perspectives, people do not arise on the morning of their sixty-sixth birthdays grumpy, demanding, or impatient. The aging process seems, however, to accentuate eccentricities, and as they age, people often become caricatures of their best and worst selves.

Many guides find senior citizens to be the groups of choice. Younger senior citizens participate in some of the most active, adventure-oriented tours available, while older senior citizens often prefer more passive, leisurely tours.

Clubs or Affinity Groups

These groups always have a common denominator, such as a shared church or interest. These groups are usually enjoyable (especially when the values or interests of the group coincide with that of the guide), as they are preacquainted and presumably compatible.

Public Tour Groups

Often the only element participants in a public tour have in common is that they decided to visit the same place at the same time. As these individuals are usually unacquainted, the guide's first and most obvious challenge is to interpret to an often diverse group of people and, at the same time, attempt to unite the group. This can be an exciting challenge for the guide: to find and interpret points of interest in such a way that all members of the group can relate. If done effectively, this often serves as a catalyst for integrating the group.

INTERNATIONAL TRAVELERS

As travel becomes attainable for greater numbers of people throughout the world, international travelers[1] become more prevalent in every country. Al-

---

[1]I prefer the term *international traveler* to that of *foreigner*, which implies a lack of acceptance and serves only to alienate. In an increasingly global society the word "foreign" is declining in usage, particularly within the travel industry.

though working with multicultural groups poses some challenges not present in more familiar or more homogenous groups, the overriding characteristics of multicultural groups are a more dynamic, provocative, informative, and rewarding experience for both visitor and guide.

The twentieth-century surge in international travel and communications has spawned a vast amount of literature, theory, and advice about how to better understand and work with international travelers. Interpreting the diverse customs, body language, and personalities of people throughout the world can be confusing, and often the slightest, most innocently conceived comment or gesture can alarm or offend visitors.

Roger E. Axtell's *Do's and Taboos Around the World* (1985) is an enlightening and often humorous reference for those who work with international visitors. In it, he highlights customs and offers guidelines for behavior in such areas as greeting, punctuality, gift giving, dress, gestures, and general protocol for regions and countries throughout the world. Resources such as these are invaluable in an increasingly intercultural world. And yet, thriving in the hospitality industry requires an understanding that extends beyond mere descriptions of behavior and personality.

The Washington International Center in Washington, D.C., has introduced international visitors to American society for several decades. In this role, they have attempted to observe and understand people throughout the world at the most fundamental level—their values. Facilitators at the center use an iceberg analogy to illustrate the difference between personality and values. Personality, as the most visible aspect, can be likened to the surface of the iceberg. People are often judged only on the basis of personality, or what can be seen of that personality—mannerisms, and style of dress and speech. Those who interact beyond a purely superficial level may come to understand more about a person's beliefs. These basic beliefs correspond to the portion of the iceberg above the water but just below the outer surface. On a deeper and more fundamental level are a person's values, corresponding to the foundation of the iceberg. Although hidden from view, values represent the core of the person.

Values are so basic and so deeply ingrained that it is sometimes difficult for people to recognize their own or perceive that they are unique. Those who specialize in training people to work with groups of different ages, cultures, or socioeconomic backgrounds stress the importance of attempting to see one's own values, beliefs, and behavior as objectively as possible, or "as others see us."

The most fundamental aspect of relating to people from other countries is attempting to understand and appreciate their values, and the best way of doing this is to explore another's values as they contrast with one's own. L. Robert Kohls, an acclaimed leader in cross-cultural research and training, created an enlightening overview of basic American values for the Washington International Center.

"Most Americans would have a difficult time telling you, specifically, what the values are which Americans live by," says Kohls, in his essay "The Values Americans Live By," an insightful and instructive exploration of the topic of values. "They have never given the matter any thought." Even if they had, they would likely assert that a definitive list of American values is impossible, he says, illustrating one of the most basic American values: "the belief that every individual is so unique that the same list of values could never be applied to all, or even most, of their fellow citizens" (Kohls 1984).

"It is not enough simply to familiarize yourself with these values," Kohls contends. "You must also, so far as possible, consider them without the negative or derogatory connotation which they might have for you, based on your own experience and cultural identity." The following are Kohls's thirteen "Values Americans Live By."

1. *Control over the environment.* Free will and the ability to overcome obstacles are important concepts to Americans. By contrast, Americans often look upon people who feel their life is entirely controlled by fate as backward and naive. In fact, "to be called fatalistic," Kohls suggests, "is one of the worst criticisms one can level on many Americans." In contrast, many societies place more of an emphasis on tradition and ritual.

2. *Change.* To Americans, change is not only inevitable and vital, but it is virtually synonymous with progress, growth, development, and improvement. Many older, more traditional cultures consider change disruptive and destructive to their way of life, and instead value stability, continuity, and ritual.

3. *Time and its control.* Time is extremely important to most Americans. Planning and managing time are more than measures of success; some would call them a national obsession. Kohls cites the many references to time in American language, "a clear indication of how much it is valued. Time is something to 'be on,' 'kept,' 'filled,' 'saved,' 'used,' 'spent,' 'wasted,' 'lost,' 'gained,' 'planned,' 'given,' 'made the most of' and even 'killed.'"

4. *Equality/egalitarianism.* Although Kohls notes that Americans differ in their opinions about how to make the ideal into a reality, he calls equality one of Americans' "most cherished values," noting that they regard it as so important that "they have given it a religious basis," believing that "God views all humans alike without regard to intelligence, physical condition, or economic status. In secular terms," he reasons, "this belief is translated into the assertion that all people have an equal opportunity to succeed in life."

5. *Individualism and privacy.* Kohls points out that Americans prize individuality and like to think of themselves as unique—to a greater extent than is actually true. As an example he cites the two-party system. With few exceptions, most Americans are either Republicans or Democrats. Americans also regard privacy as their birthright, and many strive toward privacy to a degree not valued or even known in some other cultures.

6. *Self-reliance.* Americans generally feel responsibility and take credit only for that which they accomplish themselves. The original concept of the self-made

man or woman is an American ideal, that anyone from any level of society is free to move to a higher station. In recent years self-help literature—embracing everything from *Thin Thighs in 30 Days* to *Think and Grow Rich*—has outsold almost every other genre of American writing.

7. *Competition and free enterprise.* Americans believe that competitiveness is an innate human drive that accentuates the best in people. The American economic system of free enterprise and capitalism is rooted in this perspective. Citizens from many other societies, where cooperation is valued much more highly, often find this quality in Americans offensive.

8. *Future orientation.* Americans have long believed in, invested in, and planned for the future to such an extent that many would argue that they devalue both the past and present. In some cultures, such as the traditional Moslem world, where talking about or actively planning for the future is felt to be futile and even sinful, Americans are seen as having an unhealthy obsession with the future.

9. *Action/work orientation.* Compared with many people throughout the world, Americans plan and schedule extremely busy lives. Productivity and effective time management are valued quite highly. Along these lines, Americans value their work—many, in fact, are workaholics—and feel it "sinful" to "waste time" or live idle lives. Kohls notes that the first question one American is likely to ask another is, "What do you do?"

10. *Informality.* People from other countries are struck by or even offended by the informality of Americans. The informality takes on many forms: addressing each other—even those in authority—by first name; greeting people informally, such as touching one's arm and saying "hi!"; and dressing casually for restaurants, theaters, and churches. Misunderstandings can result, for while those from some cultures might view easy familiarity as rude and insulting, to most Americans it is a compliment.

11. *Directness, openness, and honesty.* The great differences among cultures regarding this value has particular implications for cross-cultural understanding in travel. As can be seen in the popularity of assertiveness training and other self-empowerment programs, Americans value a direct approach in communication. Conversely, many other cultures find the behaviors taught in these programs offensive.

12. *Practicality and efficiency.* Americans take pride in being realistic, practical, and efficient. As an example, Kohls notes that Americans are more likely to ask, "Will it make money?" or "Will it pay for itself?" than "Will it advance the cause of knowledge?" Because of their pragmatic approach, Americans have contributed more inventions to the world than any other culture.

13. *Materialism/acquisitiveness.* Although Americans generally do not see themselves as materialistic, other cultures feel differently. By any standard, Americans have an abundance of possessions. Moreover, Americans consume more than people of any other culture and generally retain their possessions for shorter periods of time than do people in other countries.

It is important to reiterate Kohl's caveat that these are broad descriptions, and do not apply to all Americans. The goal of this exploration of human values and behavior is not to pigeonhole people but, rather, to better understand them. Moreover, the values as described here are not to be interpreted as a norm against which other behaviors are to be considered strange or abnormal. Instead, by shedding light on differences, one can enhance his relationships with others. For example, an American guide conducting a tour for a group of Japanese travelers was baffled and disconcerted to learn after a tour was finished that the group had been dissatisfied with their meals and sightseeing. Not a single person had approached the guide at any point during the tour to discuss those feelings. For Americans, expressing dissatisfaction and requesting changes are common, considered by many to be not only one's right as a customer but a sign of a sophisticated, quality-oriented traveler. Thus, when Americans work with other Americans, they usually have an instinctive sense of their effectiveness. On the other hand, Americans traveling abroad are often seen as abrasive and selfish when they voice their criticisms openly and honestly. In the case noted above, however, several deeply rooted values prevented the Japanese travelers from confronting their guide about their dissatisfaction. For one, the Japanese—and those of many cultures—prefer a more indirect approach to avoid "losing face," and any complaint voiced directly to a guide would be seen as extremely rude.

With an understanding of this deep-seated difference in American and Japanese values, a guide might ask his or her visitors for their opinions, try to be more attentive to any cues they do give, and even encourage them, while in the United States, to express their preferences or criticisms more openly.

GROUP TRAVELERS: GATHERINGS OF INDIVIDUALS

Any discussion of group travel must stress that, regardless of its homogeneity or how it is classified, a group is ultimately a collection of unique individuals. One of the challenges to the industry and to the guide in particular is to offer a more personalized level of service to group travelers. Unfortunately, condescending, substandard behavior toward groups is rampant throughout the industry. One guide related this story:

While in college I worked as a waitress in a restaurant in a popular tourist region. We called group travelers "bus people," and, I confess, served them rather grudgingly. While we loved the quick boons to our pockets, we thought of them differently simply because they came in groups. I can still hear the manager groaning, "Get 'em in and out of here." I remember the first time I saw the scenario from the other side in a similarly run restaurant, after I became a guide. Everyone raced around like Keystone Cops—never taking even a few moments to learn a little about the group or to allow the group to get to know them—obviously viewing us as a problem to be gotten rid of as quickly as possible.

I now see how much everyone loses with that mind set, and how misguided and rude it is, as it epitomizes "biting the hand that feeds you."

Unfortunately, this example is not unusual. As noted earlier, many people would prefer that no one travel in groups. Group travel is here to stay, however, and the industry must find more congenial ways to accommodate group travelers. Indeed, those who succeed in the travel industry will be those who excel in serving a wide variety of people. Thus, the guide has an important opportunity to better accommodate people who travel in groups.

The accelerated changes occurring in society and the changing character of the traveling public offer new challenges to guides. In catering to today's travelers, guides are called upon to meet these and many other challenges:

- Because travelers will come from and visit virtually every country, they will be more diverse in their tastes, behavior, and values. Guides must therefore pursue a deeper understanding of a wide range of countries and cultures.
- Because most travelers will be exposed to other cultures through television, movies, videos, and travel, guides must be able to provide a broader, more cosmopolitan perspective.
- Because they are more likely to travel and to have traveled than previous generations, travelers in the 1990s may be more discriminating and demanding about the level of service and care they receive.
- Because of increased demands on time, travelers may wish to see more in less time. Contrary to this trend, however, many other travelers are opting less for busy, whirlwind itineraries and more for in-depth, slower-paced excursions, such as archaeological tours or wildlife photography tours.
- Those who have already traveled to popular regions will be more interested in unusual or "off-the-beaten-path" ventures, providing more opportunities for guides in rural or previously overlooked sites.
- Along the same lines, the future will demand that many guides specialize in a wide variety of areas, such as nature, architecture, or foreign and sign languages.

THE RESPONSIBLE TRAVELER

Although much has been said here about the industry's responsibility to travelers, any discussion about travelers would not be complete without mention of the responsibility of travelers in today's global society. Many have observed that mankind has reached a crossroads, a point at which many of the most cherished aspects of civilized life are threatened: regionality, languages, cultures, wildlife, rich ecosystems, and even the earth itself. Consequently, travelers and the travel industry are obliged to adopt a more socially responsible approach toward travel.

Lou D'Amore, who conceived the First Global Conference, "Tourism: A Vital Force for Peace" (1990), says, "For the first time in history, we embark on a segment of the human journey with a global perspective—an awareness of the inter-connectedness of all people and all life on earth. We recognize for the first time that there are no 'foreign countries' or 'foreign people'; rather we are all neighbours living interdependently as members of a 'Global Family.'"

The roles of traveler and host are so interrelated that they sometimes seem inseparable. One guide described it this way: "Whenever I meet a group of people and begin to travel with them, I feel that I, too, am a traveler in my own terrain. As I try to see this area through their eyes, I see it in a way I never have before. I'm sure I learn as much from visitors as they learn from me." Such a realization encourages openness and exchange, creating a situation in which guides can see themselves and all travelers as fellow citizens engaged in seeing the world together.

Travel industry professionals and guides in particular can serve as a link between local people and travelers, informing travelers of local environmental and cultural concerns and encouraging them to conduct themselves in more so-cially responsible ways, in tandem with local needs and customs. In this way, visitors develop a deeper understanding, and one would hope, a stronger com-mitment to conscious, humane behavior. (Ethical aspects of travel and guiding are covered more fully in Chapter 13, "Professional Ethics and Etiquette.")

At the close of the 1988 international tourism conference in Vancouver, or-ganizers issued the following "Credo of the Peaceful Traveler," eloquently ex-pressing a philosophy that guides would do well to employ and share with travelers:

Grateful for the opportunity to travel and to experience the world, and because peace begins with the individual, I affirm my personal responsibility and commitment to:
- *Journey with an open mind and gentle heart*
- *Accept with grace and gratitude the diversity I encounter*
- *Revere and protect the natural environment which sustains all life*
- *Appreciate all cultures I discover*
- *Respect and thank my hosts for their welcome*
- *Offer my hand in friendship to everyone I meet*
- *Support travel services that share these views and act upon them*
- *By my spirit, words, and actions, encourage others to travel the world in peace*

SUMMARY

As the lifeline of tourism, travelers deserve more careful attention and under-standing from guides and the industry at large. This chapter has explored the traveler on several levels—demographic, sociological, psychological, and cul-tural. Cultivating an understanding of travelers—and in so doing, learning more about ourselves—is merely the first of many important tasks for guides.

5 *Interpretation and the Role of the Guide*

"Through interpretation, understanding; through understanding, appreciation; through appreciation, protection."
—National Park Service Administration Manual

THE PRIMARY ROLE?

"The tour guide makes or breaks the tour." So goes one of the most ubiquitous clichés in the tour and travel industry. John Stein, owner of Washington Insider Tours, puts it this way: "You can, and often do, plan a tour for the better part of a year, working with a nice budget which allows you to stay in the finest hotels and dine at the best restaurants, and all is for naught if you don't have competent guides." Says another tour operator, "No other factor is as important." Few disagree on the importance of competent guides in effecting a successful tour. But what is a competent guide? What is important about what a guide provides?

A recent informal survey (Pond 1990)[1] asked guides, employers of guides, and travelers on tours to respond to questions relating to the purpose and importance of guides, and the extent to which guides fulfill travelers' needs. Among the questions asked were:

- Why do people hire guides?
- What is the guide's primary role?
- What are the guide's most important personal characteristics?
- In presenting places, to whom are guides most responsible: themselves, the site, their employer, the region, or the tourist?

The wide range of responses to this survey mirrored other studies which indicate that guides, employers, and travelers have different perceptions about

---

[1]This survey was conducted by mail and in person in early 1990 by the author. Fifty working guides and twenty tour operators throughout the United States were contacted. In addition, over 125 visitors to Washington, D.C., were invited to participate. The questions were open-ended, allowing participants to answer freely and without any suggestions of answers. Forty-two guides, nine tour operators, and 113 visitors completed the survey.

the specific purpose of a guide. And, in this study, guides themselves had the broadest range of opinions about their role. For example, in response to the question about their primary role, guide responses included "maintaining control of a group," "disseminating information," "efficiently getting people to as many sights as possible," "teaching history," "representing my city in a favorable way," and "passing on my passion for this region."

Tour operators placed the greatest importance on public relations, citing the goals of representing the region and the tour company in a favorable way. (Interestingly, no guides in this survey cited representing the tour company as among the most important). Foreign visitors were more likely than domestic visitors to view guides as representatives of the region or country and to attach perhaps a deeper, or at least a more sociological, significance by choosing labels such as "ambassador" and "interpreter of the culture."

The age of travelers weighed significantly in the evaluation of a guide's role. Senior citizens, who travel in groups more often than do other age groups, were more likely to see a guide in a social capacity, as "companion," "leader," or "caretaker of details, situations and personalities." Younger students responded most often by saying that the guide's purpose was to teach. Likewise, most of the teachers traveling with student groups allied the guide's role with their own. "We're both here to teach students about their history and their country," one teacher offered.

Although respondents differed in the values they ascribed to various guide roles, all agreed on two issues: (1) that the guide's role varies, depending upon the setting, the visitor, the purpose of the visit, and the guide himself; and (2) that one of the hallmarks of a professional guide is the ability to carry out a wide variety of duties and functions simultaneously.

Similar attitudes regarding the tour guide's role were found in J. Christopher Holloway's study (1981) of tour guides in Great Britain. By interviewing and observing guides on motorcoaches, Holloway attempted to develop an understanding and consistent description of the sociological function of guides. He concluded that guiding "is not yet institutionalized, and remains open to interpretation by guides and passengers alike."

In his study, Holloway observed "driver-couriers" and "registered guides"[2] on actual one-day excursions. Although the guides in Holloway's study were forewarned that a tourism researcher might join their tour, they "generally assumed that a study was being made of tourists, and the passengers in turn accepted the writer as a trainee guide gaining practical experience on tours—a convenient misunderstanding which made it possible to take copious notes en

---

[2]*Courier,* a term more commonly used in Europe, is a tour manager or tour leader. According to Holloway, a courier is a guide whose responsibilities are "mainly those of shepherding and marshalling tourists and seeing to their needs during a tour." *Registered guides,* officially recognized by the British government, have completed a course of training and passed an examination given by one of England's Regional Tourist Boards.

route without arousing suspicion or curiosity." Following the tours, Holloway approached the drivers and guides, explained the nature of his research, and requested to interview them further.

As in the aforementioned survey, Holloway's study revealed that these guides hold their role as information giver in high regard—often much higher than either their employers or visitors expect or want. Holloway concludes that "the role of guiding involves a number of subsidiary and sometimes conflicting sub-roles, of which the information-giving function is emphasized by guides themselves, in their drive for professional status." Other observations from Holloway's study are featured later in this chapter.

Cohen's Pathfinder and Mentor

Sociologist/anthropologist Erik Cohen's study (1985) of the development of the role and function of the guide is perhaps the most extensive on the topic to date. Cohen refers to the development of guiding as the transition from the "Original Guide" to the "Professional Guide." He maintains that the modern guide descends from two distinct lineages, the *pathfinder* and the *mentor*. The pathfinder is primarily a geographic guide, "one who leads the way," usually a native with a firm understanding of the place but without specialized training. Examples that Cohen gives of the pathfinding role are mountain guides, safari guides, and fishing guides.

The mentor, according to Cohen, is a much more complex, heterogeneous role, such as a spiritual advisor in a pilgrimage or a personal traveling tutor. This mentor guide corresponds to the cicerone of the Grand Tour era. In Cohen's view, the role of the modern tourist guide "combines and expands elements from both antecedents, that of the pathfinder and that of the mentor. . . . The two, however, do not necessarily merge harmoniously; rather there exists incongruencies and tensions between these two major components of the modern role." Figure 5–1 shows Cohen's representation of guide roles.

The pathfinder and the mentor personify, respectively, the *leadership* and

Figure 5.1
Schematic representation of the principal components of the tourist guide's role. (*Source: Cohen, Erik. 1985. "The Tourist Guide: The Origins, Structure and Dynamics of a Role."* Annals of Tourism Research, *12:10.*)

	Outer-Directed	Inner-Directed
a. Leadership Sphere	(1) Instrumental	(2) Social
b. Mediatory Sphere	(3) Interactionary	(4) Communicative

mediatory spheres in the guide's role. Since each, according to Cohen, "has an inner- and an outer-directed aspect," four major components of the role can be extrapolated and examined: the instrumental, social, interactionary, and communicative components.

Cohen calls the "outer-directed aspect" of the leadership sphere the *instrumental component*. While "leading the way" is the basis of this component, Cohen describes other aspects within it, including (1) direction, or navigating a group, vehicle, or driver; (2) access, the capability of obtaining special access into places; and (3) control, corralling the group and holding to an itinerary while offering security and comfort.

Cohen refers to the "inner-directed aspect" within the leadership sphere as the *social component,* which he defines as that which relates to the task of bringing cohesion and morale to the group. This component requires four elements:

1. tension management of the group
2. integration, or inspiring sociability
3. humor and morale
4. animation, or inducing members of the group to participate in various activities offered on the tour

Cohen's mediatory sphere corresponds to the teacher, mentor, or guru line of origin. The outer-directed aspect of this sphere, which Cohen calls the *interactional component,* consists of two principal elements:

1. representation, in which the guide, as intermediary between the region and the visitor, "comes to represent the party to the setting, as well as the setting to the party"
2. organization, the need of the guide to work with facilities and local people in providing services

Finally, Cohen identifies the inner-directed aspect within the mediatory sphere as the *communicative component,* on which he elaborates most fully. "The principal dynamics in the transition from the Original to the Professional Guide's role is . . . away from leadership and toward mediating, and away from the outer- and toward the inner-directed sphere, with the Communicative Component becoming the kernel of the professional role." The communicative component is frequently considered to be the principal aspect of the guide's role, he says, and "it is certainly the component given primacy in the formal training of guides."

Four elements fall within Cohen's communicative component:

1. selection, the process by which the guide chooses what the visitor will and will not see or hear
2. dissemination of information[3]

---

[3]Cohen cites Holloway and others in that this is often perceived by both guides and others as the primary role of guides, taking on "an almost academic character."

3. interpretation, which he describes as "the essence of the role of the 'culture-broker,' . . . the translation of the strangeness of a foreign culture into a cultural idiom familiar to the visitors"

4. fabrication, or "outright invention or deception of guides." His examples of this include presenting fake antiques as if they were genuine, and taking visitors "surreptitiously to a false destination on the tour, but presenting it in a manner intended to convince its members that it is the one promised in the program."[4]

According to Cohen, "Interpretation, and not the mere dissemination of information, is the distinguishing communicative function of the trained tourist guide."

Having isolated the components of the guide's role, Cohen then focuses on the transition from the *original guide* (the simple pathfinder concerned mainly with instrumental activities) to the *professional guide* (the more sophisticated role, in which the communicative element is primary). The principal dynamic in the transition from the original to the professional guide's role is one away from leadership and toward mediating; away from the outer- and toward the inner-directed sphere (see Figure 5.2).

Most contemporary guides are hybrids of Cohen's original and professional guide paradigm to a far greater extent than Cohen seems to suggest. Certainly a less enlightened guide might not excel in the "mediatory spheres," and a more sophisticated guide could be a master interpreter and communicator. Guides today are expected to function, to some degree, in all spheres. A guide who mirrors Cohen's more highly evolved professional guide must also, as part of his or her work, operate in an "instrumental mode" by facilitating such functions

Figure 5.2
The dynamics of the tourist guide's role. (*Source: Cohen, Erik. 1985. "The Tourist Guide: The Origins, Structure and Dynamics of a Role."* Annals of Tourism Research, *12:17.*)

	Outer-Directed	Inner-Directed
a. Leadership Sphere	(1) Original Guide (Instrumental Primacy)	(2) Animator (Social Primacy)
b. Mediatory Sphere	(3) Tour Leader (Interactionary Primacy)	(4) Professional Guide (Communicative Primacy)

[4]One might question why Cohen treat fabrication within his discussion of the professional guide. In Cohen's view, such behavior must exist to such an extent that he feels compelled to include it as part of the communicative component of the guide. It raises the question of whether one might discuss similar undesirable behaviors practiced by unethical persons in other fields as part of the characteristics of that profession's roles. Misinformation unfortunately occurs within the profession and is discussed more fully in Chapter 13, "Professional Ethics and Etiquette."

as navigating the driver and the group, providing access to nonpublic places, and maintaining control of a group. Although some tours do have tour leaders who travel with the group expressly to handle administrative tasks, most do not. Menial administrative tasks are inescapable and are every bit as relevant for the professional guide, and indeed, are routinely regarded as extremely important by guides, tour operators, and travelers. The extent to which a guide operates more dominantly in one role or another often depends less on the professionalism of the guide than on the circumstances of a particular tour, the wishes of the guide's employer, and the needs of the visitors. It is virtually a requirement that guides not only embody all of Cohen's components but swing easily into different modes, as the situation demands.

SERVING THE TRAVELER'S NEEDS

It is not at all ironic that a field which so seeks to achieve higher professional standing lacks a consensus on the most basic questions about its practitioners' role. Clearly a gap exists, for example, between the needs and expectations of a large and growing traveling public and the perceived role of guides. Moreover, much current literature suggests that, in many cases, guides are not only not answering the desires and needs of travelers, but they are often unaware of those needs and care little about learning more about what travelers want. As noted elsewhere, many guides, driven to deliver an abundance of information, are failing visitors in ways more important to the visitor, such as offering basic hospitality, concierge-level assistance, and more personal or cultural insights.

Guides, like all players within the travel industry, must become more mindful of the goals and needs of travelers and adjust their services and products accordingly. This can be achieved through experience and by a commitment to learning more about and becoming more attuned to one's visitors. Considering the disparity between travelers' desires and what they actually experience necessitates further exploration of the guide roles and of the nature of travelers. (See Chapter 6, "Education," for a discussion of the educational status and needs of guides, and Chapter 4, "The Traveler," for an inquiry into who they are, why they travel, and what their needs and desires are.) A further consideration of travelers on the part of guides and tour planners must become a primary concern in building a respected profession. Such an understanding is important in the establishment of standards, policy, core competencies, and curricula.

Just as individuals and communities develop over time, professions also pass through stages. According to Marcella Wells, an interpreter with the U.S. Forest Service, guiding as a profession appears to be moving from childhood toward adolescence, a time in which many questions about its identity arise. Although guides have existed for many centuries, the movement toward establishing higher standards and professional requirements for guiding is relatively recent.

Tilden and the Roots of Interpretation

Holloway noted in 1981 the paucity of studies on guides and tours and expressed hope that his study would act as a springboard for others. Although little published research on commercial guiding has appeared since Holloway's study, it would be an error to suggest that the professional guide has no philosophical or empirical foundation from which to draw. It is appropriate instead to recognize that a philosophy and even an extensive body of research and literature does exist, and has for some time, within the field of interpretation. To the great extent that practitioners and researchers in the field of interpretation have tediously and carefully explored the sociological, educational, and cultural underpinnings of guiding, an overview of interpretation is useful here.

Interpretation has a noble origin. As noted earlier, the concept and practice of interpretation is rooted in the mission of the United States National Park Service (NPS) itself. Its creators believed that there were certain places so magnificent or significant as to oblige one generation to preserve them for the enjoyment of those to follow. The goal of interpretation was not merely to provide information, but rather to convey the magnificence of a place, pass on its legacy, inspire visitors, and ultimately convince them of the need to preserve park lands. The epigraph to this chapter has become an unofficial motto of interpretation: "through interpretation, understanding; through understanding, appreciation; through appreciation, protection."

William Everhart, long-time director of the NPS Interpretation program, describes the evolution of the use of the term this way in *Tourism: The Good, the Bad, and the Ugly:*

The word "interpretation" came gradually to replace the term "education," in part no doubt to avoid any suggestion that the modest appetite for knowledge that the average visitor carries with him while on vacation would be promptly submerged in a tide of completely accurate but exquisitely boring facts. But interpretation also seemed a better term to describe the function dealing with subjects that for most people were unfamiliar—geology, biology, botany. It was almost like learning a new language. The process of translating this language, the language of the earth, suggested the term "interpretation."

Many regard the field of interpretation as officially beginning—or at least as being given its most dramatic boost—in 1957, with the publication of Freeman Tilden's *Interpreting Our Heritage,* widely regarded as the classic philosophical work on the subject of interpretation. Tilden defines interpretation as "an educational activity which aims to reveal meanings and relationships through the use of original objects, by firsthand experience, and by illustrative media, rather than simply to communicate factual information."

The "objects" Tilden refers to encompass any resources and raw materials visitors might encounter: for the museum guide, they may be objects of art; for the park ranger, the shed antlers of a deer; for the city guide, monuments or architectural ornamentation.

Regardless of its type, Tilden proposed that effective interpretation is based upon six principles:

I. Any interpretation that does not somehow relate what is being displayed or described to something within the personality or experience of the visitor will be sterile.

II. Information, as such, is not Interpretation. Interpretation is revelation based upon information. But they are entirely different things. However, all interpretation includes information.

III. Interpretation is an art, which combines many arts, whether the materials presented are scientific, historical, or architectural. Any art is in some degree teachable.

IV. The chief aim of Interpretation is not instruction, but provocation.

V. Interpretation should aim to present a whole rather than a part and must address itself to the whole man rather than any phase.

VI. Interpretation addressed to children (say, up to the age of twelve) should not be a dilution of the presentation to adults, but should follow a fundamentally different approach. To be at its best, it will require a separate program.

The bulk of Tilden's book supports these six principles with examples and anecdotes accumulated from his own and others' interpretative experiences, mostly within the National Park Service program.

Since the publication of Tilden's seminal work, these principles have been distilled, refined, embellished, debated, embraced, and rejected, but they continue to be the foundation on which the field of interpretation has been built. All of the principles of interpretation and much of the related literature are explored throughout this book.

Are "Guiding" and "Interpretation" Synonymous?

As noted in the previous chapter, it is no longer accurate to ascribe interpretation solely to the National Park Service, for a growing number of public- and private-sector organizations are adopting the formal tenets and techniques of interpretation into their own programs. One major difference between the work of those who call themselves "interpreters" and those who use the term "guide" is that interpreters are often employed at a particular site, such as a national park. Guides, on the other hand, are more likely to travel with people throughout a city or region. Although this distinction would not seem to make a profound difference in the role a guide or interpreter plays, it might mean that guides, by virtue of spending more time with the same guests and accompanying them to meals and hotels, have more social and administrative responsibilities toward visitors. There are, however, an increasing number of exceptions to the distinction of interpreters as site-specific and guides as nonsite-specific.

Despite the fact that guiding and interpreting are virtually synonymous, the two "camps" have not communicated until very recently. The gap between them has prevailed in part because of the tendency for public- and private-sector operations to proceed separately. Surprisingly few guides within the travel and tourism field are familiar with interpretation, and many who are approach the field reluctantly. The trend toward increased dialogue and greater unity between the two camps will surely prevail in the 1990s.

The Role of the Interpreter   One notable distinction between guiding and interpretation that is particularly relevant to this discussion is that interpretation in the Park Service, unlike guiding in the private sector, has long subscribed to the following stated objectives.

1. To assist visitors in developing a keener awareness, appreciation and understanding of the area they are visiting;

2. To accomplish management goals by encouraging thoughtful use and reasonable behavior that minimizes impact on the resources; and

3. To promote public understanding of agency goals and objectives (National Park Service Manual).

These objectives, in effect, describe the roles of National Park Service interpreters. As employees of the National Park Service they are hired to carry out the mission of the institution.

Grant Sharpe, author of another interpretation classic, *Interpreting the Environment* (1982), examines the role and techniques of interpreters. In his essay "Evaluating the Role of Interpretation," Sharpe observes that the first of the National Park Service's three objectives is the most obvious and enjoyable task as well as the interpreter's chief role. "This is what interpreters want to do," he says, "and most do it well." See Figure 5–3.

The second objective Sharpe calls "frustrating, as is any attempt to change human behavior." Although encouraging thoughtful use and reasonable behavior toward resources have always been deemed important, he questions whether interpretation in the Park Service actually serves as a management tool.

Sharpe calls the third objective—promoting public understanding of the agency—the greatest unmet challenge, and suggests that, in light of steadily shrinking NPS budgets, interpreters "must look beyond simply helping visitors to enjoy their visit" in order to justify the cost and struggle to operate the park. "If this struggle is lost, the drama is over, and interpretation has no role to play at all."

In *A Field Guide for Evaluation*, Brett Wright and Marcella Wells (1990) analyze the dynamics of the interpretation process in order to develop techniques for evaluating interpretation. They describe what occurs in the interpre-

Figure 5.3
National Park Service rangers are trained to provide interpretation skills to a wide variety of visitors. (*Photo by Richard Freas, courtesy of the National Park Service.*)

tation process as the *interpretive component,* illustrated in Figure 5–4. Before interpretation begins, a background that impacts profoundly on the experience is already established (management objectives, legislation, etc.). Within the interpretive experience itself, visitors bring to the experience unique interests or energy levels, prejudices, learning capabilities, and preconceived beliefs about the place. Wright and Wells refer to the beliefs and attitudes that one brings to the experience as "baggage," or preconceived notions about the group and the site as well as individual prejudices and preferences. The baggage has an impact upon the experience. Wright and Wells also note that in the case of personal interpretation the interpreter/guide also brings baggage to the experience.

In order to develop a framework for evaluation, it was first necessary to

Figure 5.4
The interpretive component. (*Source: Wells, Marcella, and Bret Wright. 1989. A Field Guide for Evaluation: A Tool Kit for Interpreters. National Park Service.*)

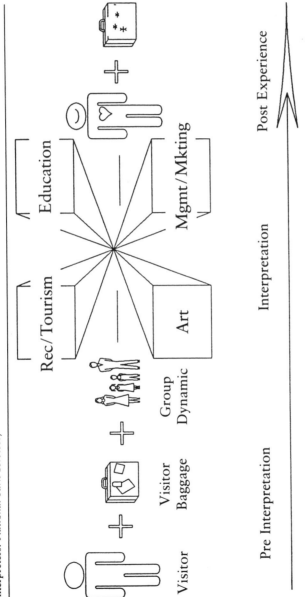

determine the roles the interpreter plays. Noting that interpretation serves a wide variety of functions, the Wright/Wells study isolated four perspectives or roles of interpretation: education, fine art, recreation/tourism, and management/marketing. Using these perspectives they explore each metaphorically, from the point of view of interpretation, the interpreter, and the visitor. To the extent that interpretation is a fine art, for example, the interpreter is an artist and the visitor an appreciator, a patron, or a critic. To the extent that interpretation is a management or marketing function, the interpreter is a manager, administrator, or salesperson, and the visitor is client or consumer. This analysis serves well the task of setting up a program for evaluating interpreters, for they could focus on the extent to which the interpreters fulfilled these functions. Additionally, it offers another perspective of the many roles the interpreter/ guide plays, such as teacher, performer, recreator, artist, manager, and so on. These will be incorporated in the discussion on the roles of the guide which follows.

FIVE ROLES EXPLORED

The following discussion examines the guide's duties and responsibilities in another way, within five easily identified roles, all of which are required in varying degrees depending on the nature of the group and the situation. The five roles are (1) the leader, (2) the educator, (3) the public relations representative, (4) the host, and (5) the conduit.

These roles are treated here as distinct functions for several reasons. One reason is simply to promote a clear understanding of the responsibilities and functions of the guide—an essential task on the guide's path toward professionalism—while emphasizing the significance of each. Another important reason is that each deserves individual attention because each requires a unique set of skills, most of which can be learned.

At the same time, it is important to recognize that all of these roles are interwoven and synergistic. In actual practice, they are inseparable. An effective educator, for example, is a leader, a public relations representative, a host, and a conduit. A true leader exhibits elements of all of these roles. And when one embodies these roles he or she becomes a conduit.

Each of these roles is described briefly below and is applied more thoroughly and practically throughout the remainder of the text.

The Leader

The leadership role inevitably finds its way to the top of any list of guide functions. Employers of guides often regard leadership as the most essential aspect of a guide's responsibilities. In fact, many tour operators are often more concerned with a guide's effectiveness with people and ability to lead groups than with the guide's knowledge or experience.

What is a leader? How does a guide act as a leader? According to *Webster's Third New International Dictionary,* a leader is "one who leads" or "ranks first," or is "a person who by force of example, talents, or qualities of leadership plays a directing role, wields commanding influence, or has a following in any sphere of activity or thought."

Such definitions, while in their own way accurate, would not satisfy many of the recent "movers and shakers" in the fields of business, management, or sociology. It would not be an exaggeration to suggest that in the 1980s—specifically the late 1980s—the definition of leadership in the business world was rewritten. Prior to that time, leadership and management were deemed synonymous, with the leader seen as the first-ranking, top-of-the-pyramid authority who makes decisions that, in a successful chain of command, eventually work their way down to low-level workers, who simply follow directions. Such popular business writers as John Naisbitt and Patricia Aburdene (*Re-inventing the Corporation*), Jan Carlzon (*Moments of Truth*), and Stephen Covey (*The Seven Habits of Highly Effective People*) regard leaders differently. They agree that the primary attribute of a leader is a strong sense of vision and an ability to infuse it in others. More important, they feel that the concept of low-level "underlings" needs to be reevaluated. Jan Carlzon, president of Scandinavian Airlines, believes these "low-level," usually front-line, workers are the lifeline of any business, for they are the major participants in what he calls the "moments of truth": the crucial, "make-or-break" moments when workers (usually front-line employees) meet customers, who quickly formulate their opinion about the business.

This concept of leadership is relevant to guiding in two ways. First, it provides a way of determining how guides, as leaders, regard their travelers. One could say that the measure of a guide's effectiveness is the extent to which visitors feel they are heard, and feel inspired and empowered to venture out on their own and experience new places for themselves. The traditional view, that the effectiveness of a guide lies in his or her ability to control a group or convince them to browse where he or she does, is quickly yielding to the philosophies of the "new leader." The "new leader" does not care to bask in the glow of his own authority, but rather, as Carlzon says, "creates the right environment," is motivated toward consensus, and "is oriented toward results more than power or social relations" (Carlzon 1987, 37–38).

This "new leader" concept is applicable to guides in another way. From the perspective of tour operators and the travel industry, guides are the front-line workers: the direct participants in the "moments of truth" in the travel business. In light of their constant interaction with the customer or traveler, guides, more so than their supervisors, have the purest understanding of whether or not they are fulfilling company goals and satisfying travelers. In Carlzon's view, guides as such are the critical element and should be empowered to make decisions and affect changes in policy where needed. Many tour operators recognize the "moments of truth" in their businesses and offer guides support and flexibility in decision making. This is referred to as decentralized leadership or the "squashed pyramid" in organizations.

Effective leadership assumes effective management. In every arena, the leader and manager must address the integral operations of the business. "Management is doing things right," says Peter Drucker, "Leadership is doing the right things (Covey 1989)." While the image of the guide as a pied piper comes quickly to mind, more is involved than physically shepherding a group. One could say that the greatest responsibility of a guide is to infuse visitors with an understanding of and an appreciation for a place.

On a practical level, however, there are many tasks that the guide as leader/manager must address. As discussed earlier, in Cohen's model the leadership sphere of the guide involves (1) the instrumental component, and the tasks included therein: navigating, providing special access, shepherding, and maintaining control; and (2) the social component, which includes tension management, integrating the group, keeping good humor and morale, and entertaining members of the tour.

In addition, the guide as leader must have many of the skills traditionally required of leaders and managers in business, such as willingness to assume responsibility, ability to organize and make judicious decisions, strength to respond unflappably to emergencies and glitches, and the skill to coordinate many administrative tasks simultaneously. Most of these leadership tasks can be performed effectively in ways other than by the traditional authoritarian methods.

Cultivating stronger leadership and managerial skills as a guide is covered more extensively in Chapter 7, "Leadership and Social Skills."

The Educator

Travel is a powerful teacher, and few activities promote the exchange of knowledge as easily, as enjoyably, and as indelibly as does travel. Under the best of circumstances, travelers interact with locals—eating, seeing, and living as they do, and, in a sense, becoming part of the tapestry of the place. No amount of classroom instruction can compare with the interaction of places and cultures firsthand.

Even the most passive of travelers is learning, and as such, travelers are students. It follows then that if travel is a "classroom" and travelers students, the guide is educator. Most guides glean particular pride from this role, and find its intrinsic rewards immeasurable. In fact, as Holloway noted, many guides, in their pursuit of professional recognition, regard their expertise and their ability to share knowledge as their most important function.

It has also been suggested, however, that some guides adopt the role of educator far too zealously, to the extent that they become self-absorbed and pedantic. Freeman Tilden repeatedly warns against this tendency, invoking Emerson's adage, "It is not instruction but provocation that I can receive from another soul." This message is so much a principal thread of Tilden's philosophy and writing that he has been accused of discounting the importance of education in interpretation. In fact, his salient message is that provocation is far more important than instruction, and that interpreters and guides often concern themselves too much with disseminating information, forgetting that people travel for many reasons other than to learn. Gabriel Cherem agrees, adding that "interpretation is the exact opposite of a lecture."

Many have written about the delicate balance between instructing and inspiring, but perhaps Anatole France expressed it best. "Do not try to satisfy your vanity by teaching a great many things," he said. "Awaken people's curiosity. It is enough to open minds; do not overload them. Put there just a spark. If there is some good inflammable stuff, it will catch fire." Too much emphasis on information and instruction can actually dampen one's desire or ability to discover on his or her own.

If guides are educators, what then do they teach? Subjects such as history, architecture, and geography come quickly to mind. In addition, guides must also be knowledgeable—and even proficient—in many other subjects, depending upon the site or region, their employer, the travelers, and the situation. Guides of many parts of North America, such as the American Southwest and the Yukon, are expected to be well informed about native Americans. Guides in New England need to have an acute understanding of early American history and regularly find themselves questioned about such diverse subjects as nineteenth-century American literature, scrimshaw, and lobsters (where and how to catch them, and where and how to eat them). Furthermore, the widespread and growing interest in nature is creating a demand for guides who can identify the birds, trees, and flowers of their region, and interpret the local ecology.

These and other subjects are only a part of what guides teach, and fall within the cognitive domain of learning. The other domains, affective and psychomotor (or behavioral), are also integral to the learning process. The affective domain includes such aspects as attitude and value formation, sparking interest, emotion, special perspective, and insight. An example of a guide operating within the affective domain is one in Tucson, Arizona, who inspires a traveler to learn more about native Americans and support their concerns; or a Washington, D.C., guide, who, through his interpretation of the Capitol and its history, sparks renewed feelings of patriotism and national pride; or an Alaska guide, educating travelers about wildlife and land use, inspiring in her travelers an appreciation for nature and an interest in conservation. Increasingly, guides are playing a prominent role in ecotourism, educating people about the vulnerabilities of their regions and the ways in which visitors can play a role in preserving them.

Within the behavioral domain fall such aspects as teaching group skills. Participatory, skill-oriented travel is increasingly popular, and examples abound: groups visiting Louisiana's Cajun parishes learn to dance and to cook classic Cajun dishes; the field of ecotourism promotes tours that educate travelers about environmental conservation and wildlife observation.

In certain sites, guides are expected to educate visitors about the rules and regulations that apply to a place. While touring a National Park, for example, visitors are prohibited from picking or removing specimens such as wildflowers, branches, or rocks. Guides conducting tours through Amish villages have a moral responsibility to convey the fact that taking pictures of Amish people violates their religious convictions. On a more subtle level, guides can teach or reinforce travel skills, including the importance of pacing oneself, eating lightly and healthfully, and packing efficiently.

Visitors to a region often look to the guide for cues about the social mores of a region: local dress, regional songs or dances, foods (and how to prepare them), and etiquette and customs. In this regard the role of educator is meshed with the other guide roles: host, public relations representative, and so forth. Mary Ann Thomas, an eighth-grade teacher from rural Tennessee, asked her guide to reiterate to her students the importance of proper behavior throughout their tour of Washington, D.C. Says Thomas:

Most of these kids have never been out of our rural county. So for them, the most educational part of the trip is not learning more about American history or government, but absorbing the shock of urban life, staying overnight in a hotel—the things we take for granted. I feel we need to teach them proper behavior—how to get by in a city, how to behave on a crowded street, in a cathedral, in a fancy restaurant, at the White House, meeting their senator. . . . These are tools to develop their confidence and their belief that they can return and survive here—maybe even become a senator!"

A guide or teacher who strives to achieve all of those goals—imparting information, impressing upon students values or beliefs, and encouraging them to learn new skills—is an effective educator. And yet, an educator may never quite know the full impact of their teaching or its value to the student.

Chapter 6, "Education," offers a more detailed look at the educational aspects of guiding.

The Public Relations Representative

To some, the public relations role is thought to be the most important aspect of the guide's work. It is also the most difficult to describe and the most controversial of the roles.

As noted in Chapter 2, many countries, sites, businesses, and other organizations employ guides specifically for the purpose of presenting a particular message or image to visitors. In this respect, as Wright and Wells have noted, guides also serve a marketing role; the National Park Service is an example of this. In parks throughout the United States, rangers and other interpreters act, in a sense, as spokespersons for the Park Service.

In some parts of the world, guides are carefully chosen by government officials to project a specific image or political philosophy and, in the extreme, even to recite a prescribed message. As government employees, such individuals are bound to the official rhetoric. Such guides are even trained to respond in specific ways to controversial or probing questions, and the most dutiful rarely stray from these responses. As democracy and the value of free speech pervades more societies, this is less common; but, in general any organization that employs guides can, and often does, exert authority over what the guide might or might not say.

In light of the personal connection they create between places and visitors, tour guides are frequently called ambassadors. Considering the often demanding diplomatic skills required of them, such an appellation seems appropriate. And yet many guides work as freelancers, taking a wide variety of jobs for different agencies. Most people, especially those in democratic countries, would agree that guides speak for themselves. This is especially true of the large number of guides who are freelancers, working for themselves. This does not mean that guiding can or should be used as a forum for guides to espouse their political, religious, or moral points of view. Most would agree that guides should remain as objective as possible.

If guides are ambassadors, who do they represent? One answer is that guides are responsible to the organizations that hire them. In few arenas is this role more clearly executed than with the National Park Service. Some would argue that a guide's first duty is to his region, especially if it means protecting and preserving an imperiled environment or culture. Certainly guides represent their regions, although it appears that guides usually take on this role more readily and more seriously than the local citizens or government would want or expect. To state this another way, guides and travelers often view guides as representatives of a place to a greater extent than do local citizens.

Other important and related questions are: Are guides expected or obliged to present their region in a favorable way? Should guides avoid showing visitors impoverished sections of their cities? Should they avoid mentioning scandals or problems of the region? Public relations implies projecting a positive image, and yet it bears mentioning that regions do not always come across favorably.

In actual practice government or agency officials rarely have real control over what a guide conveys. They may assume that guides are interpreting the region in a positive way, but such is not always the case. In fact, most guides present a naturally editorialized view—their view—of their world and home, emphasizing or omitting what they choose.

Guides can and do offend visitors, mostly unintentionally and often without ever realizing that they have committed an offense. Bad public relations—that is, interpretation that offends visitors or paints a negative picture—occurs often. Whether it is done overtly or subtly, out of callousness or ignorance, it can be powerfully damaging, and this problem must be given more attention.

Although rare, there are cases in which guides give tours of places they do not like. Fortunately, a guide who dislikes a place usually does not remain a guide there for very long. This is best not only for the city's own public relations, but also for the traveler and the guide. Enthusiasm cannot be long feigned, and when it is, the result is not gratifying for anyone.

More about cross cultural awareness and communication is covered in Chapter 4, "The Traveler," and Chapter 7, "Leadership and Social Skills." Other aspects of public relations are covered in Chapter 13, "Professional Ethics and Etiquette."

The Host

Travel is largely a social occurrence, thus the guide's role in travel embodies many social aspects. Hosts wear many hats, including those of companion, mediator, advocate, concierge, entertainer, raconteur, and others.

It may seem paradoxical that "host" and "guest" are derived from the same Indo-European root. *Ghosti* means "stranger," "guest," and "host," or more specifically, "someone with whom one has reciprocal duties of hospitality." In fact, just as giving and receiving are symbiotic concepts, so are "host" and "guest": one cannot successfully fulfill one role without understanding and partaking in the other. Impassioned guests make impassioned hosts, and similarly, the most spirited, successful guides are themselves enthusiastic, sensitive travelers.

For many guides, the role of host is an effortless joy, and is often the very reason they become or remain guides. Others, more taciturn or comfortable in other roles, find the social aspects of the job the most challenging and intimidating. A common perception is that all guides—or at least the most successful guides—are innately extroverted. In fact, the reverse is often true. As the creators of the Myers-Briggs Personality Profile point out, the *introvert* finds his support center within himself, in contrast to the *extrovert,* who requires others for his support. Such self-supported individuals are often more likely to be enduring leaders and hosts. It is certainly true, however, that individuals who are attracted to guiding and who are successful at it invariably possess the ability to be outgoing and are comfortable in that role.

The qualities of a successful host are easy to recognize and describe. A good host enjoys people and has a seemingly innate ability to create an environment in which people feel comfortable and enjoy themselves. Good hosts know how to bring out the best in people, extend a friendly hand when needed, and facilitate connections between people in a natural way. A good host is sensitive to others' needs and knows intuitively when and how to change the course of a conversation or activity if they sense that a guest is not comfortable. A good host is at the same time relaxed with and energized by people. As with all guide roles, the primary ingredient in fulfilling the role of host is that of passion and a genuine interest in travelers, locals, and all who partake of the experience.

Cohen, Holloway, and others point out that many contemporary guides, in their drive toward professional recognition and the belief that their role as educator validates them as professionals, find the social roles to be of much lesser importance or value—even demeaning at times. Such guides erroneously equate the role of service to that of servitude, believing that serving people places guides in a lower social standing. These guides fall short in their role as hosts.

By contrast, many guides strive to become the social center of attention in the experience, perceiving themselves as primarily entertainers, the "stars of the show." Such guides offer less to their guests by preventing them from experiencing the joys of self-discovery and participation.

Although people travel primarily to enjoy themselves, the importance of a guide as entertainer has been overplayed in some circles. Many guides, like comedians, measure the amount of laughter and applause they elicit to be the measure of their success. Humor in travel is both instructive and gratifying, and the ability to use it effectively is a mark of a skilled communicator. And yet, entertainment and humor are not synonymous with constant hilarity, and many guides would do well to curb their propensity toward continual joke telling. Further, for guides working in an increasingly global society, an understanding of cultural differences and the nuances of humor is vital.

The role of the host is discussed in greater detail in Chapter 7, "Leadership and Social Skills," and Chapter 13, "Professional Ethics and Etiquette." The use of humor is covered in Chapter 9, "Bringing a Place to Life."

So interdependent is the guide's role of host with all the other roles, that any discussion of it leads—as do all roles discussed above—to the last role, the conduit.

The Conduit

The guide's role as a conduit is perhaps the most important; surely it can be the most powerful and long-lasting. In a sense the role of conduit cannot be separated from any other role, for it is integral to all guide functions. At the same time, the conduit concept is so important, and is so often ignored, that it deserves separate mention.

To emphasize the guide's role as conduit is to emphasize the importance of the visitor, the local culture, and the travel experience rather than to focus on the guide's performance. In the best of situations, guides simply facilitate, or allow and encourage, events to unfold. They are the medium rather than the message.

The role of conduit is perhaps the most difficult to understand and describe. In practice, it demands the greatest level of maturity and courage, for it requires that guides subordinate themselves to the traveler and the experience. It is the most intangible and, as such, the most difficult to illustrate or teach. One could say, "You know it when it's there; if you need to have it explained, it's probably not happening." It is the innate understanding of when to be silent, when to step back, when to encourage, when to move on. It is finding the delicate balance of employing all the guide roles simultaneously. Such a lofty goal is much easier to attain than it may seem at first, for anyone who commits himself to becoming an effective educator, leader, public relations representative, and host becomes a conduit.

Paradoxically, acting as conduit is actually the simplest and most rewarding of roles, for less emphasis is placed upon the guide and what he or she knows, and more is asked of the traveler. "When we're left to our own experiences," says Stephen Covey, author of *Seven Habits of Highly Effective People,* "we constantly suffer from a shortage of data. The person who is truly effective has the humility and reverence to recognize his own perceptual limitations and to appreciate the rich resources available through interaction with the hearts and minds of other human beings" (Covey 1989).

It is the conduit-guide who learns most, forges the deepest bonds with people, and indeed, reaps the greatest rewards from guiding, for he or she creates a multidimensional, successful experience, that is greater than the sum of its parts. This is the essence of synergy.

Techniques for developing the role of conduit are covered in greater detail in other chapters, particularly Chapter 9, "Bringing a Place to Life."

Synthesizing and Applying the Roles

Guiding is not an exact science, nor should one ever attempt to pin interpretation down to prescription. Guiding is a highly individual and creative art, allowing for both style and personality. One guide might shine as host, another may strive first to teach visitors something he or she values, and both guides might excel as interpreters.

Researchers have observed that there are strains and conflicts in guiding roles. As noted, some guides resent certain roles, perceiving them as extraneous or beneath their capabilities or station. Cohen suggests that the wide variety of roles that guides are expected to fulfill, and the fact that they are required to serve in different capacities, lessens the chance that any one person could do it all. Others point out the many different expectations manifested by guides, visitors, employers, and other industry colleagues, which might result in a deeper dissatisfaction with guides as a whole. Clearly, the roles of guides and the degree to which guides are addressing their status warrants more attention.

Having outlined the various roles of guides, a clearer picture emerges of the qualities desirable in guides and their possible courses of study. Indeed, as noted by Holloway, Tilden, and others, the diverse tasks a guide must fulfill simultaneously are quite challenging. For some guides, the ability to orchestrate many details and roles concurrently is almost innate; for others, it is difficult. However, experience has shown that many of the skills required in the guide's work are teachable.

It must be noted that the five roles presented here are those pertaining to the guide's image; that is, the roles that the visitor and the industry see and expect of a professional. They are the roles that can be observed and, to some extent, taught, learned, and measured. These roles demand that guides must also work to build their identities as students, researchers, guests or travelers, businesspersons, and marketers as a foundation for the public roles described. Every educator is first a student; every host learns first to be a guest. As a public relations representative, one must first be a discerning critic of what he or she sees, hears, and reads. Says Gabriel Cherem, "Image is what you are perceived to be by others; identity is what you are."

SUMMARY

The guiding experience is complex, requiring that guides operate simultaneously in a variety of roles. The public roles outlined in this chapter—leader, educator, public relations representative, host, and conduit—embody the guide that visitors encounter. These roles may serve to illustrate a model and thus further develop the curricula and the standards to which guides can aspire in their drive toward professional recognition.

6 *Education*

"The goal of education is the wise use of leisure."

—Aristotle

INTERPRETATION AS EDUCATION

Aristotle's words hold special meaning and offer a particular challenge today, as the effectiveness of our educational systems are called into question and, simultaneously, the amount of leisure time has increased to an unprecedented level. No doubt Aristotle would favor the current trends toward devoting leisure time to travel and using travel as a means to educate.

Travel is, indeed, a natural teacher and a powerful bridge between people. Experiencing firsthand the routines, homes, natural surroundings, climates, food, entertainment, and other aspects of another culture offers profound and indelible insights not possible through textbooks or television.

In recent years, the concept of travel as a vehicle for education has become one of the most prominent trends in tourism. Recognizing the joy of travel and the power of travel to teach, consumers are seeking travel opportunities that offer more than mere entertainment. Travel planners are responding to this trend by designing tours that hold meaning beyond the journey itself.

Travel is more than simply an enlightening and enjoyable way to use leisure time; in fact, many agree that travel can be a vital tool for survival in today's constantly changing world. In the latter half of the twentieth century, technological, cultural, and economic changes have occurred so rapidly that much of what a person learns in school is obsolete within a decade of his leaving school. According to Malcolm Knowles, one of the world's leading authorities on adult learning and training, "by the time we have finished school, half of what we have learned is nonfunctional, and probably much of it is dysfunctional by the time we are 30" (Knowles 1984).

In 1972, the United Nations Educational, Scientific, and Cultural Organization (UNESCO) published *Learning to Be,* which Knowles calls "perhaps the single most important educational document of the twentieth century." According to Knowles, its central thesis asserts that we have entered "an era of civilization that is different—in kind, not just in degree—from all previous eras in history, and that to function in this new era people must continue to learn throughout their lives" (Knowles 1984). Much of Knowles's work is devoted to preparing young students for a lifetime of learning. Certainly, travel is a popular, effective vehicle for lifelong learning.

The educational potential and impact of travel cannot be overemphasized. Travel has been credited with recent strides in democratic reform, the end of the cold war, and the rapid development of many technological advances. Indeed, as people of the world travel more easily and frequently, former misunderstandings, prejudices, and barriers disappear. Inveterate traveler Mark Twain prescribed annual excursions for anyone who was able. "Travel is fatal to prejudice, bigotry, and narrowmindedness," he said, "and many of our people need it sorely on these accounts. Broad, wholesome, charitable views of men and things cannot be acquired by vegetating in one little corner of the earth all one's lifetime."

One example of the educational value of travel is evident in the burgeoning field of ecotourism. By showing travelers firsthand the impact man has on the fragile world, travel becomes a powerful tool for educating and inspiring people to do what they can to preserve imperiled habitats. Ecotourism calls to mind the interpreter's invocation: "through interpretation, understanding; through understanding, appreciation; through appreciation, protection."

Other examples of travel designed to educate include Elderhostel (a program which offers courses throughout the world for adults), the popular tradition of student exchange, and tours made to villages of one's ancestors to learn more about one's roots (sometimes called ethnic tourism).

The Guide's Unique Role

Inasmuch as travel offers a pure forum for learning for people of all ages and backgrounds, guides play a prominent and powerful role in the process of lifelong learning. As noted in Chapter 5, the guide's role is multifaceted. Depending upon the region, the nature of the group, the nature of the excursion, the amount of time available, and countless other factors, the guide's mission—and the demands on his or her abilities—vary considerably.

Despite the similarities of teachers and guides, there are great differences in both the purposes and the circumstances of their work. These differences deserve mention if guides are to formulate a clear picture of their place as educators and establish an appropriate, relevant professional path. Teachers in schools differ from guides in the following ways:

1. Teachers are formally entrusted with one of society's most important roles, for every teacher serves as a vital cog in society's educational plan for its people. As a student progresses through formal schooling—elementary, secondary, and postsecondary—each teacher is called upon to pass on the society's core knowl-

edge, skills, and values. Although guides can and do dramatically influence traveler's perspectives and lives, they generally teach independently of academic curricula in small slices of time and, thus, have less responsibility and more flexibility in their interpretations.

2. School teachers address specific age groups, from early childhood, through adolescence, and into early adulthood. Guides, on the other hand, routinely address people of all ages and most frequently work with adults.

3. The school teacher's class is usually more homogenous than a guide's group. Not only are classes usually delineated by age and sometimes by ability, but, by virtue of geography, students live in the same region and often share similar lifestyles, backgrounds, values, and socioeconomic levels. By contrast, a guide's group of travelers is often unacquainted and, in the case of a prearranged group such as a charter, is often likely to include a variety of ages, perceptions, interests, occupations, and life experience.

4. Even in situations in which students possess a wide variety of values, backgrounds, and abilities, they are generally placed with the same group for an entire term or school year. This allows the teacher sufficient time to observe and test their students' learning strengths and deficiencies, emotional character, and personal perspective, enabling him or her to tailor their approach to individual students. Guides, on the other hand, are not privy to educational records, test scores, or other information, and have neither the time nor the opportunity to utilize that information. This requires guides to be "quick studies."

5. While the teacher's primary role is unequivocally that of educator, the guide, as the leader of travelers, is hired to fulfill a variety of functions.

6. Unlike most students, who are compelled to attend school, a guide's travelers are not necessarily captive and are usually free to leave the tour.

7. Teachers, in essence, serve society. Officially, public school teachers are employed by the local government. It is generally assumed that the board of education and its teachers know best how to meet students' needs and prepare them for civilized, productive living, deciding the course and method of the students' education. Conversely, guides are hired directly or indirectly by the traveler. As customers, travelers are the ultimate judges of the experience and may determine a guide's future, as they can simply leave a tour or even have a guide fired if dissatisfied.

These differences between guides and teachers suggest that traditional educational theory and training alone is not appropriate for guides. Guides must focus on the diversity of their audience (adult learners, heterogenous and multicultural groups, etc.) and on their other roles (leader, host, public relations representative, and conduit).

In fact, many contemporary theorists suggest that, in such a rapidly changing global society, the role of conduit or facilitator should be the highest goal for all educators. Carl Rogers, preeminent psychiatrist and educational researcher, ventures even further, to say that "facilitation of learning" is the only goal.

Teaching is a vastly over-rated function. Too many people have been shown, guided, directed. We are, in my view, faced with an entirely new situation in education where the goal of education, if we are to survive, is the facilitation of change and learning. A reliance on process rather than upon static knowledge is the only thing that makes any sense as a goal for education in the modern world. When I have been able to transform a group—and here I mean all the members of a group, myself included—into a community of learners, then the excitement has been almost beyond belief. To free curiosity; to permit individuals to go charging off in new directions dictated by their own interest; to unleash the sense of inquiry; to open everything to questioning and exploration; to recognize that everything is in the process of change . . .

This is, to Rogers, the ideal (Rogers 1983). Rogers' convictions about education and the learning process are especially relevant and applicable to guiding, as are his descriptions of the qualities of the facilitator. He believes that individuals who embody the attributes of the facilitator and are bold enough to act on them are those who are revolutionizing education.

Roger Heimstra, professor of adult education at Syracuse University and author of *Guiding the Older Learner,* offers another prescription for instructors of adults: "The instructor of adults must wear at least four hats: programmer (arranges conditions to facilitate learning); guide (assists others in their educative experiences); content resource (is a master of one or more fields of study); and institutional representative (fulfills duties as a member of an institution)."

The Process of Learning

There is certainly no shortage of theory and speculation on the learning process. Over the past century, thousands of educators and researchers have devoted their careers to a better understanding of the dynamics of learning. This research has resulted in a wide range of principles and methods for learning. Until recently, however, educational theory has primarily addressed children and adolescents in the traditional classroom setting. Malcolm Knowles calls the adult learner a "neglected species," claiming that adults are often taught like children because all teaching methods are based on child learning theories. In tourism, adults account for the majority of travelers, and statistics indicate that the number is increasing steadily. In fact, guides rarely conduct tours that do not include adults; even when working with student groups, adults are present. Certainly any discussion of the educational aspects of travel must address itself to adult learning.

Given the wide variety of travelers and tours and the broad range of opinion about learning and effective teaching methods, it is difficult, and perhaps meaningless, to attempt to propose a theory or method which best serves the guiding experience. Perhaps it is more realistic and helpful to recognize prevailing beliefs about how people perceive and learn when they travel.

Theories abound about how people perceive and learn. Rather than reiterate all applicable research findings from these theories, the following is a list of learning concepts relevant to learning from travel. These ideas are drawn from classical educational theory, interpretation research, business theory, and studies of motivation, leadership, and the dynamics of travel. For the most part, they are applicable to the learning process at any age. It is important to note that these are generalizations that do not apply to all people or all situations. All of them, however, apply to some people and are useful to guides in developing more engaging interpretations. Some of the these concepts appear so simple that stating them may seem unnecessary. Yet, it is these concepts that are often the most important and most often forgotten during a guide's interpretation.

1. People perceive events and process information differently.

2. Different people may perceive the same experience in vastly different ways.

3. All ways of perceiving, processing, and learning are equally valid.

4. Learning is influenced by motivation; people are most motivated to learn about those things to which they can relate personally or for which they feel passion or love. Motivation is rooted in personal values.

5. Learning is influenced by the environment; the extent to which the learning environment impresses, stimulates, or pleases the student has an impact on learning.

6. An individual's sense of personal comfort and security has an impact on his or her capacity for learning.

7. The degree to which students will care about, believe, or remember what they are told is influenced by the way they feel about their teacher.

8. People are most likely to remember what they do, less likely to remember what they see or read, and least likely to remember what they hear.

9. People learn more easily when a greater number of senses are involved.

10. A variety of approaches to a subject greatly enhances the learning process and increases the likelihood that the learner will be interested in the subject.

11. The most effective learning occurs when the student is actively involved with the subject.

12. The process of self-discovery, or the extent to which the learner discovers on his or her own, strongly affects the motivation to learn and enjoyment in learning.

13. Learning is greatly influenced by prior experience and knowledge; in general, people are more interested in and able to grasp subjects that are familiar to them.

14. Organized (that is, chronological or thematic) instruction is an easier way for many people to learn.

15. People think and perceive and, therefore, most effectively learn and communicate in one of three ways: visual, auditory, or kinesthetic. (This concept is the basis of neuro-linguistic programming.)

16. Teaching techniques that employ all learning domains—cognitive, affective, and motor—more effectively facilitate learning.

17. Repetition often facilitates learning.

Applying Learning Theories to Guiding

Some of the concepts noted above [the theories of John Grinder, a linguist, and Richard Bandler, a mathematician and Gestalt therapist] embody the foundation for a specific learning theory or teaching method, many of which have been used successfully by guides and interpreters. For example, concept 15 (above), that people perceive and communicate either visually, auditorily, or kinesthetically, is the basis of a widely recognized theory called *neuro-linguistic programming* (NLP). NLP is the study of how verbal and nonverbal language affects our nervous system. Proponents of NLP contend that all people perceive primarily in one of these three distinct ways, and therefore, the most effective way of communicating with an individual is to match his or her manner of perception. For example, if a person perceives visually, he or she is more likely to respond to visual images, written explanations or drawings, and "visual" language—words like "see," and "visualize," and phrases like "Picture this . . ." or "I see what you mean." Neuro-linguistic programming is used to establish rapport in social situations, in management and leadership, in sales, and in education. Samuel Vaughn, interpretive specialist at the Denver Service Center of the National Park Service, employs NLP in his own interpretation and when training other interpreters. "The theoretical foundation for NLP is rather basic," he says, "since most practitioners are more concerned with discovering what works than with constructing theoretical systems. When we respond to our environment, we are responding to our images, interpretations, concepts, and assumptions about our environment," he continues. "We don't react to the world directly; rather we respond to how we see it, hear it, feel it, smell it, taste it, think about it, and remember it. We respond to our map of the world, a map that we create and modify" (Holmass and Vaughn 1988). (Neuro-linguistic programming is also discussed in Chapter 7, "Leadership and Social Skills.")

Concept 7, which stresses the importance of the relationship between learner and facilitator, is the foundation for Carl Rogers's work. Rogers contends that one of the most important conditions for learning is the attitude of the facilitator, as it is this attitude which creates the environment appropriate for learning. Rogers mentions three factors essential to the learning environment: (1) authenticity; (2) caring about, respect for, and "prizing" of the learner; and (3) sensitive, empathic listening, which creates a "freeing climate" for learners. Rogers believes these attitudes are vastly underrated and that they can be cultivated in teachers (or facilitators, as he prefers). In his view, when these attitudes are present, a natural, fertile learning environment inevitably emerges.

Over the past century, researchers and practitioners in education, psychology, business, and other fields have created countless other theories and methods of teaching or facilitating environments. By recognizing and understanding the nature of perception and learning, guides can utilize new or traditional methods or successfully create methods of their own. The keys for any teacher or learning facilitator—and especially for guides, who work in a particularly challenging, heterogeneous environment—are a sensitivity to people and a willingness to change course if the situation requires it. A diversion or story that might have delighted one group may fall flat with another. Perceiving such a response should be a clear cue to the interpreter to move on, possibly in a new direction, with a different approach. Given the wide range of personalities and circumstances guides encounter, and the fundamental duty guides have to travelers, such fluidity in one's performance is vital.

Guidelines for Facilitating Learning

The following are guidelines for creating a positive learning environment. (These concepts also lend themselves to the other guide roles.)

1. A broad-based knowledge about the region is absolutely fundamental. Many guides entering the profession for the first time are astounded by the scholastic demands of guiding. The amateur or professional historian, attracted to guiding as a way of sharing and expanding his or her knowledge of history, quickly learns that visitors are just as interested in current events, art, architecture, local politics, economics and industry, and regional natural history. Thus, guides will find themselves using many resource materials to expand their knowledge about a variety of subjects. Ideally, the guide should have a pervasive understanding of many subject areas (accumulated over years of living in a region) combined with the perspective gained by living elsewhere and/or traveling widely.

2. Guides must be committed to lifelong learning. As in many professions, new information is constantly unfolding, and travelers rely on guides to be current. Guides with interested, inquisitive natures, who are always uncovering new information, ideas, and perspectives, give the freshest and most spontaneous interpretations.

3. Enthusiasm, which emerges from genuine passion, is the single most important aspect of an affective interpreter. Without real passion, a guide's knowledge is essentially meaningless. The guide's conviction must be twofold: passion for people, and passion for the subject matter. Nothing can replace genuine enthusiasm. Most travelers will forgive a guide's lapses of knowledge or memory if they perceive a genuine concern, but nothing will more quickly offend or alienate visitors than an apathetic or unenthusiastic guide.

4. Empathy and sensitivity toward people—their needs, their beliefs and feelings, their differences, their interests—is vital for a successful learning environment. Sensitivity grows out of caring and respect for people, and is so intangible

that it cannot be easily described or taught. It is what Carl Rogers calls "prizing the learner."

5. The ability to interpret by painting mental pictures, rather than merely disseminating information, inspires people to learn. Guides have inherited—earned, many would say—a reputation for loquaciousness and pedantry. All guides must implicitly understand and repeatedly remind themselves of Freeman Tilden's principle: "The chief aim of interpretation is not instruction, but provocation."

6. Flexibility—the ability and willingness to employ a wide variety of principles and methods, and to change course midstream—is essential if guides and travelers are to enjoy (or survive) the experience.

7. Pride in serving others is another intangible and vastly underrated quality. This quality enables the guide to fully and genuinely give his or her time and energy to the travelers. The most successful and fulfilled guides are those who genuinely believe that to be a guide—to introduce visitors to their region, to facilitate an environment of learning and exchange, and to be of service to travelers—is a privilege and joy.

EDUCATING THE GUIDE

Perhaps the single most important factor in the evolution of any profession is its commitment to education and high standards. As the guiding profession evolves, it must concern itself with both its *identity* and its *image*. Identity is the collective set of characteristics of a person or a thing, including its standards and values; image is the perception others have toward it. Many people and institutions devote more attention to image building, as identity building is a more difficult and more considerable task. In fact, a positive public image usually results naturally from a solid identity. The amount of study and training required in a field usually correlates with salary, benefits, professional morale, and prestige.

As noted in Chapter 2, qualifications and educational standards for guiding vary substantially throughout the world. Travelers, guides, and industry professionals generally acknowledge a much higher standard of guiding in European countries than in North America. For example, it is not uncommon for a guide from any European country to speak several languages, have traveled widely, and hold advanced degrees. This should come as no surprise, as both requirements and training have long been held to a high standard throughout Europe. Discussions about educational programs and higher standards have only recently been initiated in North America. For the sake of comparison, it is revealing to contrast the paths to becoming a guide in Washington, D.C., and in Vienna, Austria, with a brief look at requirements in Great Britain, the Caribbean, and Canada.

Licensing and Certification[1]

Washington, D.C.   To obtain a license in Washington, D.C., the first step is to request an application from the Department of Consumer and Regulatory Affairs, the city agency that issues licenses for taxicab drivers, street vendors, and guides. After meeting a number of bureaucratic requirements—including filling out the appropriate forms, fingerprinting, passing a medical examination, and submitting letters of reference—the prospective guide is given an examination date. The examination is written, consisting of 100 questions—short essay, photo identification, and true/false. With a grade of 70 percent or higher, the applicant becomes a Washington, D.C., guide. To retain the license, guides must renew annually at a cost of $28. Other than an annual doctor's examination to assess good health, no further testing is required unless the license expires, in which case the guide must repeat the process.

It should be noted that Washington, D.C., is one of only three cities in the United States that require a license (the other two are New York City and New Orleans, where the procedures are somewhat similar) and, in effect, has one of the highest standards for guiding in the country. (Although the city of San Francisco does not require licensing, the Tour Guide Guild of San Francisco grants certification—through oral and written examinations—to experienced guides.)

Vienna, Austria   The process of certification in Vienna is quite different. Here, an interested candidate approaches the chamber of commerce, which sponsors an institute for the promotion of industry and commerce. An interview and preliminary talk acquaints the applicant with the guide system and affirms his or her ability to meet basic requirements: a minimum fluency in two languages, a basic knowledge of the city, and good health. At this point the applicant is either rejected or accepted for enrollment in the institute. In a recent year, 85 of the 150 people interviewed were accepted. Classes in a wide variety of disciplines are taught by a team of experts to those accepted into the program. Among the classes are history of Vienna, Europe and the world; architecture; history of music, art, music and drama; history of Austrian literature, politics, medicine and industry; geography; and speaking techniques. Classes are held for three hours on Monday, Wednesday, and Friday evenings. One weekend day per month is devoted to area excursions. The institute recently increased its guide curriculum from two to three years.

Every six months a guide must pass an examination—usually oral—in order to continue the program. The guide appears before the board of examiners,

---

[1]Although the terms *licensing* and *certification* have ambiguous definitions and a variety of applications, they are used here (and generally within the profession) as follows: Licensing is required by law and granted by government bodies to those who meet established qualifications. Criteria for receiving licenses tend to be minimal and objective, including paying a fee, establishing residence, passing a basic medical examination, and passing a standard knowledge-based test. Certification is voluntary and is usually administered by associations or other professional organizations, and involves more qualitative standards acknowledged within a profession.

which includes area experts and senior guides. Examinations are also required in a foreign language, and additional exams are necessary for any language in which a guide intends to conduct tours.

Great Britain The educational qualifications in most European countries mirror the high standards of Austria. Great Britain, for example, has one of the oldest, most rigorous, and most esteemed systems for guides in the world. Throughout Great Britain, "tourist guides" are legally required to wear the highly respected "Blue Badge," indicating that they are members of the Guild of Guide Lecturers and officially authorized to conduct tours by their regional tourist board. Obtaining the Blue Badge requires extensive coursework, which varies in scope and length throughout the British Isles. In London, for example, guides are required to complete approximately 320 hours, or 28 weeks, of coursework. All guides must successfully fulfill the academic work and pass written and oral examinations in order to receive a Blue Badge.

The Caribbean In recent years, countries in Central and South America have devoted considerable attention to the task of educating and qualifying guides. In 1983, at the request of the Caribbean Islands of Saint Vincent and the Grenadines, The Bahamas, and Saint Lucia, the Department of Regional Development of the Organization of American States (OAS) developed a "how-to" manual for guide training programs, which covers such topics as the role of the guide, assertiveness, communication and social skills, and voice training.

Canada Canada is also making commitments and impressive strides toward higher standards in all aspects of tourism, on both national and provincial levels. The Pacific Rim Institute of Tourism (PRIT), funded primarily by Canada's Ministry of Tourism, provides educational programs, publications, and information about all aspects of tourism. As a member of the Tourism Industry Standards and Certification Committee (sponsored by Tourism Canada), PRIT is working to develop a national approach to tourism job standards and certification. The Alberta Tourism Education Council is presently developing a provincial certification system for guides. And the Canadian Tour Guide Association of British Columbia, composed primarily of guides, is actively working toward implementing certification and higher standards for training in that province.

Working Toward Change

Although the United States noticeably lags behind most nations in developing and adhering to high standards, educational and training programs, and certification, over the past decade, guides have united locally and nationally to initiate change in all these areas. The Professional Guides Association of America (PGAA), established in 1987, is especially active. PGAA has created a Professional Development Committee to develop the first national designation for professionalism in guiding, the Certified Professional Guide (CPG). Specifics of the

CPG program and an overview of other guide certification programs are outlined in Appendix B.

Clearly, in order for guiding to move forward as a respected and united profession, communication among nations is essential. The World Federation of Tourist Guide Lecturers Associations, founded in 1983 and headquartered in Vienna, is committed to this goal. Through its biennial meetings and publications, the federation continually evaluates and attempts to improve upon the training, professionalism, and general quality of guides around the world.

Certainly, the realization of all of these tasks is a monumental goal, and one not easily achieved, whatever the commitment. Such assessment and work is especially difficult since most guides work independently and have not had policy to follow or a centralized way of communicating their needs and goals. More recently, however, guide associations are getting the necessary attention and support of the travel industry and local and national governments. Only with such support will high standards and quality educational programs flourish.

Barriers to Change

It is important to note, however, that the guiding profession is not completely unified in these efforts. Although extensive training and certain rigorous standards have been accepted by guides throughout Europe for several decades, many guides, particularly in the United States, are averse to implementing higher educational and professional standards, regulations, and certification for a variety of reasons. In a recent informal survey guides throughout the United States were asked their opinions about certification, training, and a variety of other issues. Approximately 25 percent of the guides who responded expressed disapproval of certification.

One reason guides were skeptical about certification and training is the belief that most of the qualities necessary for effective guiding are innate and unteachable, therefore rendering training meaningless. Many guides who subscribe to this belief are those who have worked quite successfully as guides for many years. "You either have it or you don't," says a twelve-year veteran of guiding. "How can you teach a person to be sensitive to a group's needs, or to be entertaining?"

A second reason for a lack of support for stated higher standards or certification is the difficulty many see in implementing them. "It would be too general to be effective regionally," one guide noted about certification. Another stated her objections this way: "In principle, I endorse the idea. In practice I wonder how valid a test could be in terms of interpretive excellence in a particular area. On what basis do you really evaluate, or certify, a guide?"

A third objection is the view, certainly valid, that such a trend would elicit a great tide of tedious administrative tasks and paperwork that at present does not exist. Some feel that such regulations would dilute the important work of the guide. Some say this would even prevent or discourage qualified people from joining or remaining in the field. One guide, when questioned about the value of guide certification, asked, "Who would pay for it? How much would that cost guides? And in a profession that is already low-paying and difficult to establish oneself in, who has the time or inclination to do even more preparation?"

Some guides expressed concern that certification and educational programs drew more attention and unwelcome competition to an already highly competitive, seasonal field. Indeed, guides can be committed to the field and to effective interpretation and still be opposed to certification; many guides are.

Another objection among those who oppose the idea of requiring higher standards is the unstated fear that, in a highly competitive business, tests and evaluations might make them obsolete. One concerned veteran guide opposed to certification said, "What I'm doing works for me, and has worked for years. I don't feel I need to be evaluated." Another asked, "Who would be evaluating me—someone half my age, with half the experience, who's taken a few courses on evaluating guides?"

It is important to note that such resistance to new policy or standards seems to be a natural part of the early evolution of most professions. People who have worked for many years in a field that requires little or no formal training justifiably believe that their "on-the-job training" qualifies them more than adequately, and are often offended at any suggestion that they pursue formal training. Proponents argue that such changes in the field are designed primarily for future practitioners and will eventually result in a stronger sense of professionalism, greater morale, and higher salaries.

Guiding is not the only field that grapples with these questions. Jeff McHugh, Dean of Students at Fairfield Middle School in Fairfield, Connecticut, and a trainer for teachers, cites the same reticence toward further educational requirements. "In the seminar I teach for Lee Canter's Assertive Discipline, the idea that teaching is essentially an intuitive art comes up frequently," he says. "We talk about the need to move from an intuitive level of functioning to a professional level of operation."

Although many of the guides who are most enthusiastic about certification are also the most experienced, there is unquestionably a palpable opposition to certification among some seasoned veterans. This opposition must be addressed, particularly since some of the harshest criticism is coming from the most senior guides. For any new standards or programs to be accepted and implemented effectively, it is essential for all to be heard in the planning process; stronger programs will inevitably emerge as a result.

It is also important to note that excellence in interpretation can and does occur in the absence of regulations. Throughout the Hawaiian Islands, for example, guides and other residents seem imbued with a sense of regional pride and an ineffable but pervasive "aloha" spirit. There are many possible explanations for this. For one, the general nature of Hawaii and Hawaiians is more relaxed and temperate than that found in many other places. Further, as tourism has long been a vital industry for the Hawaiian Islands, Hawaiians are appreciative of travelers. Hawaii's enlightened view of tourism is evident in the strong commitment that the state has made to tourism. Most notable is the popular, highly successful Interpret Hawaii program at Kapiolani Community College in Honolulu. This curriculum provides interpretive training for all tourism industry personnel in their program.

Outstanding tourism development has emerged in other regions as well. Guilds and associations in San Francisco, Washington, D.C., and New York City provide members with programs, publications, and information which serve to unite guides. In Louisiana's Cajun country, the local people, businesses, and government work together to offer consistently superior service throughout that region. The trend toward quality service could be attributed to that region's strong sense of pride and the recent surge in interest about Cajun people and culture. In Chicago, where licenses are not required of guides, one can still be assured of having a memorable tour with an erudite, impassioned architectural historian from an organization such as Architours.

If certification is to win broad acceptance among guides, the industry, and travelers, it must stand up to the scrutiny of its critics. These questions must be considered in formulating an appropriate program: Will certified guides be better qualified in any measurable ways? Are the qualifications for certification truly relevant to effective guiding? Are the qualifications challenging, so that certification is genuinely earned, or is the designation easily attained by paying a fee? On the other hand, are standards so exclusive as to be suspect, or so unattainable as to eliminate many who actually excel at what they do? These are important questions to consider in the development of a certification process.

In spite of the objections or questions about how new standards and certification can work or be applied, there is no doubt that a movement toward certification and stated standards is already emerging within the field with the enthusiastic support of many guides. In addition, the industry at large is becoming aware of and, both tacitly and overtly, supporting this trend. The wave has begun, and it seems likely that the 1990s will be marked by more educational programs and greater support for certification.

Guide Training and Certification

So much discussion has focused on certification that it is essential to clarify the distinction between certification and education. While certification is an outward measure or symbol of achievement, the essential foundation of certification is education. Guides must be more committed to learning and improving their skills than in acquiring sets of initials to embellish their resumes. Certification enhances the guide's image, but education forms his or her very identity. It has been suggested that some guides, in their desire to improve their image, are focusing more energy on certification than on education. Such a tendency would only diminish the impact of certification, for without a solid commitment to education, certification is meaningless.

In order to attempt to outline a proper educational path or curriculum for guides, several key issues must be addressed. As with teaching, a guide's education must be two-fold: training in the many subject areas which he or she "teaches, and training in the skills essential to conduct his or her work. As a working professional, a guide must have an understanding of his or her business: all the duties of the job, how and where to gain employment, how to implement a marketing plan, trends and developments in the field, and the tools of the trade. For guides, the latter include speaking, language, research, and interpretive and social skills. As travel industry professionals, guides must have a thorough understanding of their industry and their place within it. All of these skills and topics can be viewed as core competencies.

Finally, as an educator, facilitator, and representative of a region, a guide must learn a great deal about a variety of subjects specific to his region: the natural environment, geography, history, politics, and culture, including its art, architecture, literature, and more. Certainly the extent to which guides devote themselves to these topics depends upon both the guide and the region. For

Figure 6.1
Educational programs for guides have gained in popularity in recent years. (*Photo by Sharon Murphy, Today Photography.*)

example, guides of Ottawa, Mexico City, and Washington, D.C., would be expected to have a solid grasp of the schedule, policies, personalities, and nuances of the national government; guides in Alaska and Hawaii should be able to offer at least a general explanation of the geology of those states; and guides conducting tours of New England will likely be questioned about such diverse topics as the American Revolutionary War, nineteenth-century American literature, and the reason leaves change color in the fall. As each region and site is unique and imposes different demands on guides, the content of a guide's curriculum—and the instructors for such curriculum—must ultimately be determined regionally, and when applicable, at each site.

Gabriel Cherem, professor of interpretation at Eastern Michigan University, has suggested that interpreters differ only in their subject matter, and that each individual in the field should consider himself or herself an interpreter first, and a specialist second. He goes on to say that all interpreters must have the best training possible. Obtained "through professional, rigorous college curricula, through short courses, and through in-service training in interpretation," Cherem suggested coursework in interpretive methods, field studies, interpretive planning and management, and interpretive research and theory. "In addition, courses in communications, dramatics, creative writing, art, photography, public administration, landscape architecture, and industrial design can be powerful support areas for the sophisticated interpreter" (Cherem 1977). Further, Cherem cites specific examples of appropriate courses of study for particular interpreters, such as natural history, ecology, and environmental issues for the interpretive naturalist; anthropology and the study of ethnology and religion for the cultural interpreter; and local, regional, national, and world history as essential for the historical interpreter.

Is a National Curriculum Possible—or Advisable?

Certainly, it is necessary and helpful for guide training to be both subject- and region-oriented. Some guides in the United States, Canada, and Mexico are presently discussing the establishment of a national core curriculum for guides, suggesting that it is both possible and advantageous. A similar concept is already employed in England, where the National Tourist Board has established a core curriculum for guides in all regions of the country, to which local tourist boards add regional courses. Similar programs are operating throughout most of Europe and in Japan.

Outside the guiding profession, recent discussion of the topic of a national core curriculum has sparked great debate. Two of 1987's best-selling books— *Cultural Literacy: What Every American Needs to Know* by E. D. Hirsch, Jr., and *The Closing of the American Mind* by Allan Bloom—cited surveys and statistics about the "cultural illiteracy" of Americans and lambasted the American educational system for failing to meet the needs of its citizens. These books, and many of their genre, propose that a renewed priority be placed on education, particularly the liberal arts, and suggested specific topics for study.

The National Endowment for the Humanities is also committed to this issue. Recent publications include *Tyrannical Machines: A Report on Educational Practices Gone Wrong and Our Best Hopes for Setting Them Right* (Cheney 1990), and *50 Hours* (Cheney 1989), a suggested core curriculum for a well-rounded college education.

Certainly the United States is not alone in its concern for the education of its citizens, for all countries have a stake in an informed and productive society. The trend toward an awareness of cultural literacy and the literature it has spawned has a particular relevance to guides. Many feel that they, too, should attempt to establish a core curriculum that is challenging and penetrating enough to make a difference and yet is broad enough to be applicable to all guides. Surely guides, as educators, hosts, and regional and national representatives, should be culturally literate.

The cultural literacy trend is not without its critics, however. Many feel that Hirsch's model, for example, is too Eurocentric and culturally biased, and that the emphasis on specific items (*Cultural Literacy* lists 5,000 "essential names, phrases, dates, and concepts") amounts to a "trivial pursuit" approach to education. The NEH's proposed curriculum has been similarly criticized. Further, many feel its emphasis on classical literature is simply too idealistic in an age in which computers and other technology dominate.

This discussion recalls Carl Rogers's assertions that the key aim for educators today is not to teach so much as to facilitate learning, to develop individuals who are "learners in process . . . the kind of individuals who can live in a delicate but ever-changing balance between what is presently known and the flowing, moving, altering problems and facts of the future." True enough, say Hirsch, Bloom, and others, but certainly we can—and must—expect that every educated person should comprehend a basic body of knowledge.

Such heated debate about the state of the twentieth-century mind will likely persist. Meanwhile, it is essential to continue the quest of educating guides in the best manner possible, and attempting to create a national skeleton curriculum for guides has merit for several reasons.

1. In countries such as the United States, such a curriculum seems better that what is now available—nothing.

2. Even if deemed too broad or too demanding for all guides, it at least gives guides and educators from a particular region a framework from which to create an appropriate curriculum.

3. It provides a basis from which guides and educators can debate and modify.

Appendix C offers examples of core curricula. For guides in the United States there are two sections: a "universal" core curriculum (that is, those "tools-of-the-trade" topics that every guide should master) and subject areas and topics with which a guide in any region of the United States should be familiar.

Teaching Knowledge and Skills

While few would argue that subjects such as history, geography, architecture, and art can be easily taught and learned, many believe that the more important aspects of effective guiding are innate features and cannot be taught, and that personal qualities such as sensitivity, wit, and common sense do not lend themselves to classroom instruction. Even some teachers of guides agree. Gerald Wolfe, an experienced guide, professor of urban history, and trainer of many guides in New York City, says, "To a great extent, one either has it or does not."

On the other hand, Freeman Tilden said, "Interpretation is an art, and any art is to some degree teachable." One could argue that in a comprehensive observation and evaluation process problems such as misinformation, poor grammar, and ineffective speaking techniques can be cited and kneaded out of the interpreter's delivery. And those seemingly intangible, unteachable traits might be encouraged in learners who observe effective instructors with those attributes.

The final argument for educating and training guides is its alternative: doing nothing. By not pursuing education and training, the profession will surely not progress. In its early stages, certification for guides is a voluntary option. The final arbiters of the success of the guiding profession will likely be the travel industry and travelers themselves. In time, the profession may have a widely accepted or even mandatory certification process. For now, the first and most important step, most agree, is to better educate guides.

In the absence of a national or industrywide plan, a wide variety of training and certification programs for guides are emerging throughout the United States. Chicago State University and Central Florida University have incorporated guiding courses into their curricula. Community colleges such as Miami-Dade, Northern Virginia, and Los Angeles have developed certificate programs. And several proprietary schools, among them the International Guide Academy in Denver and International Tour Management Institute (ITMI) in San Francisco, offer courses for both guides and tour managers. The National Park Service has two major training centers where, ongoing programs in interpretation and other subjects are offered. (Appendix A lists those institutions known to offer seminars, courses, certificates, or degrees in guiding and interpretation.)

SUMMARY

Educating visitors is certainly one of the guide's most important and demanding roles. As greater numbers of people travel and the knowledge, sophistication, and expectations of travelers increase, the demands on guides to be effective educators and to be better educated themselves will also intensify. Education is vital in the establishment of a guide's identity (internal, or self-perception) and image (the external, or public perception). Few would disagree with these statements; however, much debate is occurring as to the level of training or testing required, the content of instruction, and the pace of the process. Although there is controversy within the profession on these issues, the greatest pressure for higher standards is being exerted by guides themselves, who are working toward implementing certification and more consistent education programs.

III. Techniques

7   *Leadership and Social Skills*

"So many guides forget the most important, most obvious bottom line: that people are here to enjoy themselves."

—John Stein, owner,
Washington Insider Tours

Mark Twain's account of his cheerless, self-absorbed Italian guide reciting tomes of information to weary, inundated travelers (described in Chapter 1) is, unfortunately, not confined to Italy or to the nineteenth century. Officious behavior seems to be a strong inclination of tour guides of every era. Travelers throughout history have noted well-intentioned, knowledgeable guides rushing to explain the origin of every object on view and to deliver to visitors all that they are promised, oblivious that the very people they are working so feverishly to please are tired, indifferent, or otherwise uncomfortable. In their quest for credibility and professionalism, many guides take their role of informant so seriously that they often overlook their travelers' enjoyment. For some guides, concern for others is innate, the most enjoyable aspect of their work, and the very reason they became and remain guides. For others, social skills are difficult to learn and to incorporate into the guiding experience.

THE GUIDE'S PERSONALITY

Most people have a fairly well-defined image of the ideal tour guide: outgoing, affable, well-informed, enthusiastic. Certainly the best guides are an eclectic composite of these positive personality traits. As noted in Chapter 2, however, guides, tour operators, and travelers often have vastly different perceptions about a guide's most important qualities.

Gabriel Cherem, professor of interpretation at Eastern Michigan University, suggests that a "gregarious or malleable temperament is more important than formal training. The ideal image of the interpretor," he says, "will be the knowledgeable, fluent, charming individual who can captivate the imagination and emotion of an audience. The personality appeal of an interpretor should be so strong as to evoke the response from the visitor, 'I want to be near that individual'" (Cherem 1977).

Several specific traits are important and highly desirable for effective guides. Others are skills that must be taught or, at least, described and demonstrated. Still others are so intangible as to be difficult to define or measure. Some of these highly desirable traits are described below.

- *Enthusiasm.* Perhaps the single most important characteristic of successful guides is passion, both for the subject matter and the travelers. This enthusiasm will not only make the traveler's experience more compelling, but will sustain both guide and visitors through mentally and physically exhausting experiences.

   Enthusiasm is usually accompanied by affability and generosity. When guides are enthusiastic about their subject or region, they are usually inclined to become more knowledgeable about it and, thus, more confident in their presentation of it.

   Enthusiasm is not easily feigned; to a great extent, a guide either has it or does not. Certainly enthusiasm is not taught or learned in any traditional sense, but many believe it can be acquired. In fact, many guides feel studying a region and guiding tours in that region has deepened their enthusiasm for that area. Peggy Wood, a Washington, D.C., guide since 1980, says, "When I moved to the area, I didn't like it at all. A friend suggested that I would like it more if I learned more about it, so I enrolled in a guide training course. And she was right; now I love it here."

- *An outgoing and affable nature.* As guides are in the business of meeting, welcoming, and working for strangers, it is essential that they be approachable, open, and comfortable in many types of situations and with a wide range of personalities. However daunting that prospect may be to some, many guides regard it as the most interesting aspect of their work.

   Cherem and others go so far as to say that individuals with highly introverted or nonpublic personalities should be actively discouraged from the field of interpretation. Others point out that introverts can survive—even thrive—in guiding, noting that shy individuals often "come alive" in front of a group. Indeed, many successful guides would describe themselves as introverts, and many eminent guides admit that addressing the public is a continual challenge. Whatever a guide's nature, it is essential that he or she possess the ability to be friendly, to initiate conversation, and to encourage others to do the same.

- *Self-confidence.* Developing self-confidence in a career requires a basic level of self-esteem combined with experience. Self-confidence enables guides to carry out their duties assertively and effectively, to put people at ease, and to help create enjoyable experiences.

- *A proactive nature.* One of the hallmarks of a true leader is the belief in one's own ability to affect change and the willingness to assume responsibility for initiating change. Such a belief is usually accompanied by a commitment to imaginative solutions and a contagious sense of optimism. This proactive—as opposed to reactive—behavior is vital for success in guiding, as guides are regularly thrust into unpredictable and challenging situations for which they must find quick, amenable solutions.

- *Sensitivity.* Extremely important, the term "sensitivity" is used here to include the wide range of human understanding required of a successful guide. Beyond liking people, successful guides are compassionate, respectful, tactful, and observant. They are sensitive to other's needs and understanding of other perspectives. Guides must be attuned to such occurrences as injuries, illnesses, disabilities, or friction among passengers. New Orleans guide and author Joan Garvey says, "People will forgive many shortcomings in a guide—even lack of knowledge about the region—but they won't forgive the guide who doesn't care about them."

- *Flexibility.* In the domain of travel, where even the best-planned itineraries go awry, flexibility and patience are vital. This includes the ability to convince others to be flexible and patient as well.

- *Authenticity.* Few qualities will offend or alienate people more quickly than phoniness or dishonesty. Most people are instinctively drawn to and trust people who are genuine and who have an honest, open aura about them.

- *A pleasant, professional appearance.* It is often said that people decide whether or not they like or value a person within the first few seconds of meeting them. First impressions are often indelible and are frequently based upon one's physical appearance. Many people may assume that those who are clean, well-groomed, and care about their appearance are on top of things and extend the same exacting qualities to their work. Moreover, people make assumptions about others, both accurate and inaccurate, based on other aspects of appearance, such as posture, weight, and stylishness.

- *Sense of humor.* A good sense of humor can bring people closer together, put them at ease, and help make the inevitable glitches of travel amusing instead of stressful and unpleasant. Since most people like to laugh, they will usually appreciate guides who bring humor to the experience. Using humor appropriately, however, requires sensitivity: a joke that makes one person laugh may offend another.

- *Knowledge.* A well-rounded body of knowledge about a wide array of topics is fundamental. Subject areas differ for guides in every region, and it is wise for guides to investigate its local educational programs. In recent years many more programs are available throughout the world on such relevant subjects as the travel industry, cross-cultural understanding, speaking techniques, and marketing.

- *Good communication skills.* The most knowledgeable and sensitive person will not succeed as a guide without the ability to communicate well. Good communication skills include articulation, eye contact, natural gestures, and a clear, pleasant speaking voice. Moreover, the absence of any one of these features can create difficulty for a guide. A nasal voice, a thick accent, annoying inflections, or a constant nervous gesture, for example, can be distracting as to eclipse the many other positive traits a guide possesses. (Communication skills are discussed in detail in Chapter 8, "Presentation and Speaking Skills," and in Chapter 9, "Bringing a Place to Life.")

- *Organization.* Time management and organization skills are underrated, essential skills. Keeping to a schedule despite delays, meeting appointments, and moving visitors along without their feeling pushed or herded is one of the balancing acts a guide must perform daily. Behind the scenes of every tour is an abundance of paperwork: instructions, maps, appointment and confirmation letters, passenger information, and bookkeeping tasks. Apart from the demanding tasks of interpretation and interaction with passengers, guides are often charged with writing and recording checks, confirming reservations, coordinating routes with drivers, and updating their agencies about the tour's status. As with so many other professions, the best measure of a guide's success is to make all of these tasks look effortless and even imperceptible. Coordinating all the tasks requires consistent planning, careful time management, and meticulous attention to detail.

- *Decisiveness.* Ultimately the guide must be knowledgeable and confident enough to make quick decisions—decisions which are sometimes unpopular or costly. Occasionally, a tour emergency may require quick, difficult decisions that involve spending a company's money or altering an itinerary. Guides often find that it is more advantageous to make decisions on behalf of a group than to use the democratic method, as voting may alienate those in the minority.

- *Good health.* Many prospective guides underestimate the rigors of guiding. Such elements as walking, long and irregular hours, different diets and eating schedules, and the stress of constantly being in the spotlight demand considerable energy and resilience.

- *Personal integrity.* As for all professionals, a strong sense of ethics is crucial to success. Guides have a moral responsibility to themselves, their employers, colleagues, travelers, and even to their regions. (See Chapter 13, "Professional Ethics and Etiquette.")

- *Charisma.* Charisma has been defined as "a personal magic of leadership arousing popular loyalty or enthusiasm." Charisma is a synthesis of many of the traits listed above and evokes the response Cherem describes as "I want to be near that individual" (Cherem 1977).

While not all guides have all of the traits described here, some level of charisma is evident in the most successful guides. Some of the traits described here can be taught, some evolve over time, and others one either has or does not. Although the "ideal guide" would embody all of these traits, having or achieving them and learning to apply them to the diverse, unpredictable experiences of guiding is extremely difficult. Indeed, as Cherem notes, "The achievement of such a level of interpretor sophistication is a long-term process. Quite frankly the interpretor should be prepared for a lifetime of personal and professional development—a lifetime of becoming" (Cherem 1977).

MOMENTS OF TRUTH

The extent to which guides operate within their roles of host, educator, leader, public relations representative, and conduit differs with the personality of the guide, the circumstances of the trip, and the composition of the group of travelers. And yet, success or failure in guiding (as in any service industry) depends upon what is now commonly referred to as "moments of truth," a term coined by Jan Carlzon, president of Scandinavian Airlines (SAS). Carlzon defines a "moment of truth" as "that precise instant when the customer comes into contact with any aspect of your business and, on the basis of that contact, forms an opinion about the quality of your service and, potentially, the quality of your product" (Carlzon 1987). As president of SAS, Carlzon inherited a fledgling company with low morale and dwindling sales. He recognized that the critical moments of truth for customers of the airline occurred not with SAS's corporate executives but rather with ticket agents, flight attendants, and other "front-line employees." Carlzon adopted a new philosophy for his company then considered revolutionary and since adopted worldwide. Since these front-line employees took part in the critical "moments of truth" for SAS, Carlzon reasoned, they should be empowered to make company decisions in the interest of serving customers. Thus, many of the annoying roadblocks one typically finds in the service industry—such as the perfunctory responses of "that's not my job," "I don't make the rules, I just follow them," or "I can't handle that; I'll have to refer you to my supervisor"—are eliminated. According to Carlzon, this philosophy places the emphasis and priority where it belongs, and addresses the most basic questions: "Is the customer satisfied with the experience?" and "Is the customer enjoying himself?" The results of this philosophy at SAS, in terms of customer response, sales, and employee morale, were overwhelmingly positive.

The moment of truth concept has registered an immeasureable effect on the service industry. Karl Albrecht, one of the leading forces in service industry training, calls these moments of truth "the anthem for service management." In a global, service-oriented economy, moments of truth will determine the very existence of many businesses.

Albrecht's Seven Sins of Service

Often it is easier and more instructive to cite poor service than adequate service. Consumers are assaulted regularly by what Karl Albrecht calls the "seven sins of service." The seven sins, as applied to guiding, are:

1. *Treating customers with apathy.* Certainly it is no accident that Albrecht listed this sin first. As noted earlier, travelers will forgive many shortcomings in a guide, but apathy is not one of them. As with any service-oriented profession, guides who are suffering from chronic apathy or burnout should temporarily or permanently seek other work.

2. *Brushing customers off.* A by-product of apathy, brushing customers off—the guide giving the impression that he or she would rather be elsewhere—alienates quickly. This is a particular challenge for many guides, for unlike many professions guiding is not a 9-to-5 obligation. Often, in fact, guides are on duty from

the morning through the late evening, and the challenge is to establish moments away from the group without appearing to brush them off.

3. *Being cold to customers.* The officious behavior described earlier, the failure to be genuine and cordial, and the inability or lack of desire to share one's self with people all express coldness toward the customer. Many travelers cite "meeting people" as the primary motivation for traveling; for them, having a cold or distant guide negates the benefits of their effort.

4. *Treating customers with condescension.* Although a condescending attitude among guides is a common complaint of visitors, most guides who commit this error are completely unaware of it. A guide who talks to tenth-grade students in the same tone as he speaks to fourth graders, or a guide who assumes that every senior citizen is hard of hearing and suffers from Alzheimer's disease unknowingly insults her guests. While the guide might be thinking, "I'll make this so simple they'll be sure to understand," the message the group perceives is "I sense you won't understand unless I make this very elementary." To state this another way, the guide indicates to the listeners that he or she is out of touch with them. Whether speaking to young, middle-aged or elderly people, oversimplification is rarely appreciated. The skilled interpreter has many ways of determining a group's level of understanding, including questioning, listening, and encouraging participation.

5. *Working like a robot.* The "I can do this with my eyes closed" attitude is conveyed more readily than many workers realize. Over the years, guiding has unfortunately attracted many robots. Canned, sing-song spiels are so common that many visitors expect them. Such behavior is offensive because it indicates apathy and boredom and is just as tiresome for the listeners as it is for the speaker.

6. *Getting hung up on the rule book.* Albrecht, Carlzon, and many others propose that service employees, before proclaiming, "Sorry, our policy is . . ." analyze the situation to see if straying from the rule book poses a detriment to anyone. Often it does not, and, in fact, challenging or bending the rules creates a better solution for everyone involved. While itineraries serve many purposes for both guide and traveler, they are rarely followed to the letter, or need to be. In fact, most companies that furnish itineraries for travelers will purposely avoid noting times to avoid having passengers (and their guide) cling to them.

7. *Giving customers "the run-around."* Many guides who see their role specifically as that of educator are offended by what they perceive as a visitor's more mundane needs or those needs that fall outside their duties. Such comments as "Your concierge can recommend the best restaurants around your hotel" or "Call room service—they should be able to help you" may be unnecessary diversions, when all a visitor wants, for example, is the guide's simple recommendation. Even in cases where a task does fall outside of the guide's responsibility or expertise, his or her handling of the situation can make the difference between a visitor getting assistance or feeling as if he's getting the run-around. For example, the guide refers a visitor to the front desk, who then refers the visitor to the concierge, who, it is soon discovered, is on a break. Frustrated, the visitor then retreats to her room, her question unanswered. The visitor perceives this as get-

ting the run-around, which began with the guide. If the guide, on the other hand, extends a few moments of time and energy by walking with the visitor to the concierge and, seeing that the concierge is not on duty, finds another solution, the result is excellent service and a satisfied customer. In a competitive, service-oriented industry such gestures are increasingly vital to a guide's success.

As mentioned previously, guides are often more worried about how knowledgeable they are rather than how effective they are. Most travelers would rate guide knowledge as far less critical than the omission or commission of these seven basic sins.

Cycle of Service

To assess whether or not a customer's moments of truth are favorable, Albrecht advises a company or individual to identify their customer's moments of truth, or those instances in which the customer comes in contact with the service and formulates an opinion. Albrecht notes that it is essential that this cycle be formulated from the customer's perspective and not that of the employee or the business.

The traveler's "Cycle of Service" (Figure 7.1), adapted from Albrecht's model, highlights the moments of truth for travelers on the first day of a tour: a group departs for a trip, arrives in a new city, meets a guide, and is introduced to the region. As illustrated, the customer's moments of truth begin well before he or she meets the guide. Once the traveler arrives at the intended destination, however, the guide becomes directly or indirectly responsible for countless moments of truth.

This cycle of service model illustrates many of the demands placed upon guides as well as the need for guides to work cooperatively with travelers and with all other players in the cycle, including tour operators, hotel and restaurant employees, museum docents, and others. Guides are travelers' constant companions. As their link to a city, region, or subject area, guides themselves are truly critical "moments of truth" for the tour industry. (Chapter 10, "The Nuts and Bolts of Conducting a Tour," explores the logistics involved in group tours.)

WORKING WITH DIFFERENT AGE GROUPS

Students

As many cities and sites around the world yield ideal learning environments for children of all ages, the number of student trips is increasing dramatically. Many schools and teachers attempt to incorporate a tour into their curricula, requiring that a guide be particularly resourceful.

For some guides, groups of young students are the most difficult to guide.

Figure 7.1
The traveler's cycle of service: the first day of a tour. (*Adapted from Karl Albrecht's "cycle of service," Service America!*)

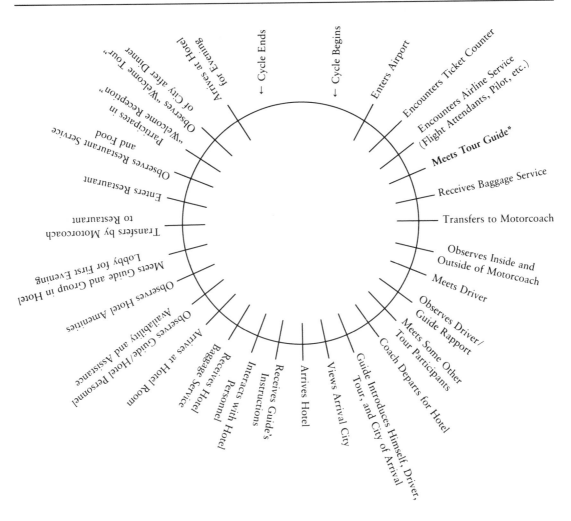

They pose special challenges in terms of discipline, motivation, and interest level. In addition, many student tours are designed to have longer hours, so as to avoid pandamonium in hotels. Students must be kept continually involved and motivated. To accomplish this, a guide must be adept at asking questions and using other creative techniques to draw students into the experience. (Some of these techniques are highlighted in Chapter 9, "Bringing a Place to Life.") However, the techniques that work for one region or one particular age group may fall flat for another group of students. For example, peer pressure can make a question-and-answer situation for students in the middle or upper grades particularly threatening or embarrassing. Thus, guides who ask questions are frequently perceived as condescending to students. Guides who are out of touch with the interests of young people will have a difficult time reaching them or giving an effective tour.

Students rarely travel without chaperones. Although guides have an opportunity and responsibility to create the ambiance of the tour, many guides prefer that the chaperone monitor student behavior. There are several good reasons for this. For one, chaperones (usually teachers or parents) are more familiar with the students and, therefore, have more insight into their abilities and behavior. Chaperones also bear the ultimate responsibility for the students. As a result, students are prepared to conform to the standards established by the chaperones. In most cases, it is not the guide's responsibility or place to alter these standards.

The extent to which a guide is expected to discipline a group of students depends upon the guidelines established between the guide and chaperones. Often teachers accompanying the students will ask that they remain silent when the guide or anyone is speaking to them and will ask guides to demand the same. Such policies make the experience much more enjoyable for most guides. Some chaperones, especially those who perceive the tour to be the students' vacation, will make no such demands on them. The unfortunate result in these cases is that the task of disciplining students rests solely on the shoulders of the guide, and if no chaperone support follows, chaos ensues. Although many guides are comfortable (and effective) with the responsibility of discipline, others are not and resent what they perceive as a lackadaisical attitude on the part of chaperones.

One practice prevalent among a few student tour companies who market directly to teachers is that of presenting the guide as a chaperone. Some of these companies market the tours as a getaway "vacation" for the teacher, even encouraging them to plan a day or evening away from the students to enjoy the area. This practice appears to be abating, however.

Fortunately, many school officials take a proactive approach to student behavior on school trips. According to Jeff McHugh, dean of students at Fairfield Woods Middle School, in Fairfield, Connecticut

The staff at FWMS has adopted Canter's Assertive Discipline classroom model for all school activities, including the annual school trip. These rules are discussed in advance with all students prior to the trip. The students also know what consequences face them if they violate the rules and are also aware of possible positive rewards that they can earn if the trip runs smoothly. The general rules are (1) follow directions the first time given; (2) always be on time; (3) keep hands, feet, and objects to yourself; (4) No littering; and (5) all laws and school rules are in effect governing drugs, tobacco, alcohol, theft, and vandalism. The rules are observable and deliberately limited to five. It is also helpful to have rules for bus decorum or for when the guide is lecturing.

The consequences for violating rules are (1) delay (last off the bus); (2) loss of trip time, (3) assignment to an adult chaperone for a period of time, (4) a phone call to parents, and (5) removal from the trip and return to parents.

It is important to let them know when their behavior is appreciated. Consequences for good behavior include extra free time in the hotel (closely monitored by adults) and special activities that can be "prebuilt" into the itinerary.

Figure 7.2
The large numbers of student groups traveling to historic and educational areas provide many opportunities for guides. (*Photo by Central Photo, Inc., Washington, D.C.*)

Such stated rules and standards and consistent expectations on the part of adults actually build a cooperative environment rather than an adversarial one, as students always know what is expected of them. Ideally, such policies emerge from the schools and chaperones, as they have in this example. When no such standards appear to exist, guides might suggest similar approaches, especially on tours lasting longer than one day.

Senior Citizens

If guides were asked to choose their favorite age group, most would likely pick—without hesitation—senior citizens. Stereotypes of senior citizens as grumpy, demanding, or otherwise difficult are largely unjustified. Although the likelihood that some members of the group will have difficulty hearing or walking is certainly greater as age increases, senior citizens are generally appreciative, eager for experience, curious, interested, and attentive, and willing to contribute much of their own life experience. Further, the pacing of senior citizen tours is often less demanding.

It is important to recognize the wide range of abilities and interests that fall under the collective label of "senior citizen." A senior citizen is generally anyone over the age of sixty (and younger by some definitions). Considering the trend toward longer, more active lives, it is difficult to generalize about senior citizens. Senior citizens run marathons, start successful businesses, and often have fuller, busier lives than they did at age thirty.

Still, there are important facts to keep in mind when working with senior citizens. All of the senses decline in the aging process. Often one's loss of sensory perception occurs so subtly, and over such a long period of time, that a person is not even aware of it. Others, self-conscious about their deficiencies, attempt to conceal them. Deafness, for example, is quite common and often overlooked. A traveler with a hearing impairment may miss much of the tour without the guide realizing it.

Rosalind Hutchinson, chairperson of the Guild of Guide Lecturers in London, suggests that most guides are instinctively aware when they need to give extra care, attention, and observation. She advises guides to keep in mind the following when guiding for senior citizens:

- Allow extra time for the tour as many activities will take longer, such as getting on and off a motorcoach, eating, and walking anywhere.
- Pause frequently and make several short stops on walking tours.
- Be particularly attentive to fatigue or any signs of stress or illness. If a participant becomes frightened or short of breath, allow them to sit and rest for at least a few minutes. (Refer to Appendix D for a review of basic safety and first aid.)
- Pay close attention to special medical problems or difficulties and pay special (but inconspicuous) attention to their status.
- Since hearing and memory problems are more common as people age, always repeat instructions, especially meeting times.

Although these and other steps are important in enhancing tours for senior citizens, Hutchinson also warns guides against patronizing or underestimating older people. "After all," she says, "[these tours are] well worth the effort. Most [senior citizens] are incredibly wise, and we can learn from them."

WORKING WITH "DIFFICULT" PEOPLE

Outrageous and humorous "war stories" of those who regularly work with the public are legion. One recently released book on the subject of "difficult people" offers "hundreds of proven strategies and techniques to get cooperation and respect from tyrants, connivers, badmouthers and other difficult people you must work with every day." The unstated presumption is that there are patently difficult people. (It would follow that all other people are "easy.")

While nearly every person could admit to moments of impatience, tardiness, or otherwise inelegant behavior, few would ever want to be typecast by those situations. Likewise, branding people as "busybodies," "tyrants," or with otherwise "difficult" epithets is to ascribe more to them than is usually known or is productive to believe. The more equitable—and productive—perspective for anyone who regularly works with the public is that people sometimes exhibit difficult behavior. San Francisco guide and tour manager Janice Holliday says, "I've learned to look beyond the personality and deal with the person."

The difference between these two cases—difficult people and difficult behavior—may seem subtle, but is in fact far-reaching for both guides and travelers. As an example, a passenger might approach a guide on the first day of a tour to report something she doesn't like. Assuming that the traveler is a "complainer," the guide unconsciously adopts a defensive stance ("Here she goes. . . . I need to let her know that I'm not going to put up with constant complaints. . . .") without giving the traveler an opportunity to voice her concern. Thus, the guide begins the trip frustrated and with an annoyed passenger, and the traveler begins the trip with the perception that the guide is cold, short-tempered, and indifferent to the passengers.

If, however, the guide operates from the belief that this is a reasonable person who is momentarily unhappy, the encounter begins on an altogether different note. The passenger perceives and appreciates the guide's concern, and feels grateful for the support. Thus, a spirit of cooperation is established from the outset of the tour.

This is not to suggest that some people will not exert difficult behavior repeatedly. Guides, like all those who work with people, encounter those who complain, those who are late, or those who attempt to dominate others. The incidence of difficult behavior is, however, relatively infrequent. Moreover, poor behavior handled with compassion and reason can be converted to model behavior. It is rarely a coincidence that some guides have consistently content, well-behaved groups while others have repeated problems with lateness, discourteousness, and even "mutiny."

For all the horrifying and amusing stories guides share about difficult passengers and difficult groups, it is the guide who is largely responsible for the ambiance of a tour. Creating an atmosphere of harmony and mutual trust is the first task a guide must address upon meeting a group. In the initial moments of meeting, visitors will scan the guide for cues about his or her attitude, personality, capability, and any other indications about the kind of experience they will have. If such intense scrutiny seems daunting, a few facts are worth noting:

1. People travel on tours primarily to enjoy themselves. As one tour operator puts it, "This isn't brain surgery. Relax and enjoy yourself, and your group will, too."

2. Most people would like to see the guide succeed.

3. No one expects perfection. In fact, many perfectionists put people on edge. As piano virtuoso Vladimir Horowitz once said, "Always there should be a little mistake here and there—I am for it. The people who don't do mistakes are cold like ice."

Keeping these concepts in mind and adopting an optimistic, proactive attitude can help guides establish rapport, develop and maintain cohesiveness among tour members, and deal with challenging situations as they arise.

Establishing Rapport and Cohesiveness

Rapport—the sense of connectedness and mutual trust—is a popular subject of much current psychological literature. Many psychologists and human relations experts advocate learning techniques for developing rapport. Among the most popular of these learning techniques is neuro-linguistic programming (NLP), which is based on the premise that people perceive primarily in one of three ways—visually, auditorily, or kinesthetically. Those who practice NLP believe that highly effective communication and rapport can be learned. By recognizing which of these three ways others perceive, guides are better equipped to deal with a variety of personalities. For example, if a person is "visual," they will respond to visual stimuli and to visually oriented language (words such as see, show, visualize, horizon, appear, examine). Those who are "auditory" will respond to sounds and to auditory language, including words such as say, hear, scream, and articulate. "Kinesthetic" types will respond to sensory stimuli and words like touch, feel, hold, grasp, and pressure. NLP practitioners recommend that those who work with groups of people consciously utilize all three modes, increasing the likelihood of reaching everyone. Many NLP practitioners liken matching communication modes to speaking the same language.

Creating rapport and a harmonious, cohesive environment—as opposed to merely controlling a group—is a primary goal of a leader and a guide. The following tips can help guides build rapport and maintain cohesiveness and order.

1. Be prepared. The importance of knowing one's subject cannot be overstated. Seeing that a guide is comfortable and fluent in his or her role and region garners respect and ease among passengers.

2. Adopt an attitude of friendliness and positive expectancy, and take responsibility for creating and maintaining harmony.

3. Let visitors know that their enjoyment is of primary concern.

4. Respect others and be a careful, concerned listener. Establishing an environment in which each person feels free to contribute is more interesting and beneficial to everyone. In this way, people are more likely to approach the guide with questions or minor issues before they become major problems.

5. Give clear instructions. Saying, "We'll be leaving in about ten minutes" practically guarantees a late departure. A clearer, more effective approach is to say, "We will be departing at eleven sharp. According to my watch, it's now ten-forty."

6. Don't give ultimatums that cannot or will not be enforced. An example of this is telling people they will be left behind if they are late. Will they? Although leaving behind a chronically late person may be extremely tempting (and unanimously popular with other tour members), it should never be done without considerable warning and care.

7. Follow through on promises. It is best to be conservative with promises and not to mention places and events that passengers may not be able to see.

8. Avoid playing favorites, making a conscious effort to treat everyone the same. This can often be difficult, as guides, like all people, have a tendency to interact more with those who have similar interests. Quiet individuals are easier to overlook and can be more difficult to draw into a group. It is usually the more challenging passengers who monopolize the guide's time, and by indulging those passengers in all their complaints and problems, the guide denies the remainder of the group adequate time and attention.

9. Exemplify the desired behavior. By arriving early for every departure, avoiding gossip, not telling or laughing at insensitive jokes, not talking while others are talking, and otherwise embodying the traits of a model traveler, the guide provides a constructive paradigm. Guides should resist any urge to confide in passengers during a tour.

What If . . . ? Working Under Difficult Circumstances

The joy (and horror) of guiding lies in its unpredictability. No two individuals, groups, or tours are ever the same, and the range of situations, from humorous to challenging, can be staggering for a new guide.

The most serious glitches are those involving safety, such as medical emergencies and motorcoach breakdowns. (These are discussed in greater detail in Chapter 11, "Travelers with Special Needs," and Appendix D, "Basic Safety and

First Aid." Most of the problems, however, center around personalities. Perhaps the most common situations guides encounter are complaints about some aspect of the tour: the hotel room is too small or too close to the ice machine or elevator, the food is inadequate, or the schedule is too hurried. Handling complaints requires patience and diplomacy as guides are sometimes placed in the awkward, very delicate position of having to face guests who are, in fact, being given less than what they bought. As guides are normally hired by and representatives of tour operators, they must speak on behalf of the company. Since most companies agree—at least nominally—with the adage "the customer is always right," it is the guide's dual (and sometimes contradictory) duty to render compassion and genuine concern to the guest while defending the company.

Although tour operators always provide ways for guides to reach them (at their offices during the day, and with a company representative at all other times), guides are expected to do some troubleshooting, and placing a call to a tour operator is not always the best first step.

In the case of customer complaints, guides should ask themselves these questions:

1. What exactly is the complaint? Sometimes simply listening to the guest's full story is enough to placate him or her. Or by listening, the guide may discover that the complaint is the result of a cumulative problem that deserves more attention. In any case, all deserve to have their grievances heard.

2. Is the guest's complaint valid? While being assigned the room near the elevator can be less than ideal, such a complaint does not warrant a refund or an upgrade to a suite, nor is it a reason to notify the company. On the other hand, a leaky roof is unacceptable, and the guide should press the hotel into providing another room as quickly as possible.

3. Can the situation be resolved easily? If so, how? Often a complaint can be quickly resolved with no cost to the company or passenger. At other times, an issue involves much negotiation on the part of the guide on behalf of both the company and the visitor. If possible, it is often best if the guide can meet privately with another industry representative so that both feel free to fully discuss all ramifications and possible solutions. If the complaint cannot be resolved by the guide during the trip—as in the case of a billing or refund issue—there is no need for the guide and passenger to spend unnecessary time and energy during the tour trying to resolve it. By letting the visitor know that he is documenting the events for the tour operator and providing the visitor with the proper name and number of a person who can help him or her after the tour, the guide has fulfilled his duty.

Finally, in all cases of passenger problems or complaints, guides should document the situation and report it to the tour company.

Dealing with Chronically Late Passengers

Chronically late passengers are a common bone of contention between guides and tour passengers. A few suggestions are worth noting. Lateness is, in essence, a lack of courtesy, and when the schedules of many people are at stake, it is essential for guides to establish firm policies on promptness. This will win the respect of those who are consistently on time, and those who care less about punctuality will at least respect the policies.

As noted above, giving firm times is vital so that 9:00 will not be interpreted as 9:09. Although leaving behind a late person is a tenuous strategy, it is sometimes reasonable and justified. If a group is spending the night in the same town or city, the guide might handle a stop by clearly establishing the report time, and adding, "If you are not here at three o'clock, we'll assume that you have decided to remain here and wish to make your own way back to the hotel." In this way the guide provides a very clear option, and discussing it in terms of the group ("we") makes it a collective policy, providing an involved audience to help make the decision when the time of reckoning arrives. The guide can make the point even stronger by adding, "If you wish to make your own way back to the hotel, the best way is to take a taxi. Remember that we're meeting for dinner tonight at six-thirty." In this case, the guide has not only given a clear proposition, but has also provided an easy contingency plan.

Finally, a note of encouragement about "difficult" people. The range of personalities and problems guides encounter is vast and fascinating. Like difficult people, difficult situations are a matter of opinion and attitude, and those who expose themselves as monopolizers or complainers or who are chronically late are actually a very small percentage of people. "Difficult" people quickly make themselves known to all in the group, and many guides find they do not need to be heavy-handed with such passengers, as other passengers will often take matters into their own hands and reprimand them themselves.

Dealing with "Difficult" Questions

On the whole, the more experienced the guide, the more likely she is to welcome questions, even (especially) challenging ones. Those new to guiding often fear questions or are caught off guard by them. Whether a question is difficult depends upon the individual guide, but some questions are perennially difficult for guides. These include:

1. *Questions for which a guide does not have an answer.* For many guides, particularly novice guides, the most dreaded situation is being asked a question they cannot answer. Many guides measure their success by how much information they have, and not knowing the answer to a question diminishes their sense of self-worth and professionalism. As every guide eventually learns, there will always be new questions or questions that one cannot readily answer. (If not, it could be that the material is too familiar, and that the guide is no longer learning, in which case stagnation or burnout may not be far behind.) Once a guide begins to feel secure in his knowledge, such questions will not register to him (or others) as evidence that he is deficient. Many of the most successful interpreters and guides welcome questions they cannot answer as an impetus to learn something new.

Certainly the appropriate answer to questions for which the guide has no answer is "I don't know." Paradoxically, it can build one's credibility, as people value honesty and believe that they can trust the factual information the guide is able to provide.

In some cases, however, a simple "I don't know" may not be sufficient. An educated guess is sometimes acceptable, provided the guide has an approximate idea and indicates that she is guessing, though "I don't know, but I'll find out" is usually better. The guide can then use spare moments to look up the answer or consult someone else. Another solution is to say, "I don't know. Does anyone else know?" In addition to providing quick answers to questions, this allows others to participate.

2. *Questions whose answers are controversial.* This category includes questions about politics, religion, local scandals, or pending criminal cases. Guides are continuously confronted with these kinds of questions, as visitors often view guides as insiders and value their point of view. The long-standing maxim about avoiding the topics of sex, politics, and religion is advisable for guides, as one can never be sure of the political view or affiliation of everyone in a group. At the same time, there is a middle ground between absolute avoidance and sharing some personal views, which allows some of the guide's personality to emerge. In democratic societies, everyone is entitled to his or her own opinion, and, within reason, guides can share their own views, provided they qualify statements as their own opinion and remain open to the opinions of others. Visitors will often appreciate a guide's openness.

Appropriate responses to controversial questions include: "That's being debated here as we speak. Some feel . . . and others believe . . ." Another tactic is to return the question: "What do you think?" Often this will end the discussion. If not, it at least serves to invite other opinions, and people generally enjoy voicing their opinions. Sometimes, particularly in cases where local scandals have become national news, an individual or group will relentlessly press for the guide's personal view. In such cases, calling forth "Of course, I don't discuss my political views . . ." provides an easy exit. Guides are not obliged to answer questions or to become "chameleons," adopting the points of view of each of their groups.

3. *Questions that are, in the guide's view, too personal.* Clearly there are questions that no one should be asking and no one is obliged to answer. Questions such as "How much money do you make?" or "Why don't you have any children?" fall into this category. Sometimes personal questions of this nature can catch guides off guard to the extent that they forget that they do not need to answer. The challenge rests in dodging such questions gracefully.

Sometimes a question which the guide perceives as "too personal" may be intended as a gesture of concern or friendliness. Children, for example, often ask very personal or inappropriate questions. And certain questions are considered "too personal" in one culture and matter-of-fact in another.

Sometimes by simply eluding these questions sensitive questioners will discern that they have overstepped their bounds. Another solution is to respond with a depersonalized answer. For example, with questions having to do with salary and working conditions, perhaps the questioner is genuinely interested in guiding as a career. In such a case, a comfortable answer might be, "The salary range for guides in the United States is from x to y, and in big cities or places with high demand or high costs of living, the scale is on the higher end."

One guide suggests responding to inappropriate questions with a disbelieving look and "Pardon me?" In this case, merely having to repeat the question to an obviously startled person will often cause the questioner to swallow the question with, "Never mind." If not, at least the guide has created a few extra moments for determining a response.

If none of these tactics averts a personal question, the guide might respond by saying, "I prefer not to answer that," and move on.

4. *Questions that shed an unfavorable light on the guide or some aspect of the region.* Often people will pose these questions rhetorically, just to see how a guide will respond. Guides are not often given due credit for their commitment to their role of public relations representatives for their regions. On the whole, local governments and businesses would be pleased to see the extent to which most guides zealously defend their region and seek to present it in the most favorable way possible.

Kevin Delany trains people to appear before the media for The Executive Television Workshop, Inc. His clients—CEOs, journalists, politicians, and other well-known personalities—are often asked "difficult" questions before large audiences. Delany's advice to them is, "Don't ignore the question. Acknowledge it, and as quickly as possible create a bridge into the positive side or positive points you really want to stress. Then dwell on those positive points." For example, when asked how they tolerate the Louisiana humidity, some guides point out the resulting lush, green environment and add that, all things considered, they wouldn't rather live anywhere else. New Orleans guide Joan Garvey, when asked about trash in the city, said, "We get so many houseguests that we don't always have time to clean up the house."

An important key to responding to such questions is to refrain from a defensive response. Humor is extremely helpful. Former Mayor of New York City John Lindsey, when asked how he could tolerate breathing the air in his city, quipped, "I never trust air I can't see."

In the case of a complicated question or one that would not be of interest to everyone, it is sometimes desirable to divert the question to a later time ("Maybe we can take a few moments later to talk about that").

To summarize, these tactics are helpful in responding to questions:

- Welcome questions.
- Be gracious, even when the question is "difficult."
- Never belittle a question as stupid or trivial.
- Never feel obliged to answer a personal question.
- Acknowledge a controversial question, then move on to more positive points.
- Use humor when appropriate.

CROSS-CULTURAL UNDERSTANDING

In an increasingly global society, guides are called upon more and more to conduct tours for people from other cultures. Certainly all the basic tenets of positive human relations discussed elsewhere apply to working with anyone. And yet, truly understanding others requires stepping outside of one's own perspective or values. In fact, as Karl Albrecht points out, simply being a nice, concerned person is not entirely sufficient. The golden rule, "Do unto others as you would have them do unto you" assumes that all people prefer to be treated in the same way. George Bernard Shaw believed the key to good relations was to "do unto others as they would have done to themselves."

The following are guidelines that may help those in the service industry develop a multicultural perspective:

1. *Learn about the people and cultures of the world.* It has never been easier to learn about the world. Through the media, literature, school, and meeting international neighbors and visitors, one can learn much about the values, habits, and preferences of others.

2. *Travel.* Nothing offers a better means for truly understanding other cultures than travel. By eating others' foods, walking in their streets, listening to their music, and experiencing their daily concerns, travelers come to understand people on a level not possible through reading.

3. *Learn a language.* Learning and using another's language is one of the most basic and effective gestures toward forging positive cross-cultural experiences. Whether traveling in a foreign country or meeting guests in one's own country, learning another's language and attempting to converse in it is an act of courtesy and an expression of interest in another's culture. Certainly learning a foreign language is a long-term commitment. Even learning basic expressions, such as "Welcome," "please," thank you," or "may I help you with that?" in the languages of visitors makes a big difference.

4. *Participate in specialized cross-cultural training.* Cross-cultural training literature, courses, and seminars are now widely available to help those who live and work in multicultural settings, addressing both general cross-cultural contact and that which is specific to certain cultures. Such training is vital to guides as it enhances travel experiences and engenders goodwill.

Cross-cultural counselors recommend these basic guidelines for working with different cultures and languages.

1. Speak slowly and distinctly—at least until the level of understanding is established—and periodically ask listeners if they understand.

2. Be mindful of voice volume. Often speakers have a tendency to speak loudly to someone who does not understand them.

3. Encourage listeners to question what they do not understand, or interrupt if they need to have something repeated. Begin by using simple words and phrases

and short sentences. At the same time, be mindful of a person's understanding of the language. If they have a firm grasp of the language, overly simplistic language may appear condescending or insulting.

4. Encourage and reassure visitors in their use of the language.

5. Be patient and do not assist others attempting to use a foreign language unless they request help.

6. Speak in terms of positives rather than negatives. For example, tell a group what is expected, and omit telling them what not to do.

7. When an interpreter is present, speak to the listener and not the interpreter.

SUMMARY

As both a leader and a host, the guide accepts the challenge of creating a harmonious, cohesive atmosphere in which people can be comfortable, learn, and enjoy themselves. This requires a basic understanding of human nature and an attitude of respect, optimism, a willingness to serve, and a great interest in people and in one's region.

8   *Presentation and Speaking Skills*

"It is often said that people judge you during the first five seconds of simply looking at you, and again during the first five seconds after you begin to speak. These dual aspects of your person—your appearance and your voice and speaking ability—can make a crucial difference in your career and in your life."

—Lillian Brown,
Your Public Best

In virtually every survey ever taken on phobias, "speaking in front of a group" is cited as the most commonly held fear. Somewhere below it fall more predictable items such as death, snakes, and fire. From this one can surmise that most people would rather face snakes or fire, or even die, than speak in front of a group.

Public speaking does not have to be so formidable; in fact, most people who address groups will agree that public speaking can be extremely energizing and enjoyable. Moreover, the kind of public speaking a guide performs is not nearly as daunting as lecturing at a podium in an auditorium, for example. Indeed, if a guide is effectively interpreting a place, the visitors and the site itself are the prime attraction and the guide is merely the link between them. Intimidated guides might do well to remind themselves that when they are sharing the spotlight with the Grand Canyon or the Golden Gate Bridge, the visitor is usually much more interested in the latter than in them.

Overcoming the fear of speaking before a group is essential for guides. Not only is this possible but it is one of the rewards of guiding, for many guides credit guiding with curing them of that greatest of fears.

WHAT MAKES A SUCCESSFUL SPEAKER?

What is it that makes some people delightful, even mesmerizing, to listen to, and others monotonous and pedantic? It is sometimes easier to describe the components of a poor presentation than to pinpoint what makes a presentation memorable. Certainly no one likes to listen to a speaker who uses trite or arcane language, who mumbles or lisps, or who talks condescendingly. As noted earlier, the initial moments before a group are critical, as people often decide immediately whether or not they will listen to or value what a person says. How does a speaker inspire confidence and interest?

Generally, people are attracted to speakers who are enthusiastic, natural, and comfortable with their audience, their topic, and themselves. A spontaneous, solicitous, relaxed style draws listeners, while an unenthusiastic or tense style makes people wonder why they are there and daydream about making an exit. The Reverend Jesse Jackson, a master speaker, says, "Nervous speakers make people nervous."

For the novice speaker, such qualities as naturalness and serenity before a group are much easier to describe than to put into practice. As with any skill, the more adept the speaker is, the more effortless his or her work appears. Even some of the most accomplished and seemingly confident speakers admit to regular bouts of nervousness and the need to continually monitor and hone their communication skills.

How does one overcome the fear of speaking before groups? In short, speaking at ease requires feeling at ease. And one of the most important keys to feeling at ease in front of a group is being prepared. Preparation is not to be confused with the memorization of canned spiels, an unfortunate habit of many guides. True preparation boosts a speaker's confidence and ensures that he or she is comfortable and spontaneous with the subject. On the other hand, unprepared speakers are crippled, and the experience is uncomfortable and meaningless for both speaker and audience. Behind all great presentations—even seemingly spontaneous ones—is usually a long history of hard work and practice. Mark Twain once said, "It usually takes me more than three weeks to prepare a good impromptu speech."

Another essential key to combatting nervousness is to have a genuine interest and desire to share a subject with the group. Ron Hoff, author of *I Can See You Naked: A Fearless Guide to Making Great Presentations,* says, "Shift, as quickly as you can, from self-consciousness to audience-consciousness. Put yourself in their shoes. It's the best way to beat nervousness" (Hoff 1988). In moments when either preparation or desire is lacking, the other will usually carry the speaker.

Finally, experience will inevitably help develop confidence in speaking. All who are new to public speaking should find comfort in the knowledge that overcoming nervousness takes time and practice. With practice, guides find that they need less time to prepare for each tour and that they enjoy tours rather than fear them. Even experience does not entirely cure speaking jitters, however. And, according to Janice Holliday, "Even though you become less fearful, the edge that adds to an enthusiastic approach need not be lost or overcome."

In time, most guides gain confidence, overcome nervousness, and become more relaxed, spontaneous, and effective as speakers.

BODY LANGUAGE

The body is a powerful communicator with a language of its own. It is said that body language, including posture, movement, gestures, eye contact, and dress, has an even greater impact than the spoken word, and when a speaker is sending mixed messages, listeners will believe what they see rather than what they hear.

Posture

Posture reveals much about a person's self-esteem, health, and level of interest in his or her surroundings. Tense, stiff posture can be just as unappealing as a slouched posture. The ideal posture is centered and erect but relaxed. For some, good posture is a natural, lifelong habit. Others with habitually poor posture must consciously remind themselves over time in order to improve it. The benefits of good posture include more efficient breathing, better health and appearance, increased energy, and a stronger, clearer voice.

Simple exercises to improve posture can be practiced almost anywhere and at any time. To achieve natural and ideal posture, you should stand or sit up, hold your head high, and inhale deeply. Your stomach should expand while inhaling. While exhaling, allow your arms to fall to the side and relax your shoulders; your stomach should visibly deflate while exhaling. Your head should remain high, with the jaw parallel to the floor. Continue to breathe deeply for a few minutes, remaining conscious of head and shoulder placement and of breathing and stomach movement. Proper posture allows an overall feeling of relaxation and centeredness.

This excellent exercise was a favorite of actor George Schmitz:

Stand against a wall, placing heels and shoulders flush with the wall. Relax in that position. Then, using the wall as a springboard, walk away. This sends a message to your body of strength, security, and confidence, Schmitz would say, as the wall is always behind you.

Body Movement and Gestures

Gestures (the movements of the body, face, and hands) are powerful communication tools. The most effective movements and gestures are purposeful and natural. Tentative or nervous movement and unnatural, affected gestures can erode the confidence or trust people have in a guide. Moreover, unconscious, repetitive movement or gestures can be extremely distracting and even belie the speaker's spoken message; as noted above, people tend to focus on body movement and gestures when receiving mixed messages. A good way to become aware of one's body movement and overall speaking image is to participate in videotape sessions in which experts evaluate all aspects of speaking style. Despite an initial discomfort, guides usually find this experience enlightening and instructive. For many, simply being made aware of awkward speech or speaking manners is a catalyst for changing the behavior. (Learning to spot and overcome ineffective gestures and nervous habits is covered at the end of this chapter.)

Eye Contact

One of the most important speaking techniques, making eye contact is daunting for the novice speaker and is difficult for many to learn. Once mastered, however, eye contact becomes an invaluable and even energizing tool for speakers, as it provides needed connection and yields immediate feedback and support. Many experts recommend that speakers systematically look at every member of an audience, which a guide can easily accomplish on tours. John F. Kennedy, widely regarded as an outstanding speaker, is said to have taken this one step further by talking to one eye at a time.

Making eye contact in such a deliberate manner is difficult for the nervous novice who has many things to keep in mind at once. At the outset, it might be less taxing to simply remember to vary the direction in which one speaks, and to choose a few people to look at, preferably those who seem to be most interested in the talk. Some listeners—sometimes intentionally—give negative feedback, such as listening with a furrowed brow, looking at or doing something else while listening, or appearing not to listen at all. These are distractions an already ill-at-ease speaker might best avoid. Conversely, obviously interested listeners who nod and smile in recognition and agreement provide welcome support for uneasy speakers. Once a guide is more comfortable, he usually finds that all feedback is helpful in gauging commentary, and even those who react somewhat negatively present a welcomed challenge or valuable information about the presentation. As with other speaking skills, learning to use eye contact comfortably and effectively takes time and practice.

THE VOICE

The Greek philosopher Galen called the voice "the mirror of the soul," and many have noted that the voice also reflects one's state of health and level of confidence or conviction.

It is surprising how many people have never really listened to their own voices. Even those who speak regularly as part of their work are often unaware of how they sound and are averse to listening to their voices or to having them evaluated. Others, aware of a nasal, scratchy, or otherwise unpleasant quality in their voices, feel resigned to it, believing that the voice is a fixed feature that they cannot control or change. In fact, nearly all the elements of a voice can be improved upon with proper attention, skill, and practice.

The voice is the speaker's most valuable commodity and, like a musical instrument, it must be cared for and kept in tune. Travelers often listen to a guide's voice for eight or more hours a day or for several days at a time. Unfortunately, many guides have unpleasant voices. Guides and other speakers owe it to themselves and their listeners to cultivate as clear and as pleasant a speaking voice as possible, and this can be achieved through evaluation and practice.

Good voices are natural, pleasant, expressive, and easy to hear and understand. The qualities of a voice are determined by one's health and muscle tone, temperament, vocal habits (formed in early childhood and altered throughout one's life), and the physical makeup of the voice mechanism (the size and shape of the mouth, nasal passages, and vocal bands). Because it is created within the body, general health directly affects the voice. In fact, among the most common areas of tension and illness for stressed or inactive people are those that help to create the voice: the throat and the stomach.

Understanding how to use and improve the voice requires a basic understanding of the physiology of the upper body. Voice coaches often make a simple analogy between the upper body and an inflated balloon, with the bulb of the balloon representing the lungs filled with air and the neck of the balloon the vocal passageway, or the throat and voice box. By forcing the air out of a balloon, sound is produced when the air vibrates against the balloon's neck and inner surface. Similarly, when a person exhales, sound is produced as the breath pushes upward through the lungs and against the vocal cords, causing them to separate and vibrate. This vibration is called *phonation*.

Just below the lungs is a thin, umbrella-shaped muscle called the diaphragm, which separates the chest from the abdomen. It is the upper abdominal muscles that are the true source of the human voice. During inhalation, the diaphragm contracts and the abdomen expands and fills with air. During exhalation, the diaphragm relaxes and air is pushed out of the abdomen, passing through the lungs and throat to create sound. Relaxed, deep breathing is essential in creating clear, easily heard vocal sounds.

Although breathing begins in the first moments of life and remains the most basic involuntary function, voice coaches and yogis contend that most people are not breathing properly, or at least not in such a way as to preserve and enhance their health and their voices. Simple changes in one's breathing can vastly change the pitch, volume, and overall quality of a voice as well as the posture, energy level, and overall image of the speaker.

The following exercise illustrates proper breathing:

Lie on the back with shoulders relaxed (or if unable to lie down, stand with shoulders relaxed). Exhale and press the lower back to the floor, placing hands lightly on the abdomen. Inhale slowly and deeply, then exhale slowly and deeply. Repeat. The abdomen should expand visibly during inhalation and deflate during exhalation. Continue inhaling and exhaling. While exhaling, sigh audibly, noting the way in which air is pushed from the abdomen and through the lungs and throat. Do this several times. Next, create a vocal sound, noting the way the air is controlled in order to produce specific vocal sounds.

One can feel the abdomen pulling in during proper breathing, speaking, or singing. In contrast, shallow breathing creates weak, breathy sounds and strains the vocal cords unnecessarily. Shallow breathing also accentuates a thin, nervous voice while fuller breaths can hide nervousness.

The voice has several key characteristics, including pitch, resonance, and volume, which can be developed to enhance one's overall speaking image.

Pitch

Pitch is the high or low quality of a voice, or the musical note at which a person utters a sound, created by the frequency of vibrations in the larynx (voice box). Although pitch is largely a factor of one's physiology (men have longer and thicker vocal cords than women, resulting in a lower pitch) it can be altered to a great degree. People generally make natural associations with different pitch levels. For example, higher pitches are often associated with femininity, excitement, nervousness, helplessness, and enthusiasm. Lower pitches connote deliberateness, control, and rationality. Middle-pitch ranges are more neutral and if not varied become monotonous. Most people have a fairly wide natural pitch range, but many unconsciously suppress their natural range and speak at one pitch level. Experts recommend using at least a full octave of range when speaking, allowing the musical qualities of the voice to emerge. Most speakers, and women especially, tend toward speaking in too high a pitch, which not only lacks authority but can also be harsh and unpleasant.

Finding one's natural and comfortable range is a simple process. The easiest way is to begin by uttering aloud, "Ah" at the most comfortable level. Then, sing the next note downward on the musical scale, and continue doing this until singing lower begins to strain the voice. From here, sing upward to the point of the highest unstrained note. These notes represent one's natural pitch range. Although most people only use their vocal range when singing, incorporating this natural range of musical notes into one's speech greatly enhances speech. The most pleasant voices sound natural and conversational and have a wide range in pitch.

Resonance

Resonance is the "resounding" quality of a voice that singers and speakers work on regularly. The two most common problems with resonance are nasality and denasality, terms which are often confused. *Nasality,* more common among women, is one of the most common, and most annoying, vocal habits. Although nasality is sometimes caused by physical problems, it is more often the result of vocal tension or of too much air being pushed through the nose. Only when uttering "m," "n," and "ng" sounds should air be pushed through the nose. One can determine whether his or her voice is too nasal by putting the thumb and index finger over the bridge of the nose and saying, "Manner," "nanny," and "running." When saying these words, the nose will vibrate. Continuing to hold the fingers over the nose, say "yoke," "brother," "sell," and "yell." If the nose still vibrates, nasality is present. The basic relaxation exercises described earlier combined with a conscious effort to open the mouth wider often eliminates the nasal sound. To illustrate the importance of opening the mouth, place two fingers on the bridge of the nose and repeat the words above, "Yoke, brother, sell, yell," first with clenched teeth, then with teeth apart and mouth opened wide, and again, with clenched teeth. When teeth are clenched, the nose vibrates and a nasal sound results.

Denasality is the "cold-id-the-dose" quality, occurring when not enough air is passing through the nose. The result is that the consonants "m," "n," and "ng" become "b," "d," and "g," as in "badder" for "manner" or "sig" for "sing."

Denasality usually results from physical problems such as a severe cold, enlarged adenoids, or other obstructions. Except in the case of a passing illness, it is often necessary to seek professional help in correcting denasality.

Volume

Volume is the loudness of sound. The ideal qualities of good voice volume include not only the ability to be loud, but also to control volume, adjusting it to the space and group, and to produce volume without straining the vocal cords.

Many people, particularly women, have problems producing voice volume and assume that projecting their voices necessarily results in hoarseness or even laryngitis. In fact, hoarseness is a clear indication that a person is not speaking properly. Learning to project the voice extends back to the most fundamental elements of speaking: relaxing, proper breathing, and using the abdominal and diaphragmatic muscles.

Learning how to increase voice volume without straining the vocal cords is enlightening to many. Everyone has witnessed a speaker attempting in vain to get a message across to someone who is hard of hearing. Upon failing to be heard the first time, the speaker repeats, using the same vocal tone and quality but with more intensity (bordering on yelling). Unsuccessful the second time, the same pattern is repeated, continuing until the speaker is shouting, annoyingly loud to people nearby and even out of normal hearing range, but still, sadly, inaudible to the hearing-impaired person. The result here is often that all are frustrated and a bit embarrassed, and still, the message is not conveyed. Unfortunately, hearing-impaired people will often feign understanding, merely to prevent such scenes from developing. With a growing number of senior citizens traveling, guides need to be more aware of potential communication problems as a result of hearing loss.

Depending upon the extent of the hearing loss, a simple solution exists. Usually, if the speaker merely breathes properly, pulling air from the abdomen, he or she creates a lower, louder sound that the listener can hear. To illustrate this, practice uttering sounds by using shallow breaths created only with the upper body, such as "la, la, la, la . . . ." Then change to a deeper, abdominal and diaphragmatic breathing pattern and repeat, "la, la, la, la . . . ." The latter sounds will naturally be lower, louder tones that are much more pleasant and much easier for hearing-impaired people to hear. Moreover, sounds produced in this way preserve the vocal cords. For this reason, accomplished speakers are more likely to get stomachaches than to lose their voices after long speaking engagements.

The ideal solution to projecting to a larger audience is, of course, a microphone. (Microphone techniques are discussed later in this chapter and in Chapter 10, "The Nuts and Bolts of Conducting a Tour.")

Caring for the Voice

As with any precious commodity, the voice requires continual care. Those who rely on their voices for their livelihood—such as singers, speakers, and guides—need to be especially mindful of protecting their voices. According to Dr. Lillian Glass, a well-known voice coach and the author of *Talk To Win,* common irritants to the voice include smoking, excessive use of alcohol and other drugs, clearing the throat often, sleeping with the mouth open, talking loudly or too much, shouting, and screaming. In addition to breathing properly, Glass recommends these tips for caring for the voice: keeping the throat lubricated, drinking plenty of water, limiting consumption of dairy products, and using steam (such as in a hot shower) as often as possible. Voice coaches also recommend generally limiting the use of the voice as much as possible and advise singers and speakers to space engagements so that they can rest their voices regularly. This practice is not realistic for guides and other speakers whose work is seasonal. Not surprisingly, guides are most likely to strain or lose their voices during their busiest times, when using the voice is a necessity.

What should a person do if he or she starts to lose his or her voice? Experts contend that the only responsible solution to laryngitis is to stop talking completely, until the vocal cords have healed and the voice returns. This means canceling any business or social engagements that require using the voice and not talking to anyone. This is often difficult for most freelance tour guides, as they earn money only during the touring season and only when they are talking. Moreover, a guide's schedule is often booked six months or more ahead of time, and finding replacements on short notice can be extremely difficult.

To a voice expert, however, these responses are lame when compared to the consequences that result from taxing already damaged vocal cords. Indeed, talking with damaged vocal cords can cause permanent damage to the voice. This is the reason why professional speakers and singers will cancel shows, even when 10,000 people have already purchased tickets.

Being instructed not to talk prompts many people to do what they perceive as the next best thing: whisper. In fact, whispering is actually extremely detrimental to vocal cords as it places more strain on them than does diaphragmatic speaking and breathing.

With the knowledge that many speakers who begin to lose their voices will not abide by the most responsible behavior—not talking at all—the following tips are important to keep in mind: avoid whispering, talk as little as possible, get plenty of rest, gargle frequently with lukewarm water, drink water or citrus products such as lemon or lime juice, and avoid dairy products and caffeinated and carbonated drinks.

LANGUAGE AND DICTION

One of the benefits of recording and listening to one's own speech is that it attunes the speaker to idiosyncrasies he or she would not otherwise hear. In addition to the voice itself, aspects such as pronunciation, articulation, and choice of words form the basis of vocal style, which contribute to the success or failure as a communicator. It is vital for a professional speaker in any field to become attuned to their visual and spoken idiosyncracies.

In most civilizations—and especially among educated people—mastery of one's language, including such oft-dreaded components as grammar, pronunciation, and articulation, is a point of virtue. For many people, credibility fades along with poor use of the language.

Since most people hesitate to point out or correct a speaking error, the best way to become aware of and correct problems is to have expert speakers or colleagues who will honestly listen and evaluate aspects of your speech. The following are important characteristics of vocal style.

Vocal Variety

Successful, charismatic speakers have an ability to vary qualities of the voice and style of speaking. The most fundamental source of vocal variety is enthusiasm. A person who is not genuinely enthralled with his subject will often revert to dull, monotonous speech. Working on the technical aspects of the voice without reassessing one's commitment to the experience is akin to putting a Bandaid on a headache. To ensure vocal variety a speaker should listen to recordings of his or her voice and be mindful of the pitch, volume, intonation, and other vocal aspects.

Intonation

Intonation is the melody of speech. It is a personal, sometimes colloquial quality that often offers a window to such aspects as a speaker's geographic background, personality, and enthusiasm. Ideal intonation is natural and varied, never singsong or stereotyped; many guides are guilty of the latter, however, as a result of rote memorization or repetition, and most travelers find this distracting and annoying.

Articulation

Articulation is the muscular process of producing clear and distinct speaking sounds. Good articulation is considered one of the hallmarks of eloquent speaking, and of all speaking characteristics is one of the easiest for people to modify. One of the best ways to improve articulation is to record one's voice and listen carefully and critically. Some of the most common offenses include dropping or slurring the endings of words (as in "gonna" instead of "going to," "dint choo" instead of "didn't you," and "yea" rather than "yes"); mumbling or failing to open the mouth when speaking, and simply talking too rapidly. Some speakers add vowels, consonants, or extra syllables to words. (Common examples of these include adding "r" as in "i-dear" rather than "idea," or "ath-e-lete" rather than "athlete.") Proper articulation is a means of assuring that the speaker is understood by everyone, including the hearing-impaired, those farther behind in a group, and those straining to understand the language. Articulation should never sound affected or condescending, as is the case when speakers overarticulate.

Vocabulary

Having a good vocabulary is more a matter of using basic words appropriately and colorfully than dazzling people with large but little-known words. Guides must always be mindful of their audiences and choose words that communicate effectively to them. Using unfamiliar words can offend or intimidate listeners. Sometimes words are too arcane or sophisticated for the background or age level of a group, are jargon (which only a few outside a field may understand), or are examples of local vernacular or slang which should be either explained or avoided. Choosing lively and colorful words can create more engaging interpretations, as is discussed in Chapter 9, "Bringing a Place to Life."

Grammar

Unless one has been exposed only to the "king's English" throughout his or her life, the rules of proper grammar become rusty and require occasional rejuvenating. As regional representatives and constant communicators with a wide variety of sophisticated audiences, tour guides would do well to submit themselves to an occasional evaluation and refreshing by grammarians. Toastmasters, the international organization for public speaking, appoints a grammarian as a standard procedure for every session.

Having stated this, some latitude is essential. Proper grammar is merely one attribute of a professional speaker or guide. In fact, language is a living aspect of the human experience and, as such, its rules change over time and with continuous usage. Moreover, one of the beauties of language is the great variety in its use, and not every region embraces the "king's English." In many regions, the finest interpreters are those who know only the local vernacular, which breaks many of the rules of standard grammar. Most travelers would probably rather have a native "ungrammatical" personality who captures the essence of the place than a guide from outside the region who can merely describe the place, regardless of the propriety of his or her grammar.

The ideal may be an ability to converse in both "languages"—the "king's English" and the local vernacular. To cite one example, Henry LaFleur is an extremely articulate native Cajun guide who, to the delight of all his charges, spices his interpretations with his family's Cajun French.

Pronunciation

People rarely win kudos for pronouncing words correctly, though everyone seems to notice when they are mispronounced. Mispronouncing words can irk listeners, immediately calling the speaker's intelligence into question and eroding his or her credibility.

In languages that are spoken by millions of people and that vary throughout countries and among regions, "proper" pronunciation is anything but an exact science. Many experts prefer to distinguish between "standard" and "appropriate" (rather than "correct") pronunciations. Some dictionaries offer two or more pronunciations that are generally accepted by cultivated speakers. Although it is wise to avoid using words whose pronunciations one is unsure of, the only way a speaker can steer clear of mispronunciations is to become aware of them.

Regional Dialects   Regional dialects are the differences in pronunciation, inflection, and enunciation within one language that vary from region to region. In any country these dialects can be so strong as to instantly identify the speaker's home region, and in some countries, a person's accent will indicate his or her social standing.

In recent decades, many national politicians and media personalities have hired speech coaches to help rid them of strong regional dialects. Although speech coaches themselves are divided in their opinions about the need for this, few educators recommend it for guides and interpreters. Provided one's dialect is understandable most visitors appreciate any indication that their interpreter is a native and, therefore, an insider. Moreover, some regional dialects—notably in the United States, those from the South, Boston, and New York—seem to characterize the local experience as much as any attraction or event.

Foreign Accents   Slight foreign accents are almost inevitable for a non-native speaker, and most people find them charming. On the other hand, thick accents can interfere enormously with the communication process. Those who guide in a foreign language have a duty to their employers and to travelers to be able to communicate easily with them. Guides who have studied a language and feel comfortable speaking conversationally will often bill themselves as bilingual or multilingual, only to be humiliated and overwhelmed by their first multilingual tour. Speaking for several hours at a time about the many elements of a place—architectural, historical, political, and technical—requires a surprisingly high level of fluency. Multilingual guiding also requires extra care in pacing and planning. For these reasons, multilingual guides require additional training and usually earn slightly higher salaries.

Rate of Speaking

Rates of speaking depend on many factors and vary considerably from one language to another, from one region to another within a language, and from one situation to another. One of the most common complaints among listeners is that a speaker talks too rapidly. Rapid speech is especially common in urban areas, but all guides must be mindful of a tendency to speak too fast if they work regularly with people from outside their own region, whose native language is different from their own, and with those who have hearing deficiencies.

It is said the average rate of speaking in public is approximately 125 words per minute. One way to monitor one's speaking rate is to read a passage as if saying it conversationally, time it, and see how closely it approximates the 125 average range. With regular monitoring and practice, it is relatively easy to curb problems with rapid speaking. Using pauses and varied rates of speech is a powerful way to enliven interpretations (discussed more fully in Chapter 9, "Bringing a Place to Life").

Recognizing and Overcoming Annoying Habits

Many speakers unknowingly and unintentionally sabotage their performances by their own distractions. Fortunately or unfortunately, most people will not tell a speaker about his or her annoying habits. Instead, listeners will simply make an effort to tune out or even to leave an interpreter to avoid enduring the experience.

Examples of common annoying habits of speakers are: playing with hair, jewelry, or clothing; persistent "um"s and "ah"s; jerky eye movement; hyperbole; overuse of slang or colloquialisms; and overuse of pet words or expressions such as "you know," and "like," or superlatives like "incredible" or "this is my favorite. . . ." One traveler noted that his guide's tendency to become distracted by his surroundings was also distracting to him.

As with so many other idiosyncrasies of speaking, learning about one's own requires that guides see themselves speak on videotape or ask a coach, instructor or colleague to give them an honest evaluation. Most people are unaware of the image they project to others, and through constructive criticism are pleased to be shown their quirks and learn how to control them. Just as bad habits are formed through practice over time, unlearning them, or acquiring new habits, requires time and practice.

Affectations   People usually respond negatively to phoniness and affectation, such as using arcane language, very formal pronunciations, or foreign words and phrases. It is far more effective and inviting to hear a speaker use language with which his audience is comfortable.

Microphone Technique

Few experiences can be as uncomfortable as having to endure a blaring commentary, a fuzzy voice, or recurring feedback over a public address system. So disturbing are these conditions that most listeners would rather the speaker put down the microphone and say nothing.

On motorcoaches, these annoying situations often occur without the guide knowing it since many passengers do not like to complain. If possible, the guide should check the microphone for volume and quality before passengers arrive, which can be done with the help of the driver. Once passengers are seated, the guide should check the sound again before departing and request that anyone who cannot hear or is unhappy with the sound to let him know. It is also advisable to encourage passengers to inform the guide immediately if a problem with the sound develops.

Often the difficulties are the result of faulty (or nonexistent) equipment, and depending on the nature of the problem and the length or nature of the excursion, it may be necessary to alert the motorcoach company to the situation. Although it is rarely desirable to delay the start of a tour, a company representative may be able to deliver a working microphone to the group.

Sometimes microphone problems are due to the shortcomings of the user. A microphone enables the speaker to use his or her own voice at its most natural volume. Oddly enough, however, many guides need to be reminded that they need not talk loudly into a microphone. To the public speaker who always uses a microphone or to one who never has this seems obvious. But to a guide who speaks to people continuously, both on and off a motorcoach, with and without a microphone, the point must be made that while projection is vital when talking to the group without a microphone, projection can be deadly when combined with a microphone.

Feedback occurs when the user is either standing too close to a speaker or other metal object or not pressing firmly enough on the microphone button. When using a microphone, it is essential that guides use a firm and constant pressure on the level to avoid feedback and to avoid the annoying result of having one half of a sentence transmitted and the other half lost. Since this is more difficult than it seems, many guides and drivers put elastic bands around a microphone to hold its button in the "on" position.

In general, microphones are becoming less of a problem, as newer motorcoaches are equipped with more sophisticated amenities and motorcoach companies are responding to the requests of tour operators and guides for more reliable microphone systems. Many motorcoach companies are now purchasing lavalier microphones, which hook around the speaker's neck or are attached to a blazer or shirt, allowing the guide or driver some mobility. Microphones often "disappear" and tend to break easily, and a few companies and guides purchase and carry their own microphones. This practice is rare and not always necessary or useful, as not all microphone systems are compatible. Portable microphones are becoming more popular and more competitively priced, and many guides choose to carry them, particularly when addressing large groups in open, outdoor areas.

Listening

No discussion of speaker skills should exclude the importance of listening to one's audience. At its best, speaking to a group is a symbiotic experience, and speakers are only as effective as their audiences perceive them to be. For the speaker, listening can take the form of diligent attention to the questions, attention span, posture, eye movements, and gestures of the group. The "listening" speaker will wish to interact with the group, both asking and answering questions. Guides who actively and attentively listen to travelers and learn to alter their approaches in response to them are not only more successful interpreters, but tend to enjoy themselves and learn more in the process.

Ending

Finally, many speakers (guides not excluded) have difficulty knowing when or how to quit. As noted in the previous chapter, conclusions and parting moments provide opportunities as the most powerful and memorable parts of interpretations, but at times are the weakest. Speaker guru Ron Hoff states that the secret to any presentation is to "tell them what you're going to tell them. Then tell them. Then tell them what you've told them." Although interpretations are different in many ways from speeches some of the same principles apply, as well as the adage, "If you don't have anything worthwhile to say, say nothing at all." Guides and other speakers often tend more toward drama and loquaciousness than restraint and can be uncomfortable without providing a dazzling ending. The simplest closing, however, is usually the most effective: "Thanks for coming to _____. I enjoyed traveling with you, and I wish you well."

SUMMARY

Guides are essentially public speakers, and must possess the ability to communicate in an engaging way. It is therefore essential that guides have a basic understanding of speaking techniques and an awareness of the images that they project to travelers. By focusing on skills such as proper posture and breathing, care and use of the voice, use of a microphone, and proper use of language, and on overcoming distracting habits, guides will gain poise, confidence, and effectiveness.

9   *Bringing a Place to Life*

---

*"On the street whatever comes to my mind I say it if I think it will be
good. . . . And the main requirement for that is mood. You gotta be
in the mood. You got to put yourself in it. You've got to feel it. It's got
to be more an expression than a routine."*
— Kingfish Smith, as told to the Federal Writers' Project in 1938

Kingfish Smith was not a guide in any traditional sense. He was, however, a
superb interpreter, for he understood how to engage people spontaneously with
his surroundings. Powerful interpreters who can capture the essence of a place,
person, or idea and infuse it in others abound in many fields. Virtually anyone
in any field is a potential interpreter, including writers, filmmakers, sculptors,
songwriters, architects, teachers, singers, cartoonists, naturalists, interior designers, and fashion designers. Ken Burns, acclaimed creator and producer of
"The Civil War" and other television documentaries, uses impeccably researched
first-person accounts to interpret places, personalities, and eras. James Michener has explored and interpreted a staggering number of places by using well-
developed characters and delving into the history, geology, architecture, and
other aspects of a region and era with remarkable detail. The National Geographic Society's Mr. World, wearing his emblematic "map-of-the-world" cape,
"raps" to students throughout the United States about the pleasures of geography and far-off places.

At the core of these and all other successful interpreters is passion for a
subject, a desire to share it with others, and a wide array of communication
techniques that they have honed over time. Like master artisans, seasoned
guides conduct themselves with seemingly little effort and a palpable sense of
joy, so that anyone observing them feels drawn to the place, the experience, and
the guides themselves. Grant Sharpe, author of *Interpreting the Environment*,
calls effective interpretation "an affair of the heart—the heart of both the interpreter and the listener.

"Successful interpretation," Sharpe continues, "is a balancing or juggling act,
a graceful and smooth ballet of interaction between your interpretive presentation and the mind of the listener" (Sharpe 1982). Comparisons of interpreters
to jugglers, dancers, and artists are common, for interpretation is both an art

Figure 9.1

Unlike other forms of public speaking, guiding allows the speaker to turn the group's attention away from themselves. Here, Janice Holliday, tour manager and San Francisco guide, conducts a tour. (*Photo by Sharon Murphy, Today Photography.*)

form and a performance. As with all forms of art, much more is occurring than first meets the eye. Although certain "raw ingredients" are essential in all art forms, mastering them requires an inexplicable union of intuition, sensitivity, passion, and skill.

Lively, appealing interpretations are not always the result, however. Instead, the images of guides that often first come to mind are Mark Twain's "necessary nuisances," from *The Innocents Abroad,* his hurried, self-absorbed guides, tied to rigid itineraries, intoning their memorized spiels to disinterested travelers.

And it is not only dull, canned spiels that offend. Overzealousness can be equally annoying and ineffective. In *A Little Tour in France,* Henry James noted, "It was not to be denied that there was a relief in separating from our accomplished guide, whose manner of imparting information reminded me of the energetic process by which I have seen mineral waters bottled."

Arthur Frommer calls typical sightseeing "an activity as vapid as the words imply. We rove the world, in most cases, to look at lifeless physical structures of the sort already familiar from a thousand picture books and films. We gaze at the Eiffel Tower or the Golden Gate Bridge, enjoy a brief thrill of recognition, return home, and think we have traveled." Most of the vacations taken by Americans, says Frommer, are "trivial and bland, devoid of important content,

Figure 9.2
Sometimes interpretation takes the form of acting, as with these costumed interpreters who impersonate well-known historic characters. (*Courtesy of the J. A. Wagar Collection, Department of Recreation Resources and Landscape Architecture Colorado State University.*)

cheaply commercial, and unworthy of our better instincts and ideals" (Frommer 1990).

Frommer proposes that travel is "scarcely worth the effort unless it is associated with people, with learning and ideas. To have meaning at all, travel must involve an encounter with new and different outlooks and beliefs. . . . At its best, travel should challenge our preconceptions and most cherished views, cause us to rethink our assumptions, shake us a bit, make us broader-minded and more understanding" (Frommer 1991).

All guides can play an important role in promoting travel that is deeply enriching, challenging, and synergistic, a "smooth ballet" between themselves and visitors in which all are positively changed by the experience.

CREATING MEMORABLE INTERPRETATIONS

What is it that makes some tours and interpretations mesmerizing or motivating or both, and others dull, pedantic, or otherwise uninteresting? How do guides ensure that their interpretations are lively and interesting?

Although there are no firm rules for creating enlightening, enjoyable, or memorable interpretations, there are many identifiable techniques and qualities that can enhance the process. Travelers, regions, and guides are unique, and each combination lends itself to a singular experience and style of interpretation. A story that delights one group, for example, may fall flat with another. One site might be ideal for hands-on activities, while a sacred place or a fragile environment might call for quiet observation. In any case, guides must respond to their visitors' interests and whims and be agile and flexible enough to change course immediately if necessary.

Although much of this talent is intangible, the following are essential qualities and guidelines for creating sparkling interpretations. Many of these are used by artists, storytellers, performers, and interpreters of all kinds; some of these are based on Freeman Tilden's six principles; others are drawn from entertainment, storytelling, business, marketing, and education.

Passion for Site or Subject Matter

The first essential ingredient for making any place or personality come alive is the guide's continued sense of delight in and awe of it. Enthusiasm is immediately discernable and is highly contagious. When met with an impassioned interpreter, a visitor is far more likely to care about a place and to feel inspired to learn more about it. Freeman Tilden went so far as to say that if he had to distill his six principles of interpretation into one, "I feel certain that the single principle must be Love" (Tilden 1957).

Certainly a guide need not be enamored of every aspect of a place to make it come alive. The key is for guides to share what they love about a place. It may be a natural feature, and how their understanding of that feature enlarges the visit there. It may be a fascination with a contemporary or historical personality who, in the guide's view, indelibly altered the region or embodied the region's ideal. Or it may be the guide's personal feelings about or memories of a place shared genuinely, that strike a chord of kinship or pleasure in the visitor.

Sheldon Caplan, a long-time tour guide and tour manager from Waterford, Virginia, says, "Guides should talk about what they know and love. If your interest is in nature or Civil War history, share that. My own love is architecture . . . and it's my way of seeing and explaining a place. When you talk about what you love, your own enthusiasm inevitably will spark an interest in them."

Passion for People

Karl Albrecht calls apathy toward visitors one of the "seven sins of service," and New Orleans guide Joan Garvey observes that it is the one quality visitors will not forgive. Visitors sense immediately whether a guide cares about them, and if they feel the guide does not, they will respond with the same lack of sentiment for the guide.

One could go so far as to say that mastering the art of interpretation has as much to do with one's ability to connect with people as it does with one's knowledge of a topic. A guide who is honestly interested in visitors will seek to learn more about them, find out why they are traveling, where they have enjoyed traveling before, and what their interests are. In doing this, the guide can more easily draw visitors closer to the place and make them feel welcome. When problems arise, guides who have already inspired respect in and shared enjoyment with their visitors will find that they have greater compassion, as the visitors will willingly place their trust in these guides. Understandably, guides who genuinely like people tend to have happier, more comfortable charges.

Enhancement of the Relationship Between Site and Experience

This quality, which embodies Freeman Tilden's first principle, is an outgrowth of the previous one, passion for people. "The visitor's chief interest," says Tilden, "is in whatever touches his personality, his experience, and his ideals." The most comprehensive history of a site has no meaning whatever if the visitor feels no relationship to it. In *Where's the Me in Museum: Going to Museums with Children,* authors Milde Waterfall and Sarah Grusin focus on the need to let children enjoy museums in their own way. "By removing pressure and adult preconceptions, the way is cleared for children to find their personal "ME's" in museums," they say. "When a museum-goer recognizes part of himself in the museum, he has found a *Me.* There are *Me's* inside paintings and *Me's* riding rhinos. There are *Me's* who hide between the lines of the Declaration of Independence and *Me's* who keep dreams alive while hanging from a ceiling" (Waterfall and Grusin 1989).

U.S. Forest Service interpreter Marcella Wells and others at the Wetherill Mesa use familiar items to provoke visitors into thinking about how archeologists have used artifacts to deduce aspects of the Anasazi lifestyle. Following a short introduction, a typical tour begins with the interpreter asking members of the audience to choose one thing they would want to leave behind for archeologists 800 years in the future to illustrate what their life was like. Responses vary, and include things like photographs, eyeglasses, a car, tools, my little brother, and so forth. The guide then talks about what archeologists find during excavation and how those things tell them about the way the Anasazi lived 800 years ago.

As an example, the interpreters explain that the doughnut-shaped items made from fibers of the yucca plant are found occasionally in the ruins. As the hike resumes, visitors are asked to contemplate probable uses of these yucca-fiber doughnuts. Throughout the tour other items are used to illustrate how material remains suggest a way of life for these ancient cliff dwellers, and how, at first glance, these items can lead to misconceptions or uncertainties about how the Indians might have lived.

When the interpreter asks the audience about how they think the yucca-fiber doughnuts were used, their responses include: a hairpiece, a bracelet, a frisbee or game piece, a plant starter, a filter for water, and so forth. It is then explained that archeologists theorize that the Anasazi used the doughnut to balance round-bottomed pots full of grain or water in storage.

To reinforce the idea that what we leave behind often illustrates how we live, the interpreter then describes a scenario in which an archeologist returns to the visitor's house 800 years in the future and finds in the yard a broken plate, the rusted remains of a car or a washing machine, several bent and rusted utensils, and several plastic twist ties (which the interpreter then pulls from his or her pocket). Visitors are then asked to speculate on what an archeologist of the future might conclude—are they earrings, jewelry, tools, or game pieces? Amused, the audience realizes that archeologists piece together information about a culture from material remains, but can only speculate about the lifestyle of their users.

Emphasis of Interpretation Over Information

Many guides and other interpreters mistake information for interpretation, believing that being called a "walking encyclopedia" is the highest compliment they could receive. In fact, information is merely one ingredient of interpretation. Tilden's third principle of interpretation reads: "Information, as such, is not Interpretation. Interpretation is revelation based upon information. But they are entirely different things. However, all interpretation includes information."

Effective interpretation is a matter of distilling and selecting information. The dimensions of a building or a statue, or the date on a cornerstone become meaningless trivia if they are not connected to an interesting story. One guide recalls a teacher who brought her eighth-grade class to New York City. No doubt expecting an avalanche of dull information, the teacher greeted her with, "Please, no dates or statistics. We're here to enjoy ourselves."

Details such as dates, however, add spice or can even become the highlight of a story. Guides may find it helpful to ask themselves, "Why should they care about this? What meaning does it have for them, or for their lives?" or "What made this place (or person, or era) fascinating to me?" Most would probably agree that it is usually not important or interesting, for example, for visitors to learn the exact lifespan dates of presidents or other famous figures. But such information can actually be fascinating, as in the following interpretation:

Of all his great accomplishments, Thomas Jefferson regarded writing the Declaration of Independence as his most important. In his later years, Jefferson harbored a dream of living to see the fiftieth anniversary of its signing and shared this dream with his friend (and one-time enemy) John Adams. In the years following their presidencies, the two men corresponded regularly, occasionally mentioning their mutual goal of living to the fiftieth anniversary.

After long illnesses, Thomas Jefferson and John Adams both died on July 4, 1826, on the day of the fiftieth anniversary of the signing of the Declaration of Independence.

Adam's last words were "Jefferson survives." In fact, hundreds of miles away, Jefferson had died a few hours before him. Thomas Jefferson was 83; John Adams was 90.

In this case, the exact date, July 4, 1826, is integral to the story, and the ages of the subjects further illustrate their commitment to their goal.

Willingness to be Personal and Authentic

"Objectivity is overrated," one guide notes. "People really want your 'insider's' point of view." For better or worse, guides are often one of the only individuals a visitor gets to know in a region, and a guide's personal touches and perspectives are often the most meaningful part of a trip.

John McCaffery, a retired FBI agent who became a part-time guide, remarked, "It's surprising to me, but it's definitely true: the more personal I make my tours, the more interested the [visitors] become. They really want to know what I love to do here, what I think about Washington."

Still, it is important that guides learn how to strike a balance between being personal and maintaining a necessary distance. Guides who are too personal or "chummy" are often perceived as unprofessional.

Many people agreed that Glacier Bay was the most memorable place on their fourteen-day tour of Alaska and that the highlight of the trip was when National Park Service interpreter Maria Gladziszewski read to them from pages of her journal. Drawing on the writing of her favorite naturalists and philosophers, she read, "The power of this place is staggering, beyond description, mysterious, unspeakably pure and even sublime. . . . The awesome, raw power and tremendous expanse of this place can catch you off guard, can throw you off your everyday balance. And here—every now and again—the experience of *aha!* happens."

Ability to Create and Tell Stories

Stories make places and people come alive. Says master storyteller Laura Simms, "You can visit a place time and time again and remain endlessly an outsider, but when you know its stories, you are no longer a visitor. You become a participant. New Zealand was so prosaic for me until I began to learn its stories. Then it burst alive to me like a fruit. Now I *participate* in the history of that place."

For many guides, the prospect of storytelling is intimidating. Moreover, the very concept of telling stories tugs at their valued perceptions of themselves as accurate historians, for the word *story* carries for many the connotation of falsehood.

Certainly, truthfulness and accuracy are essential virtues for guides, and intentionally misinforming or sensationalizing are grievous. And yet interpreters, like all artists, inherit a license to embellish and intensify, provided they let their listeners in on their digressions. All too often, guides will completely abandon the vibrant and telltale (but unprovable) anecdote or legend in the name of accuracy, when, in fact, the legend has a powerful meaning to convey.

Nowhere is this proclivity to cling to only the substantiated facts more apparent than in the retelling of history. "No, I'd never tell people that; it's a myth," was a common response when guides were asked whether or not they share with their groups a well-known city legend.

In fact, life itself can be seen as a vast collection of stories. Authors Joan Garvey and Mary Lou Widmer prefaced their highly regarded book, *Beautiful Crescent: A History of New Orleans,* with this: "History is a story, and as a story, differs with the story-teller. The story-teller's point of view becomes the attitude with which the history is related. For this reason, the following chronology is *a* history . . . and not *the* history. . . ." Garvey and Widmer go on to say, "We maintain that there is no definitive history, only stories told with more or less documentation" (Garvey and Widmer 1984).

Allan Gurganus ventures further and even celebrates this point throughout his interpretive novel, *The Oldest Living Confederate Widow Tells All.* Gurganus (1989) precedes the novel with an interpretation which is, by his own admission, inaccurate:

A word to the reader about historical accuracy. In testimony collected from former slaves during the 1930's Federal Writers' Project, many recalled seeing Lincoln in the South during the Civil War. Fanny Burdock, ninety-one, of Valdosta, Georgia, remembered, "We been picking in the field when my brother he point to the road and then we seen Marse Abe coming all dusty and on foot. We run right to the fence and had the oak bucket and the dipper. When he draw up to us, he so tall, black eyes so sad. Didn't say not one word, just looked hard at all us, every one us crying. We give him nice cool water from the dipper. Then he nodded and set off and we just stood there till he get to being dust then nothing. After, didn't our owner or nobody credit it, but me and all my kin, we knowed. I still got the dipper to prove it."

In reality, Lincoln's foot tour of Georgia could not have happened. In this book, it can. Such scenes were told by hundreds of slaves. Such visitations remain, for me, truer than fact.

History is my starting point.

With history as the starting point, man has created stories, legends and myths to remember, enlarge, embellish, and celebrate life. Acclaimed mythologist Joseph Campbell called myths "the world's dreams, . . . stories about the wisdom of life. Myths tell me where I am" (Campbell and Moyers 1987). And finally, myths enable us to feel "the rapture of being alive."

Too often, mythology is associated only with the ancient cultures; however, no culture, era, city or region is without its myths. Henry LaFleur, guide and owner of tour company Louisiana Rendezvous, freely shares the rich mythology of his Cajun heritage with his visitors. "As Andy Edmonds [author of *Let the*

Good Times Roll! The Complete Cajun Handbook] points out, 'Many Cajuns believe that when God declared the seventh day a day of rest, He came down to the Bayou . . . and never left.'"

San Francisco guide Janice Holliday notes the locally well-known story about Coit Tower being created in the shape of a fire hose in honor of its patron, Lillie Hitchcock Coit. So many guides have repeated this story that it has become "fact." "The truth," Holliday says, "is that the architects had no thought whatsoever about fire hoses when they created the fluted tower building." The story is amusing, however, and serves as a memorable metaphor for the building.

Sometimes the known facts are there, but the interpreter takes liberties with their translation. John Francis Marion, historian, author, and Philadelphia guide, said, "I'm a daydreamer in history. When I read history I project myself among the historical figures and it becomes a story. A great friend once said 'Get your facts straight and then do whatever you want'" (Naff 1987).

As guides cannot ignore their obligation to truthfulness, it is necessary to distinguish between fact and fiction. One way is to preface the unprovable or questionable legend with, "Legend has it that . . ." or "As the story goes . . ." or "My favorite story about him is. . . ."

Ability to Ask Provocative Questions

The ability to ask questions is an invaluable interpretive skill. By inviting visitors to participate, interpreters involve them in the experience. Asking provocative questions is more complicated than it seems, however, and not all questions enhance presentations. Gerald H. Krockover of Purdue University and Jeanette Hauck of the Indianapolis Children's Museum have analyzed four questioning levels and their impact on listeners.

1. *Cognitive memory questions,* which rely on recall, memory, or recognition, elicit the "lowest level of thought on the part of the person responding." Examples of such questions are, "What style of architecture is this?" or "What kind of tree is this?" Unfortunately, many interpreters rely only on these kinds of questions.

2. *Convergent questions* require putting together facts and concepts to obtain the best or correct answer. Examples include "How is this animal like that one?" or "What is the difference between . . . ?"

3. *Divergent questions* involve predicting, hypothesizing, and inferring, and allow for many "correct" answers. Examples include "If you had to choose one word to describe this era, what would it be?" or "What kinds of items would the first colonists have had on these ships?"

4. *Evaluative questions,* the highest level, require respondents to make value judgments, formulate opinions, or defend their point of view. Examples include "If you were a colonist in 1776, what do you think you would have done? Why?"

or "Which of these paintings do you prefer? Why?" (Krockover and Hauck 1980).

Krockover and Hauck illustrate that the respondents' answers will usually be only as provocative as the question itself. In formulating questions, interpreters should use a variety of questioning levels, allow adequate time for responses, and never ridicule a response.

Finally, asking questions in interpretation is not always the best approach. Questioning can be extremely successful for young children, for example, but can fall flat with adolescents or adults, who might find it condescending or feel intimidated by having to speak publicly.

Ability to Relate the Parts to a Whole

This is Freeman Tilden's fourth principle of interpretation, along with the concept that interpretation must address the whole person rather than any phase. This is not to say that every interpretation must answer or address profound philosophical issues. "I say 'a' whole, not 'the' whole," Tilden proposes. "'The' whole soars into infinity, and the time we can spend with our listener . . . is all too brief" (Tilden 1957).

The most vivid illustrations of the whole are found in details. The naturalist interpreter might use the example of a honeybee on an apple blossom to illustrate the symbiotic relationships in nature. Drelis Fujah interprets her heritage through her compelling "Lifeseeing Tour of Chicago's Black Community." Fujah has chosen music and the church, which she calls "the carrier[s] of black culture," to portray the culture. "Music is an important form of religious expression for African-Americans," she says. "To go back in any historical line of ascent in black music leads one inevitably to religion (i.e., spirit worship), for the cultural characteristics and simple style of slave spirituals are at the root of all black music (Blues, Gospel, Rhythm & Blues, Jazz)." Exploring the many churches, she contends, illuminates this world, which the tourist rarely sees. "The church is a place where Black people move in almost absolute openness and strength, and is one of the few places full expression of African-American culture has remained constant."

Profiting from Humor

Used judiciously, humor is one of the most effective and universally appealing communicators. On the other hand, it can be extremely awkward and offensive. Many guides erroneously feel that the funnier they are, the more popular they will be with travelers. While it is true that people love to laugh, working hard at being funny usually backfires.

It is important for guides to recognize the subtleties of humor. Some guides equate wit and humor with constant joketelling, when in fact a wry approach based on the truth is often more humorous and sophisticated. Guides who attempt to keep their groups constantly laughing can be annoying to visitors. After a tour of Martha's Vineyard, for instance, more than one person felt exhausted and disappointed by their guide. "He's a frustrated comedian," said one woman. "I have no idea whether I heard anything that's true about the whole island. He tried to make everything into a joke. And he never came up for air."

Finally, it is extremely important that guides understand the power of humor to offend and alienate. Tastes in humor are not universal, so it is best to be extremely conservative with it when working with multicultural groups.

The following are guidelines for using humor:

- Be yourself. If you are uncomfortable telling jokes, for example, avoid them. Nothing is more pathetic than someone trying to be funny and falling flat.
- *Never* tell ethnic jokes or make light of another's region, language, customs, or beliefs.
- Remember that few people judge the quality of a guide by how humorous he or she is.
- On longer trips, a guide might invite passengers to share with the group some of their favorite stories. Many of these will provide conviviality and humor.

Using Clear and Colorful Language

Words are extraordinary tools of communication that enable interpreters to paint pictures or transport visitors from the real to the imaginary. It is common for guides to overlook their use of language, or to believe that a strong vocabulary is an extensive, scholarly one. In fact, the simplest words—those that even a young child would understand—are usually the best.

Some guides have a tendency to adopt unnatural or archaic language when giving tours, using words, phrases, or sentence structures they would never use in their ordinary conversation. As an example, "And to your right, towering exaltedly to a height of five hundred fifty-five feet five and one-eighth inches, stands the Washington Monument. . . ." Such overdramatization is unnecessary and usually falls on bemused ears.

One powerful technique in language is the use of metaphor. Author and guide Joan Garvey's description of New Orleans in its three major incarnations—French, Spanish, and English—is itself colorful. But her use of metaphor makes it unforgettable. "For as long as people have written and spoken about New Orleans," she says, "they have referred to the city in the feminine. As I see it, when she was French, she was treated like a mistress; when she was Spanish, she was a housekeeper; and, finally, when she became part of America, she was wanted and loved, and treated as a bride." Such a vivid metaphor both encapsulates the history and makes an indelible impression on the traveler.

Knowing When to Be Silent

Often the most appropriate and powerful interpretation is silence. Silence can set a tone of reverence or reflection, or give visitors time and space to absorb and assess a place themselves. Silence also permits travelers to rest mentally, a healthy option of doing or hearing nothing for awhile, a concept that many guides forget. A reprieve from a guide's interpretation also grants visitors time alone with a place and enables them to make discoveries on their own. Silence is not the absence of interpretation, but is, in fact, a vital part of it.

Unfortunately many guides fail to understand that many places do not require or lend themselves to any verbal interpretation. Even the most eloquent interpretation can smother a visitor's experience, as when a guide feels the need to describe exquisitely beautiful or dramatic scenery. Tilden characterizes this blunder as "gilding the lily. Not only is the lily destroyed, but the painter has made a confession that he does not understand the nature of beauty." Tilden advises two tactics when dealing with aesthetic experiences: "first, to create the best possible vantage points from which beauty may be seen and comprehended; and second, to do all that discreetly may be done to establish a mood, or sympathetic atmosphere" (Tilden 1957).

Sacred sites, such as cemeteries and cathedrals, must also be handled thoughtfully. Despite the popularity of Westminister Abbey and Arlington Cem-

Figure 9.3
Sometimes sites or scenes are best experienced in silence, requiring little or no commentary from the guide. (*Photo courtesy of the National Park Service.*)

etery, their primary function is sacred, and the guide has a duty to respect that. This means refraining from interpretation that might interfere with another's visit and, when necessary, informing visitors of the appropriate behavior. Similarly, places that evoke emotion, such as war memorials, are by nature intended to remain quiet places of reflection and mourning, no matter how frequently visited. One traveler visiting the Punchbowl Cemetery in Honolulu remarked, "We just had to get away from our guide. She wouldn't stop talking!"

A final note about silence: it is often wise for a guide to omit mentioning or raving about those places or events that the visitors cannot experience because of timing or poor planning. Such comments cause visitors to wonder about the other sites they might be missing or to begin to feel they have taken a second-rate tour.

Knowing When To Stop

Many guides seem to suffer needlessly from the fear of leaving something out. The great English stylist Macaulay noted that in any art, including everything achieves a less, rather than more, truthful result. Tilden brilliantly illustrates the concept of "less is more" with a personal analogy:

I got a taste of this wholesome injunction years ago when I had a country house that needed wooden shingles. I hired an old cunning carpenter of the neighborhood to do the job, and then I was seized with the ambition to try my own hand at laying a square. The experienced eyes watched me for a few moments. Then he said, 'Would ye take a little advice: The way you're doing, you'll split the shingles. Never give the nail that last tap' (Tilden 1957).

Similarly, many guides are guilty of attempting to deliver all the facts they know, thereby overloading the listener with information.

Learning when to quit is a hallmark of a great performer; "leave them wanting" is a golden rule of show business. The perfect time to leave is at a peak, not the point at which the performer has used his or her last trick. Instead, knowing that there is so much more to see and do ensures that an audience will want to return.

Commitment to Learning

The surest way for guides to keep from becoming stale and to retain their ability to inspire others is to maintain a sense of wonder and awe about their subjects.

For a clever, lively interpreter, virtually every kind of knowledge, material, or art form can be braided into an interpretation. Guides whose primary resources are generic guidebooks not only cheat their visitors, but limit themselves as well. There has long been a tendency for guides to digest reams of information and statistics and feel they are prepared to give engaging interpretations only to find their visitors are indifferent.

The telltale signs indicating that a guide needs to explore his or her subject more deeply include (1) the feeling that one could conduct a tour without really thinking about it, (2) a loss of interest in the subject, and (3) being unable to remember the last time he or she has learned anything new about the subject. One who feels truly impassioned about a place usually needs no prompting to find interesting and relevant information; indeed, it can be found virtually everywhere.

Those wishing to learn more about the essence of a place might start with guidebooks or encyclopedia, since so much factual information can be found there. Other resources should avail themselves through interest and intuition. Biographies and autobiographies of prominent or intriguing personalities are invaluable resources. Fiction, essays, poetry, or any literature written in or about a region can shed light on it. Guides of New England who have not read Hawthorne, Thoreau, Emerson, and Melville, for example, are missing subtle and profound insights that visitors might already possess by having read their work. Novelist James Michener offers detailed interpretations representing years of research in the regions he covers, blending the geological, geographical, historical, and cultural aspects of a place in a clarifying and enthralling way. Any city guide could benefit by studying architectural reference books or reading William Whyte's *City: Rediscovering the Center,* in which he analyzes the social life of city streets. Books or essays written by a region's visitors—even (and especially) those who did not like it—provide objectivity that many guides often lack. Notable examples for guides in the United States include Charles Dickens's *American Notes,* Francis Trollope's *The Domestic Manners of Americans,* de Tocqueville's *Democracy in America,* or Mark Twain's often acerbic and always searing accounts of the many places he visited. Contemporary examples include the works of Jan Morris, Paul Thoreaux, or Alistair Cooke. Field guides, books by or about local humor or humorists, old maps and census reports, and photographs and artwork all provide powerful insights into a region. The staggering success of Ken Burns's television documentary "The Civil War" illustrates the power that first-person research plays in portraying an era and its people. For guides, such activities as making frequent trips, exploring local stories in depth, reading literature that diverges from the ordinary or from one's own point of view, and making a habit of talking to locals and visitors all offer first-person perspective to the interpretation of a region.

INTERPRETING DIFFERENT THEMES

Ideally, an interpretation synthesizes the diverse worlds of virtually all branches of knowledge. Interpreters in a particular city or region are routinely asked questions about that region's history, architecture, natural science, and current politics, for example. At other times, interpreters must conduct tours with a specific theme. In recent years, specialized tours have been gaining in popularity. The following are guidelines for interpreting nature, history, art, and architecture, as well as a brief discussion of incidental interpretation.

Interpreting Nature

A knowledgeable naturalist can walk ten steps in a forest, meadow, or even a city park, and comprehend what an untrained person cannot. And, as all of nature is interconnected, an interpretive naturalist can begin virtually anywhere—by describing the land and its flora, by talking about a region's rock formations, by examining a leaf or insect, or by pointing out bird species or animal tracks—leading to discussions about larger themes. To avoid overwhelming their visitors, many interpreters prefer to choose particular themes, such as the local ecology, the cause and effect of an unusual phenomenon, or an overview of the changes that occur during a specific season (see Fig. 9.4).

Reading and interpreting nature should draw on all the senses. Many people never learn to appreciate nature beyond its broad, visual impact. A bird's song not only identifies a species but tells the naturalist about its behavior. The rustling of leaves can indicate the size and proximity of an animal. A fragrance can

Figure 9.4
Effective guides often show visitors aspects of a place they would likely have missed if they traveled on their own. (*Photo by Richard Freas, courtesy of the National Park Service.*)

lead the way to a grove of peaches or a wall of honeysuckle. The texture of a snake for someone who has never touched one can be surprising and intriguing. The sense of touch applies not only to what the fingers feel; the climate, winds, and humidity levels indicate much about a region.

Although it is best for those who are most experienced in nature to interpret it, it is important for all guides to keep in mind that the subject of nature can be woven into most interpretations. In recent years, nature and the imperiled earth is on the minds of many people, and guides who are accustomed to focusing on a region's other aspects can enhance their interpretations by incorporating a discussion of some of the region's natural characteristics. The natural phenomena of urban areas are often overlooked. For example, the New York City area is a mecca for bird watchers throughout the country, yet most guides there rarely mention birds on their tours.

Fortunately, many resources are available for guides who wish to increase their understanding of nature. Field guides who specialize in interpreting a region's flora, fauna, and other natural phenomena, are excellent resources for learning about an ecosystem's specific elements. Many local birding and hiking clubs or nature stores offer regular interpretive walks that can be useful in developing a better understanding of a region's natural beauty and history.

Interpreting History

History is one of the most common subjects of interpretation in any region, and the historical interpreter's task is to make the events of the past interesting and meaningful to the contemporary visitor. Historians, philosophers, and other academicians have long believed that the teaching of history is vital to living productively in both the present and future.

Unfortunately, many have been alienated by the vain attempts of history teachers who forced them to memorize dates and facts about the wars, movements, court cases, and statistics of the past, most of which have been forgotten. One of the advantages guides often have over school curricula is that they are able to work within the day-to-day context of the events. Being able to show visitors the homes, furniture, and personal possessions of a noted participant in history often provides a more memorable interpretation.

Another effective technique in the telling of history is to focus on the personal stories of historical figures. Indeed, many who are passionate about history were inspired by an initial fascination with a person or an event in history that seemed to have a relevance to their own lives. Most of the people chronicled in history texts are fascinating, often rebellious characters whose antics are at least as entertaining as those featured in today's celebrity news magazines. By humanizing historical characters and sharing the stories of their lives, guides can create historical heroes and role models.

Interpreting Art

Art is an especially intimidating subject. Often as a result of an academic and personal mystification, many people are doubtful about their ability to create and, oddly enough, to appreciate art. Perhaps too many adults were dragged to museums as children and encouraged to appreciate forms of art that they did not understand and that did not appeal to them. In one sense, museum browsing is like shopping. If one is forced to browse in room after room filled with items of no interest or appeal the shoppers will quickly become bored.

In their book *Where's the Me in Museum: Going to Museums with Children*, the authors point out that museums seem to "command a certain reverence that has hindered both children and adults from enjoying the museum adventure." Further, they outline "The Museum-Goer's Bill of Rights and Responsibilities," in which they counter prevailing notions about how one should feel or behave in a museum. Many of these suggestions are important for guides to bear in mind as they attempt to interpret art and museums:

- We have the right to our curiosity and therefore are able to identify our own treasures.
- We have the right not to like a museum or an exhibit.
- We have the right to be confused by what we find in museums.
- We have the right to be bored if there is nothing that seems interesting.
- We have the right to take the time we need to look and think while in a museum.
- We have the right to want to go home.
- We accept the responsibility for listening to other opinions besides our own (Waterfall and Grusin 1989).

Rather than attempting to influence others' appreciation of particular styles or pieces, interpreters of art might instead encourage visitors to find pieces that appeal to them and ask them why. Further study can proceed from there, with discussion about the artist's life, style, techniques, and goals in his or her art.

Interpreting Architecture

To the uninitiated, architecture may seem to consist merely of static buildings; those who understand it believe that it is one of the greatest of all human achievements. Architecture is the art and shelter of one time cemented and hammered down for the ages, revealing the clues to a culture, its prosperity (or poverty), and the mood of the time. Goethe called architecture "frozen music." The architect, architectural historian, and any person who learns even a little about architecture can look toward the rooftop of virtually any building and see some of the "music" of another time. The interpreter of architecture should strive for that goal.

As with other themes, it is essential that the interpreter of architecture understand some of the subject's fundamental elements and terminology. A basic course or field guide can acquaint a guide with the differences, for example, between Federal, Georgian, Victorian, and Beaux Arts styles. Rather than merely pointing out various architectural styles, a guide might show visitors how they can explore various parts of a city and know which areas were most prosperous during a certain period. Or a guide might discuss the ways in which a style of architecture reflects the character of the time in which it was developed. For example, during the Gilded Age, an "if you have it, flaunt it" philosophy reigned, and the homes of that era are appropriately massive and wildly ostentatious. The public buildings of the Greek Revival period, on the other hand, are classically styled structures, more serious, simple, and staid, reflecting the political and social values of the government's leaders.

Incidental Interpretation

Incidental interpretation includes all the subtle but meaningful messages that a guide sends but does not—in fact often cannot—control. This constant stream of powerful statements flows from a guide unconsciously. The elements of incidental interpretation, which are more likely to be noticed by travelers than by guides, include such aspects as the guide's tone of voice, pacing, his or her manners and mannerisms, the way in which he or she interacts with colleagues and with other travelers, and the significance he or she bestows on a place.

For example, people are often more affected by a guide's passion for a subject than they are by the actual information he or she presents. A guide might express that a certain place or historical event or character altered their lives or their way of thinking. Such a statement is often more important to travelers than the reasons the guide had for feeling that way.

Filmmaker Ken Burns, producer, writer, and director of the PBS documentary series "The Civil War," is one of the country's most celebrated and effective interpreters of history. One of his favorite relics from the Civil War period is a letter written by Major Sullivan Ballou to his wife prior to the Battle of Bull Run. In an interview about the documentary, Burns spoke of the letter. "Would you like to hear a bit of it?" I have it right here," he said, as he opened his wallet and gingerly removed and unfolded the timeworn letter. "I always carry it with me." Burns's reading of the letter offered a riveting interpretation of one man's love for his wife and his dedication to the cause of the war. The incidental message was just as powerful: that Burns cared for the letter more than almost any possession. Guides are continually sending such messages, whether they realize it or not.

Sometimes the message that the traveler receives is not one that the guide would like to be sending. As noted earlier, people will believe what they see a speaker do, when what is said and what is done appear to be in conflict.

A guide who recommends a wax museum and is seen rolling her eyes and snickering at it to the motorcoach operator has certainly said more by her actions than by her words. Visitors might respond in different ways to such behavior. While some may be amused by her irreverence, others might understandably feel insulted, wondering, "Why is she not being honest with us?" or "Can we really trust what she's telling us?"

Another way in which guides interpret incidentally are by simply giving priority to a topic or a place. One Louisiana guide devoted much time recounting stories about Huey B. Long. After the tour one participant said, "I never had any interest in him or Louisiana political history because I always wrote him off as a simple scoundrel. But he was fascinating, and I can see that he really did do some positive things for the people of that state."

After four days of informative touring in and around Vienna, the visitors realized that they had never heard their Viennese guide mention the Austrian president's home or even his name. Questioned about this, the guide immediately changed the subject. In this case, the guide's deliberate and obvious exclusion of a topic said much about her feelings and drew attention to and created speculation about them.

A guide's realization that he or she interprets incidentally should not be intimidating. It is important, however, for a guide to recognize that travelers can perceive much that he or she genuinely feels, and that the most memorable interpretations are derived from all aspects of a guide's delivery, not only those for which he or she prepares.

SUMMARY

Even more important than having an advanced understanding of one's subject matter is a guide's ability to make the information come to life. Although many believe that such an ability is innate, there are many interpretive techniques that can be learned. Guides can at least be made more aware of these techniques, with the goal of eventually incorporating them into their work. In general, guides can be assured of more dynamic interpretations if they talk about what they love, remain interested enough to continue learning, and tune in to their visitors and attempt to involve them in the experience.

IV. Management

10 *The Nuts and Bolts of Conducting Tours*

"Mastering the mechanics of tour conducting frees the guide and allows self-expression and creativity to become an integral part of the tour experience."

—Catherine Shilts,
president, PGAA

Conducting a tour is much like leading an orchestra or directing a theatrical production. Although the many details are meticulously planned, the actual production is always a unique, creative experience. Conducting a tour combines many skills, among them those of an archeologist, a storyteller, a teacher, a manager, and a diplomat.

There is no typical tour, and one of the joys of guiding is that no two days are ever the same. Whether guides work at a specific site or conduct tours over a large geographical region, their "audience" might be one person or forty, a family or a senior citizens' group, executives or farmers, or visitors from the Soviet Union, Japan, West Africa, New York City, or Iowa. Some guides meet with a group for less than an hour; others travel with the same group of people for anywhere from two to thirty days. Countless factors can alter the tone of a tour, such as the sites themselves, individual personalities within a group, the season, the weather, the group's itinerary, the length of a visit, and the mode of transportation. Groups who are tired or hungry or on the twelfth day of a two-week tour are more likely to be inattentive or phlegmatic. Moreover, the specific interests of a group or a guide often dictate the focus of the tour. Some guides specialize in a particular subject or site and others find that their work embraces all of the variables mentioned above. Often, guides who are trained in one "mode" or who work most frequently, for example, on walking tours, are less effective and sensitive to the needs of travelers on a motorcoach. Such nuances, all of which dramatically alter tours, are discussed here.

Tours that cover a large geographical area and last one week or more traditionally have been conducted by tour managers. Tour managers meet groups, check them into hotels, and attend to the smooth operation of the tour, working as a liaison with hotels, restaurants, and attractions. When the group arrives in a particular city, local guides (also called city guides or "step-on" guides) then conduct tours of that city, and with guides who work for specific sites conducting brief, on-site tours at particular stops along the way. Although this practice is still followed widely, other methods are emerging. Most notably, the distinction between the role and work of tour manager and tour guide is, for a variety of reasons, becoming less pronounced in many regions. Many passengers prefer the in-depth interpretation a single guide can offer throughout an entire tour. This is especially true in regions that have attractions of historical and natural significance at nearly every turn, such as New England. Many guides naturally learn the skills of both functions simply because they have chosen to remain in the business for years or decades. As tour guides and tour managers come to regard their positions as long-term, professional careers, they are more eager to increase their expertise to include both roles. Many companies are also welcoming this trend, as it is more time- and cost-effective, allowing them to hire, train, and oversee fewer people. Guides and tour operators also often prefer the continuity that having one guide provides.

As the travel industry continues to grow, becoming more sophisticated and service-oriented, travelers expect a more responsive and adaptable professionalism from all guides; that is, they expect tour managers to interpret areas, and guides to offer the high quality of personal attention traditionally associated with tour managers. Many who work as both guides and tour managers concur. Catherine Shilts, president-elect of the Professional Guides Association of America (PGAA) and the chairperson of its Professional Development Committee, says, "As a professional who strives to have extensive knowledge regarding the areas we pass through and convey that information to my passengers, I consider myself a tour guide who also manages the necessary details."

GENERAL TOUR PROCEDURES

Pre-tour Planning

As in any production, executing a tour involves much backstage work and careful planning over a long period of time. Most tour operators and destination management companies[1] plan tours approximately a year in advance. During this time they must construct an itinerary and price structure based on the number of participants, group interests, and availability. In addition, the tour planner must contact, negotiate, and make bookings with the hotels, restaurants, and all other attractions included in the tour. (Policies regarding the booking of guides vary widely depending upon the region, the company, and the nature of the tour. In order to secure their first choice of guides, some companies book

---

[1]The term *tour operator* will be used in this chapter to refer to any company (destination management company, travel agency or association, etc.) that sponsors and plans a tour, except where procedures differ. For further clarification about the different kinds of tour operators, see Chapter 3, "Tourism."

and send contracts a year or more in advance. Others book and confirm guides much closer to the dates of tours, at the point when their clients pay their first installments. Bookings, contracts, and cancellations are discussed in greater detail in Chapter 12, "The Business of Guiding."

The amount of information available to guides at the time of booking varies as well. Some companies send itineraries immediately to ensure that the guide is fully aware of all aspects of the tour. Certainly, it is advantageous that guides have any confirmed information as early as possible. Learning well in advance that an itinerary includes a stop at a historic home, winery, or any site with which the guide is not familiar gives the guide an opportunity to visit the site during the off-season and to read any related or relevant literature. With advance information, companies can also feel assured that a guide has time to prepare. And at that point, guides have an obligation to either commit to learning the site or relinquishing the tour so that the company can find someone with expertise in the area.

Such advance notice in booking is the ideal, however. Cancellations can and do occur, and depending on the tour operator's policies, groups can cancel up to a week or two prior to a tour. In the case of convention tours, public tours for independent travelers, and other shorter tours, bookings and cancellations can occur up to the moment a tour begins. Since cancellations cannot be predicted, and because they can be devastating to a guide's livelihood, many companies delay booking some types of tours so that they can offer their senior or preferred guides replacement work in the event of having to cancel. Some companies offer guides a cancellation fee, ranging from full payment to 20 percent and based on how close to the scheduled date the tour was cancelled. More often, however, cancellations leave guides with no income and not enough advance time to schedule other tours. Obviously, the game of booking can be a precarious one for the freelance guide.

As early as possible, guides should obtain a group's name and as much information about them as is available. Details such as where they live, their approximate ages, their affinity (a school class trip, a local senior citizens' group, a national organization, a group of independent travelers) help a guide tune into the group as individuals, making the tour more rewarding for all. At the time of booking, guides should also clarify the payment and expenses covered for the tour and request an itinerary, both the company's itinerary for the guide and the literature about the tour that the travelers receive, if they are at all different.

One of the overlooked but most time-consuming aspects of a guide's work is the important briefing period required prior to a tour. Tour planners spend many hours consulting with clients and learning about their priorities and idiosyncracies, making reservations, and anticipating the timing for driving, sightseeing, dining, and browsing. All of this information must be conveyed to the guide, which can take from 15 minutes to a few hours in the days or weeks prior to a tour. Some companies require that guides appear in person for briefings and are willing to pay for their time; others conduct briefings over the telephone or by mail and consider this time, whatever the length, to be "unbillable" time in preparation for the job.

Immediately upon receiving an itinerary, guides should read it, map out and visualize the actual operation of the tour, and check for inconsistencies in the literature as well as allowances for timing in travel, dining, and sightseeing. Because they are aware of actual driving times and the kinds of delays that might occur in particular places, tour planners often rely heavily on guides and drivers to inform them as soon as possible upon noticing any problem areas in an itinerary. This allows sufficient time not only to change plans and reservations but also to change the travelers' itineraries. This is especially important when it becomes necessary to eliminate something on a tour, so that travelers do not arrive with expectations that conflict with reality.

To some tour operators, itineraries are sacrosanct, and guides are never permitted to alter them unless specifically told to do so. At the other end of the spectrum are companies that offer passengers and guides purposely vague itineraries (with no times listed) and expect guides to use their own judgment and contacts and create much of the tour as they go. Most companies operate between these extremes, making reservations for meals and most attractions and relying on guides to confirm information directly with vendors as the tour progresses. Almost all require that guides contact them before making significant changes, especially those that involve additional expense for the company, or emergency decisions that affect the health and safety of tour participants. Since all guides must inevitably make decisions on the company's behalf and alter itineraries to some degree, many companies prefer to hire only experienced guides.

Paperwork and Bookkeeping

At some point prior to the tour, the guide receives paperwork from the tour operator. For shorter tours, the paperwork is presented on-site or arrives two days to one week ahead; for longer tours, companies usually send it one to two weeks prior to the start of the tour. The amount and type of paperwork and bookkeeping depends upon the complexity of the tour, the guide's role, and company procedures and policies. Typical items for shorter tours include passenger lists, with persons in charge noted; detailed itineraries; confirmation letters from any restaurants, hotels, or attractions on the tour; checks or vouchers for payment; accounting sheets for all expenses; telephone numbers for vendors and tour operator representatives; rooming lists; luggage tags; and forms for documenting all emergencies or problems. In addition, some companies have forms for guides to evaluate vendors, including the motorcoach and driver, the hotel and its staff, and so forth. For extended tours, forms and paperwork are usually more complicated.

The First Day of the Tour

The hours just before a tour begins are important. Before leaving for a tour, it is advisable for guides to confirm arrival times. For example, if a group is arriving from a long distance—by air, train, or motorcoach—the airline, transportation company, or tour operator may have up-to-date arrival information. Flights or trains are often delayed or even cancelled. Guides should also check weather reports for the day or days in which the group is traveling. Guides also need to bring itineraries; passenger lists; checks or cash; any paperwork the company has provided; and anything else the company requires.

Guides should also bring important telephone numbers, including those of the sponsoring tour operator, motorcoach company, motorcoach dispatch office, and any restaurants or attractions that the group will be visiting. When the guide is meeting an unknown driver, it is also wise to take maps in case the driver is unfamiliar with any of the scheduled stops on the tour. Guides who are not yet fully comfortable with the planned sites or region should take along notes or reference materials in case they need to refresh their memories. Some guides regularly carry compact first-aid kits. In any case, guides should be aware of the necessary procedures and telephone numbers for emergencies. (Safety and emergency procedures are discussed in Appendix D.)

Tour attire and accessories vary widely among regions and companies. Some companies provide complete uniforms, required on all days of a tour. Others have uniform colors or styles or company trademarks, such as badges, name tags, scarves, or umbrellas. Because many people dislike name tags, some companies have eliminated them; others require them only on the first few days of a tour, until people get to know each other and the guide. Most companies require guides to wear some form of identification. Some companies offer a distinguishing sign so that travelers can locate the guide on the first day. Dress is discussed further in Chapter 13, "Professional Ethics and Etiquette."

Arriving at the Tour Site

Guides should plan to arrive at least twenty minutes prior to the start of the tour; when meeting a group out of town, some companies recommend or require reporting 30 minutes to one hour ahead of the expected arrival time. Those minutes are vital to a tour, and the most reputable tour operators require (and pay for) guides to be there early.

There are many reasons why guides should arrive early to the tour's meeting place. Planning an early arrival allows extra time for unexpected delays along the way. Once arriving at the site, it is wise for guides to have time to relax so that they feel and appear at ease and ready when the group arrives. Such an image instills a feeling of confidence among tour participants. Being available when the first people arrive allows time for guides to have casual conversation and gain a sense of the personalities of the group, so vital to interpretation. Moreover, there are important tasks that need to be taken care of in the moments before the tour.

If the place of arrival is an airport or train station, the first task is to check the arrival terminal to confirm the actual arrival time and arrival gate. Once this is established, if the guide is not familiar with the airport or train station, he or she should walk to the gate, establish a meeting/waiting site for the group, and note the location of the baggage claim area. Airports and train stations vary as to the waiting procedures. Many train stations will permit guides to wait on the platform; others require everyone to remain in public areas outside the gate. Although some airports do not check for tickets, most airports prohibit anyone without a ticket beyond established security points.

Once arrival information is established, the guide should meet with the prearranged ground transportation. For motorcoach, van, or limousine tours, the guide must meet the driver and review the details of the tour. This is discussed at length below (see "Working with Motorcoach Operators").

Meeting Groups

First impressions are critical. Many people immediately appraise the guide's personality as a way of evaluating the success of the tour, unconsciously registering a lingering assessment of the guide in the first moments. An impression of the guide as nervous, disheveled, underconfident, unenthusiastic, tired, or disinterested can be extremely damaging to the mood of the tour. People like to meet a guide who is cheerful, confident, enthusiastic, caring, and professional. These are in general the qualities of someone who is suited to the work, prepared for the tour, and genuinely interested in people.

Most guides agree that the initial moments are the most difficult and stressful aspect of tours. In some cases, the company or person who hired the guide will be present to introduce the group leader and group to the guide. More often, a guide will meet a group alone, which requires that the guide approach a group of strangers, introduce himself or herself to the members of a group, and begin the tour.

Ideally, the guide is provided with the names of people in the group and, sometimes, the person in charge. If there is a person (or persons) in charge, the guide should immediately ask for and confirm the initial strategy with them. As an example the guide might say, "Mr. Jones? I understand you're the leader of this fine group. Do you think we should head straight to the hotel, or are you eager to see a little of the area first?" If there is no designated person in charge, it is important for the guide to assume that role.

When meeting at an airport or train station, a guide should introduce himself or herself briefly, offer a friendly greeting, inquire about their trip, and give brief but clear instructions as to the immediate procedures. From the outset it is critical to be mindful of a group's needs while keeping them moving efficiently. As it is difficult and ineffective to speak at length to groups at loud and hectic airports and train stations, it is best to keep group instructions and introductions to a minimum until the group is situated elsewhere. As an example:

"Hello, everyone! Welcome! How was your flight? Good." If they have already had a horrendous experience, the guide might say, "Oh, no! Well, you can relax now, and leave all your worries to me." And then, "I'm really looking forward to talking with you more, but for now, I thought we'd go straight to the hotel, where you can get settled. Here's what we need to do: The baggage will be arriving on the lower level at 'Carousel B,' which is straight ahead and down the escalator. I'll lead the way. Once we're there I'll designate an area where you can put your bags when you identify them, and, when we have all of them, we'll proceed to the motorcoach. There are rest rooms in the baggage area which you're free to use, but please remain in the area, as we hope to be leaving the airport as quickly as possible."

Don Cross, British guide and author of *Please Follow Me,* advises guides to "Remain slightly aloof—friendly but not gushing . . . radiate assurance, self-confidence and command" (Cross 1991).

Meeting people at train and bus stations is similar to meeting them at airports. One exception is that groups traveling by train often board and disembark as a group, and baggage for a group is often handled collectively by red caps. For this reason, it is important for a guide meeting a group traveling by train to check in with the train office to see if special arrangements have been made for them. Often the guide is escorted directly to the track where the group arrives, and the group's baggage is loaded and driven directly to the waiting ground transportation.

Depending upon the tour operator's arrangements, either the guide is responsible for finding and tipping a skycap or redcap for carting luggage, or passengers will carry their own luggage or tip a handler themselves.

Setting the Stage Guides should concentrate on tuning in to visitors immediately: Are they tired, hungry, agitated, or eager to get going? The first day—specifically, the first few minutes and hours of a tour—sets the stage for the remainder of the trip.

Groups often mirror the mood or behavior of their guide to a surprising degree, so it is critical that the guide exemplify the behavior he or she wishes the group to display. For example, guides should arrive to all meeting places early and begin activities on time. If a guide is lackadaisical about time and timing, the group will quickly imitate that behavior.

On tours lasting more than a day there are usually certain policies or goals that the guide should establish, and it is most effective to convey them to a group early in the tour and to do so in a positive, nonauthoritarian way. Tour manager Ron Wesner stresses certain points to groups by inviting their responses. An example might be: "We all want to be able to see and do everything that's scheduled. And no one wants to be sitting on the coach waiting for one or two people each morning, right? So, why don't we all agree right now to be considerate to everyone and not keep anyone else waiting. O.K.?" No one would not agree to that, says Wesner, and by establishing these ground rules, they have more or less made a pact.

Stressing the cooperative effort involved in traveling with a group is important. Regulations and tight schedules seem far more palatable when expressed as something that everyone must endure together. Guides should also encourage passengers to express any concerns or questions as they arise. Questions make a tour more interesting for both guides and participants, and addressing concerns is wise so that they do not fester into more serious problems.

Finally, guides should make clear their wishes for the tour's success and the tour members' enjoyment. Telling a group, "I want this to be the most memorable trip you've ever had" will go a long way toward instilling a good feeling.

Visiting Restaurants and Attractions

Most tours involve visiting attractions and restaurants. Moving around with forty people is more complicated and cumbersome than individual traveling. When arriving at public buildings, memorials, or parks with no admission procedures or fees, groups can enter en masse. At most places, however, it is usually wise for a guide to ask a group to remain outside while he or she alerts the management to the group's arrival. This prevents the opportunity for any uncomfortable situations, such as lost reservations, to be observed by the group. As most stops on tours are scheduled, the guide will confirm the group number, pay the entrance fee if necessary, and inquire about any current information or regulations the group members should know.

Those who work in restaurants and at attractions are, in a sense, the guide's colleagues, and it is important that guides work cooperatively with all businesses and their employees. Doing this creates a pleasant ambiance that reflects on the guide, the tour, and the region. Moreover, guides can be assured that whenever they bring groups to a place of business where they have had a positive encounter, they will again be treated well.

Altering Itineraries

"The best laid plans of mice and men. . . ." Itineraries do not always unfold as planned. Traffic, weather, long queues, a late or ill passenger, motorcoach breakdowns, or unexpected but interesting incidents can all cause delays of any duration. Sometimes a delay prevents a group from participating in a planned event, and at times even planned events fall through for unforeseen reasons. For instance, one of the main attractions of a tour is closed due to a broken water main or a presidential visit on the day the group is in town. When it becomes clear that the group will need to omit a promised attraction, for whatever reason, the guide is often placed in an awkward position. Most people will accept unavoidable "act of God" events, and the few who do not are often silenced by the majority who do. When the omission is substantial and is clearly the result of poor planning or negligence on the part of the tour operator or guide, people will often demand substitutions or refunds or will press to fit in the missed event regardless of cost, and in spite of any other events they would have to miss.

While democracy is desirable for running countries, it can be disastrous for running tours. While it seems logical to have tour members decide how to make changes, taking votes often backfires. Unless the group vote is unanimous, certain members will feel slighted. It is usually best for a guide to simply make a decision based on his or her own judgment about the importance of an event and the general feelings and statements of the group. "Voting is so tempting," says Janice Holliday. "But I have never heard of or experienced a vote that didn't backfire."

Evening Activities

Although tour managers are always included in a group's evening activities, the procedure for tour guides varies. When a guide is hired to be with a group and a meal is included in their planned evening, it is normally the custom for the guide to join the group for dinner. Sometimes corporations or affinity groups will request a private meal but will want to schedule sightseeing afterward. In such cases, companies usually provide a meal or a meal allowance for guides on duty.

Some tour companies strongly recommend that guides do not socialize with tour members during nontour activities, and there are good reasons for this. For one, guides who socialize with one or a few people on the tour might be viewed as "playing favorites." Second, the tour manager has an already full schedule. At the end of one touring day and before the start of the next, the tour manager must attend to paperwork and planning. And finally, guides deserve and need time away from their charges to rejuvenate. It is easy for novice guides to get caught up in doing too much for their guests, denying themselves time for rest. The intensity of leading and interpreting for a large group makes it essential for guides to take care of themselves and allow plenty of time for rest during a tour.

A Local Guide Should Know . . .

One never knows what a visitor will ask for or need, so a guide must have a lot of information on hand, such as:

- The location of nearby medical facilities and local emergency procedures
- Banking availability

- Currency and exchange rates, or, at least, knowledge of how to find them
- Telephone and postal service information
- Information on purchasing tickets for transportation, including air, train, subway, and local and regional motorcoach
- Current theater information
- Information on procuring taxis, including fees and where to stand
- Shopping information, including where to buy what and a store's hours of operation
- Restaurant recommendations, including cuisines, locations, price ranges
- Local tipping customs
- Safety tips, including those areas that people should avoid after dark and those considered very safe
- Any unusual customs or helpful suggestions about an area

MODES OF TRANSPORTATION

Walking tours, bus tours, and auto and limousine tours all offer unique opportunities and challenges in timing, pacing, and lecturing. Tours that feature various means of transportation (known in the travel industry as *intermodal tours*), provide many advantages and challenges. A tour of Cape Cod, for example, might include flying into Boston and traveling to the Cape via motorcoach. Once on the Cape, one might take the train from Sandwich, the ferry to Martha's Vineyard, or a dune buggy ride in Provincetown. All are very different ways for visitors to see places, and all offer unique challenges for a guide.

Walking Tours

Most tours involve walking to some degree. Many travelers insist that nothing can replace the closeness that walking provides. Walking tours enable people to use all their senses and give them opportunities for close contact, which motorized tours can lack. Even the least adventurous cruise or motorcoach tour offers segments (or should) for exploring on foot (see Fig. 10.1).

Often, large urban areas and colossal buildings are more congenial at the pedestrian level than by motorcoach. New York City is a good example of this. Overwhelming by many standards, even for the well-traveled, New York can be more intimidating by car or motorcoach, from which point everything seems fast-paced and daunting. Although the same can hold true for the traveler on foot, New York, like many cities, has countless surprises for the pedestrian, such as stunning window displays, unexpected parks, and inimitable delicatessens. To have visited Manhattan and not strolled down Fifth Avenue or in Greenwich Village, Chinatown, or Harlem is to have missed the New Yorker's New York. The same can be said of sculptures, gardens, and sacred places in

Figure 10.1
Guides should attempt to incorporate walking tours into any tour, as the close proximity provides opportunities that driving by cannot. Washington, D.C. guide Catherine Androus offers her perspective on Frederick Hart's sculpture at the Vietnam Veteran's Memorial. (*Photo by Deborah Androus.*)

any town. Anyone who has ever visited the Vietnam Veteran's Memorial in Washington, D.C., would agree that viewing it from a motorcoach 50 yards away is to entirely miss its impact.

Guides should always encourage visitors to experience places on foot, except when travelers have limited mobility or when walking in a particular area would put them in danger. Ideally, when a tour involves heavy or moderate walking, participants of a walking tour have been forewarned and are properly prepared. If a guide is with a group for several days, he or she should inform the group during an early review of the itinerary which day involves much walking. When long or difficult walks are scheduled, groups should be encouraged to wear their most comfortable and well-worn (never new) walking shoes. Guides should, in addition, be mindful of local weather reports and update travelers regularly about them.

Before Departing   Guides should try to assess the personality and mood of a group: How well do they know each other, do they get along well, how much do they have in common, are they physically fit, are there any mobility problems, where have they been and where will they go on this tour, how far into the tour are they, are they tired, cranky, excited, relaxed . . . ? These are questions that guides should be mentally asking themselves before the tour departs. If there is a group leader, these questions can be directed to him or her. Otherwise, it is advisable for a guide to converse with the group casually to discern its mood.

Before departing, the guide should set the stage for the tour by briefly describing its nature and significance. An example of this might be, "I understand that some of you saw the city from the top of the John Hancock Tower. Today we're going to get a closer glimpse of Boston life by walking through the heart of the city on the Freedom Trail. We'll be seeing. . . ."

For practical and psychological reasons, guides should describe the route of the tour, including the distance and time involved. If the tour is circular, it is helpful to mention to the group the scheduled return to the starting point. If the tour begins in one location and ends in another, it is necessary to give specific instructions as to where and when it ends and how to return. Guides should mention whether and approximately when breaks are scheduled, so that people can mentally prepare for rest rooms, shopping, photography, browsing, or resting. One sure way for a guide to lose an audience is not to mention these points. After only 30 minutes into the tour, people will begin to look at their watches or talk amongst themselves.

Outlining the game plan also helps the guide establish necessary control over the group, since members of the group will be less likely to stray away to drinking fountains or rest rooms. An example of such an opening is: "Our tour today will cover approximately three miles and take about four hours. But we'll be breaking it up with several stops and a break for lunch at Faneuil Hall." Tours that involve little walking and much standing can be even more exhausting, so it is a good idea to vary standing and walking when at all possible.

If the terrain is rough, such as cobblestone streets or a high footbridge, participants should be advised and, if possible, given the option to sit out a rigorous segment. "This walk will provide you with your aerobic exercise for the day. It's fairly rigorous. If you have doubts about it, feel free to wait for us here. We'll be back in about 45 minutes, and there are some interesting galleries and stores here that you might prefer. For those of you who are going, please be careful and let me know if you need to slow down or stop." On all walks, guides should be diligent about pointing out uneven walkways or steps or any potential obstacles.

Sometimes gentle or humorous reminders encourage participants to be better sports: "To think people have been walking on these cobblestones for centuries. . . . I guess we can handle it for a few minutes." Jeff Jerome, curator of Baltimore's Poe House and guide of the Westminister Church catacombs says, "Catacombs were not designed for tourism; they were designed for dead people. So I do need to give you a few guidelines for seeing them safely. . . ." Before entering darkened or dimmed areas guides should allude to easily recognizable hallmarks. Many guides purposely wear bright colors or eventually create their own trademarks, such as an unusual hat or umbrella.

It is important for guides to stress that participants in a walking tour must stay together. This is particularly critical on busy streets or in large buildings. A guide might tell a group, "If you need to stop for any reason, let us know."

Counting, repeatedly, is critical. Few transgressions are more unforgivable to tour operators than losing a tour passenger.

Setting the Pace   It is desirable in most countries and with all companies for guides to begin tours on time. This is a courtesy for those people who arrive on time and are eager to see and learn as much as they can.

Walking tours offer a guide the opportunity to compromise. It is a good idea to begin on time, remain stationary, describe the route of the tour, and time frame and breaks, and then provide a background of the area. In this way, those who arrive late can still join the tour, and those who have arrived on time have not had to wait for latecomers. As mentioned earlier, groups will mirror the guide's own behavior to a great degree, and always beginning on time sets a precedent for the remainder of the tour.

In the case of a family tour or a small, closely acquainted private group, however, the group itself often dictates the pace and tone of the tour to a great degree. In other words, if a private group has hired a guide, the guide is often obliged to work within the parameters set by the group. On the other hand, guides are expected to be mindful of appointments and travel times and to give gentle reminders when necessary. If the group is particularly slow and lax, the guide might point out, "Of course, we can take as long as you like here, but if you want to see the show, we'll need to leave here by two-thirty, at the very latest."

Browsing time can dramatically enhance tours. Allowing people time and space on their own in a place creates the opportunity for a more lasting personal experience. Allowing free time also eases some of the tension of a walking tour in a busy place where it is more challenging to keep a group together. Street crossings, street musicians, street peddlers, traffic, intersections, and tour members who are photographers, dawdlers, or simply curious travelers can be seen as distractions that work against a smoothly timed walking tour. In fact, these diversions embody the advantages of the walking tour experience. Rather than admonishing the group to move along without stopping to experience the nuances of street life, allowing extra unstructured time often offers interesting, indigenous experiences.

Indeed, one of the joys of walking tours is the close interaction people can have with a place, whether it be a cave, memorial, art museum, or urban ghetto. All too many guides regard the tour as their personal show and forum and prefer to keep a tight rein on their groups in public places, which prevents guests from experiencing a place personally. Places that lend themselves well to free, unstructured time include public parks, memorials, museums, and gardens.

If a walking tour includes a visit inside one or more large buildings, it is advisable to spend some time outside the building explaining its background, design, and layout. A building's architecture can tell much about the organization's history and the era in which the building was built. Relating the outside of a building to what they will see inside enhances the experience.

Guides are usually among the best walkers in a group. Often there is a collection of brisk walkers who surround the guide, while the remainder of the group lags behind. Guides must be sensitive to their own tendency to walk faster than average. It is usually advisable for guides to slow their pace and to stop periodically to allow stragglers to catch up to the rest of the group. If there are one or more participants who lag far behind a group, it is the guide's duty to ascertain whether the slow walking is due to physical problems or mere dawdling. In the case of the latter, the guide might remind the group to stay together as much as possible. "Please let us know if you feel we need to slow down the pace."

If a tour member has considerable problems walking, a private conversation with them may be necessary. Such a conversation must be handled tactfully to avoid offending the visitor. The guide might mention points in the tour that will involve considerable walking, and if the guest seems receptive, offer a wheelchair or the option of staying behind for a less demanding activity. Some people with mobility problems prefer that a group not wait for them, and when they begin to fall behind, welcome having a guide move on. It is important for the guide to be mindful of the participant's level of independence and comfort as well as the comfort of the remainder of the group.

One of the most common and most annoying blunders guides make is the tendency to interpret while walking, thereby eliminating from the experience those who are not close to the guide. This is of particular importance with larger groups, as many are likely to be out of earshot while on the move. Inevitably, guides will be asked questions or will hear or share interesting anecdotes when walking from one spot to another, and these should be shared with the entire group when everyone is stopped and gathered together. There are several ways to handle this. If a traveler asks a question that requires a short answer, the guide might answer it, and when the group gathers, say, "Someone just asked whether or not we. . . . We do, and. . . ." If the question requires a longer explanation, the guide can say, "That's a good question, and I think everyone might want to know about that, so I'll explain it in a minute." If the guide has shared a story, he or she might say, "I was just telling Susan and Joe that. . . ." If a member of the group has shared an interesting and relevant story, the guide might say, "Do you mind if I share that with the group?" And when the group gathers, "Steve had an interesting experience. . . ." This is a courtesy that people greatly appreciate, as no one wants to feel that they are missing the guide's casual, off-hand remarks.

Inclement Weather For walking tours it is especially important to be mindful of weather reports and to account for weather in planning a walk. Most guides carry umbrellas when there is even the slightest possibility of rain, and it is important to warn participants also if the likelihood of rain exists.

Except when poor weather poses safety risks, guides should be conservative about actually cancelling a tour due to inclement weather. What may seem to a guide or to some passengers to be unbearable or severe weather conditions may be easily tolerable for others. When people have spent money and traveled distances to experience a place, they are often willing—and prepared—to endure the inconvenience of rain or heat. On the other hand, if an electrical storm is looming, or if the day's walk features a long, uphill climb with senior citizens in 97°F heat, the wisest decision is to offer alternative plans and explain the reason.

Motorcoach Tours

The most common motorized transportation for guided tours is the motor-coach. This is the most economical way in which to hire a guide, and the most efficient, as up to forty-five people (and more on double-decker coaches) can participate at once.

In recent years the terms "motorcoach" or "coach" have been used within the tour industry to distinguish larger, heavier, restroom equipped vehicles from school or city buses.[2] Motorcoaches vary greatly in size, style, and amenities. European coaches tend to be lighter and quieter and have larger windows than American coaches. European coaches and more modern American and Asian coaches have stairwell jumpseats or "courier seats," which are met with mixed reviews by guides, drivers, and passengers alike. Those who prefer the stairwell jumpseats feel that they allow more private conversation between the driver and guide. Another advantage offered by jumpseats is that they leave both front seats available for passengers on tours. Others argue that stairwell jumpseats place the guide out of sight of passengers, so that they are unable to make important eye contact. Some guides complain that they allow no room for their maps,

---

[2]In this text, the term "bus" will not be used; "coach" and "motorcoach" are used interchangeably. "Motorcoach operator," "coach operator," and "driver" are also used interchangeably. It is suggested that guides also use these terms, which are in keeping with current industry standards and evoke positive connotations.

Figure 10.2
Motorcoaches offer special advantages and challenges for tours. Grant Doyle of Educational Tours of Inverness, Florida, conducts a tour. (*Photo by Deborah Androus.*)

notes, and usually extensive tour information. Both drivers and guides note the loss of personal space, and guides often complain that stairwell jumpseats are drafty. Moreover, some jumpseats do not have seat belts and many guides feel particularly vulnerable using them.

Working with Motorcoach Operators   Drivers and guides are teammates, and fostering professional, amicable relationships with drivers is one of the most important aspects of a guide's work. Although the duties of drivers and guides are distinctly different, their roles overlap. Ideally, the relationship between driver and guide is synergistic, with each making the other's work easier, less stressful, and more rewarding.

The relationship between driver and guide can vary somewhat, depending upon the nature of the tour. When the guide's company has hired the motorcoach company, the guide is responsible for following and making any changes in the itinerary and conveying this information to the driver. When the motorcoach company hires the guide, the driver gives instruction to the guide. When guides and drivers have been hired simultaneously by the same company, they often share the responsibility. In all cases, however, it is essential that driver and guide work together as a team.

Building good relationships takes time and commitment. The following are suggestions for guides for creating better working environments with drivers.

1. Empathize with drivers by fully understanding their job. Many guides take a driver's work for granted. As drivers point out, this is especially true when the driving is flawless. Driving a motorcoach is not an easy task, however, particularly in urban areas, inclement weather, or places new to the driver. The responsibility that drivers have is staggering, as they hold the lives of passengers in their hands. Adding such challenges as enduring heavy traffic, maintaining the coach, getting directions, finding parking spaces, and the many other tasks a driver has, it is difficult to understand how most drivers maintain their calm demeanors. Ed Schaffer, long-time driver and guide in Washington, D.C., and owner of tour company The Guide Post, feels that everyone would benefit if all guides, as part of their training, would ride with a driver and learn exactly what is involved in driving a motorcoach. For example, many guides will give a driver ten seconds' or thirty yards' notice to make a right turn, unaware of the space and time a driver needs in order to do so. Many guides have no concept of the bookkeeping tasks a driver has. On longer trips, many guides freely ask a driver (in front of a group) to do extra driving, unaware that there are harsh legal restrictions limiting the number of hours they work. A driver's many tasks usually make his days at least two hours longer than the actual tour. Simply learning what the driver's job entails, Schaffer says, can make a major difference in the working relationship between driver and guide.

2. Find ways to make a driver's job easier. Most drivers are conscientious about the cleanliness of their coach, and many spend an hour or more a day cleaning it. Guides should point out to passengers the cleanliness of the coach and remind them not to leave litter around their seats. Guides working with out-of-town drivers who are somewhat unfamiliar with an area might plan to spend extra time with the driver before the passengers have arrived to make sure he or she is comfortable with routing, driving, and parking. "I find that by pointing out the good work a driver has done at a particular section of a tour or at the end of a difficult day, and asking the passengers to join in in a big 'thank you' brings major rewards," says Janice Holliday, making "team effort seem effortless."

3. Allow extra time for the driver. Motorcoach companies usually require their drivers to arrive (or "spot," in the industry jargon) at least fifteen minutes earlier than the actual start of the tour, and most drivers will arrive earlier than that. Spending extra time with the driver is invaluable for a number of reasons: it provides an opportunity to discuss thoroughly all aspects of the itinerary and ease any concerns the driver has, particularly if he or she is unfamiliar with the region; it permits the guide as well to share concerns and ask questions about the tour; and it allows time for casual conversation. This ensures a relaxed start to a day and a certainty among the passengers that the driver and guide are a team.

4. Share with the driver any insights you might have about passengers on a tour, and ask the driver to do the same. For example, a driver might notice some unrest among certain passengers, and the guide can follow up on it. Or the guide might notice that a passenger is limping and instruct the driver to take extra care when that person boards or disembarks from the coach. Again, it is vital that

the driver and guide work together and rely on each other, and any support they can provide for each other is helpful.

Unfortunately, adversarial relationships between drivers and guides are not uncommon. Guides are often intimidated by drivers, especially experienced ones who have likely worked with the most talented guides. Drivers who often work without guides and are very knowledgeable and experienced in the region sometimes resent being instructed by guides. And the stress of the work combined with the many glitches that can and do arise can easily create tension. For this reason, it is important to be diligent about maintaining a positive relationship.

When a guide reaches a motorcoach prior to a tour, he should check the coach for general cleanliness, the restrooms to make sure they are fully equipped and clean, and, finally, the microphone. If any of these items are unsatisfactory, the guide should note it and report it to the company. Before the guide or driver allows anyone to board a motorcoach, it is important that an appropriate seat be reserved for the guide. If the coach does not have a courier seat, the seat behind the driver is usually designated.

When a guide meets a driver, he or she should ask the driver's name and the way he or she would like to be introduced to the group. As soon as the group has boarded the motorcoach, the guide should introduce the driver, preferably by more than just his or her name. "This is our driver, John Smith, who will be with us throughout the tour. John [or Mr. Smith, whichever the driver prefers] is an experienced driver in Seattle, and he knows this city better than just about anyone."

Sometimes a guide will join a group that is already on the coach. This is especially true of longer tours in which the guide joins a group briefly as a "step-on guide" or when the group has traveled from their hometown by motorcoach. In such a case, the guide should introduce himself, greet everyone, and proceed after making sure the microphone is working properly.

Before the coach moves, the guide and driver should have discussed the route and destination, and other relevant facts such as pace and timing. For example, if there is a particular building or site where the guide would like the driver to pull over or pause, or a city block the guide would like to pass by very slowly, the driver should be made aware of this at the outset. If the route is unfamiliar to the driver or involves many turns, it is advisable for the guide to draw a map or list the instructions as reference for the driver, especially if the guide will be talking about the region. Guides should always be aware of the driver's comfort level in an area and take extra time and care if there is any uncertainty.

One of the hallmarks of a competent guide is the ability to talk smoothly to passengers while giving instructions to the driver. Some drivers listen carefully to the guide's commentary, and are especially adept at following a guide's instructions when they are included in commentary ("After we turn right at this corner, you'll see . . ." is sufficient for some drivers). Other drivers do not listen to commentary and wish to be told directly. It is always wise to give pointed instructions directly to a new driver, rather than to incorporate them into the commentary.

Honesty between guides and drivers is critical. When there is a particular site that neither the driver nor the guide has seen recently (or ever), it is important for them to share that. And any professional guide or driver appreciates the gesture of helping the other out quietly and discreetly, rather than making one appear inexperienced to visitors. For example, when giving a driver instructions, the guide should turn around and talk to the driver, making sure the microphone is off. Any turns should be indicated well ahead of time (ideally, a minimum of at least one city block) so the driver has time to change lanes or signal to those behind. Guides should also be aware of the height restrictions on motorcoaches, which occasionally prohibit them from entering low bridges or tunnels or from driving on certain highways.

Fostering an amicable relationship with drivers reduces the stresses of the work, creates a more pleasant environment for everyone, including visitors, and assures that if problems do arise there is a partner willing to help solve them.

Guidelines for Motorcoach Tours   In conducting motorcoach tours, guides must keep the following in mind:

1. Most people on the coach cannot see what the guide, the driver, and the two fortunate people in the front seat see. Such a statement seems so obvious as to be unnecessary to mention, but guides routinely neglect to indicate which side of the coach they are speaking about, assuming that all can see their hand gestures. Most motorcoach passengers cannot see anything but what is immediately in front of or beside them. When pointing things out on a coach, guides should be careful to speak of the passengers' right and left, rather than their own. One oft-committed guide error is in talking about sites a city block ahead of their location. This can be effective if the site is extraordinary and the guide hopes to arouse enthusiasm before the passengers can actually see it, but in general passengers in the middle and rear of the coach prefer to hear a description of a site as they are driven past it.

Many novice guides find successful timing on a motorcoach to be one of the most difficult elements of mobile interpretation to achieve. Since the length of a motorcoach guarantees that none of the passengers will see the same thing at any given time, timing is admittedly a challenge. For buildings or scenes that are particularly significant or beautiful, it is best to have the driver pull over to the side of the road if at all possible. In this instance, a skilled and considerate driver who attempts to synchronize his or her driving with the guide's commentary is a godsend. Drivers also claim that some guides' commentaries are easier to follow and coordinate their driving with than others.

2. All guides must know how to use the coach's fire extinguisher, first-aid kit, and emergency exits, and should make sure that all storage areas above passengers are closed and that all baggage is safely stowed or secured before the tour begins.

3. Make sure passengers know the name of the motorcoach company and the color, number, and any other distinguishing features of the coach so that they can always find it. At popular sites, there are usually dozens of coaches, often many from the same companies.

4. Passengers should be advised of all regulations regarding standing, eating, drinking, and smoking on coaches. Although it is now illegal to smoke and drink alcoholic beverages on public motorcoaches, those who charter motorcoaches are often free to enact their own policies for smoking, eating, and drinking. A charter tour company may, for example, permit eating and drinking and prohibit smoking, but policies vary widely. When no tour company policy exists but the driver prefers to prohibit eating, drinking, and smoking to maintain the coach's cleanliness, guides should clearly explain this to passengers at the outset. In any case, people are usually agreeable to these regulations, provided they are presented judiciously and that time is set aside for stops at regular intervals to accommodate these comforts during a tour.

5. Due to differences in the configurations of motorcoaches and as a result of tour guides' preferences, there are no firmly established rules about where guides sit and stand during the course of a tour. It is standard (and in some cases required by law) for a guide to have his or her own seat, preferably very near the driver, for obvious reasons.

Many guides stand beside the front seats and just behind the driver, facing the passengers and turning when necessary to talk to the driver. This enables most passengers to see the guide clearly, and permits the guide to make direct eye contact with visitors. Disadvantages to standing include fatigue (especially if the tour is lengthy); possible obstruction of the view from the front of the coach for many passengers; and the likelihood of an accident as a standing guide is vulnerable to being thrown about on a moving, turning coach. Sitting on the front seat, facing forward, is far safer and more comfortable, but inhibits eye contact with passengers.

Some guides kneel on their seat, allowing them to face backward. Although this position is not a particularly dignified one and many companies prohibit it, it does have advantages: it allows the guide to make eye contact with all passengers; and it is one of the safest positions, as the guide can easily hold on to the back of the seat for support. Most guides find that combining all three stances offers the best opportunity for visibility, safety, comfort, and effective communication with passengers. In any position, it is imperative that the guide maintain a firm handhold, as losing one's balance on a motorcoach is not only undignified but dangerous.

6. Except on very brief tours, it is also advisable for guides to walk about the motorcoach periodically, to talk casually with passengers and to view the coach and the tour from their perspective. Many people are far more likely to ask questions or raise concerns when speaking directly to a guide than when speaking in front of the group.

7. For a guide on a motorcoach, a microphone is an essential piece of equipment. Since a microphone is usually set up near the driver and has a cord of

limited length, a guide's movement is often limited to the first two seats when speaking on a motorcoach. Guides should test microphones immediately upon boarding the coach, and encourage passengers, especially those in the back of the coach, to indicate when the sound is too high or low. (Using a microphone is covered in Chapter 8, "Presentation and Speaking Skills.")

Driver-Guiding

Although driver-guiding is actually illegal in some countries, it is conducted regularly in many places, including North America. Hiring driver-guides is more cost-effective for tour companies; in the view of many passengers, they provide a more personalized service. Others believe that driver-guiding is less safe, as both driving and guiding require concentration and focused skills. Opponents of driver-guiding also feel that such tours are not as informative, since the driver-guide must remain with the vehicle and is unable to conduct walking tours or tours inside buildings. Some driver-guides work for companies that own or lease motorcoaches or vans, while others own and use their own vehicles for tours.

Van and Automobile Tours

Family tours and small group tours (those with less than 10 participants) are becoming increasingly popular today. Many baby boomers, who are well-established in their careers and financial status, are traveling with their young families. Industry experts predict that this trend will continue to increase through the 1990s, making automobile and van tours a growing market for guides. Frequently individual travelers or groups of family or friends prefer the convenience, comfort, and intimacy of having a guide in their car or van. This is already popular at many sites, such as the battlefields in Gettysburg.

As with limousine tours, discussed below, auto tours require that guides adapt to the whims of the individual or group. On the other hand, auto tours offer great flexibility and control, as it is much easier to maneuver several people in a car than forty in a motorcoach. On the whole, auto tours can be one of the most satisfying of travel experiences.

Whether to use one's own automobile for tours is a question guides should not take lightly. Many guides would not agree to it under any circumstances, and this may be the wisest practice. Certainly, if a guide's car is used for the tour the guide should be the driver. Laws vary from country to country, and in the United States, from state to state, but in most places a chauffeur's license is required in order for anyone to legally drive passengers for hire. It is the guide's responsibility to understand the insurance and motor vehicle operating regulations that apply to his or her policy and region.

Liability is a critical issue here. The key variables are the automobile involved (the guide's, the visitor's, or a rental) and the driver (the guide or visitor). Guides who use their own vehicles should, of course, incorporate a fee for the use of the car, usually comparable to or slightly less than the rental cost of a similar car. The fee must represent the cost of the car and its upkeep, licensing, and insurance. Expenses for gasoline, tolls, and parking charges must also be included in the cost of the tour. Guides who might find this concept tempting should try to imagine the dreaded but possible scenario of the car breaking down. If the car is rented, the frustration, anger, and blame are thrust onto a faceless rental agency, and the guest must concede that it was "just one of those things." Of course, in that case the guest understands that the exclusion of any sites or attractions that might result from a breakdown is beyond the guide's control, and that the guide is still entitled to full payment. If the car belongs to the guide, however, the guest might feel that what he or she bargained for was a working automobile and a confirmed itinerary assuring specific sites. It is easy to see the concessions that a guide might feel forced to make should this happen. All things considered, it is probably best for a guide to avoid using his or her car for sightseeing. Whenever a vehicle is used, however, driver-guides must be absolutely certain that they are covered for accidents and liability, and that their clients have signed a waiver of liability; this point cannot be stressed enough. (Chapter 12, "The Business of Guiding," covers liability issues in greater detail.) It is also wise to establish ahead of time who is responsible for moving luggage.

In urban areas, where driving can be a harrowing experience for anyone, guests with a personal or rented car will often ask the guide to drive their own car. There are advantages and disadvantages to this. The ideal is for the group to have a calm, unflappable driver who is knowledgeable about the city and adaptable to the pace of the guide. Visitors usually do not fit that description, however. While talking and driving at the same time are challenging, talking about the surroundings and instructing a frenzied, frightened driver is often far more difficult. A city guide, on the other hand, not only knows the exact location of the site, but is accustomed to the layout of the city, the one-way streets, and the traffic flow. With experience, a city guide can artfully manage both driving and commentary, paced perfectly.

Limousine Tours

To the novice guide, a limousine tour might seem to be the choicest of assignments. Although giving a tour in a limousine certainly has a cachet that a motor-coach tour does not, limousine tours can be, in fact, the most difficult of tours.

People hire limousines for a variety of reasons. Efficiency and convenience are key, especially in urban areas. Having a driver deliver his or her passengers to the front door and return on cue eliminates the hassles of traffic and finding parking spaces for both the guide and the group leader. People win limousine tours as prizes as a way for their sponsors to present a first-class look at a region. But many people hire limousines for the "VIP" allure or because they enjoy the status and attention that driving one's own car does not provide. The glamour of such an assignment quickly fades for the guide, however, as the reality becomes clear: limousine tours can be extremely demanding, as limousine passengers often expect red carpet treatment at all times.

To begin with, an expectation (sometimes implied but often explicit) exists that because a person has gone to the expense of hiring a limousine for sightseeing, the tour should be conducted entirely on his or her terms. Guests might also feel that inherent in the hiring of a limousine is the concept that they should not be subject to any of the indelicacies of travel, such as waiting in lines, having to dash through rain, or huddling with other guests in public buildings for standard, clipped tours. It seems incongruous for a person to emerge from a $100-per-hour stretch limousine in diamonds and mink and wait in the rain in an hour-long queue. Much to their dismay, limousine tour guides are sometimes asked to do much scurrying around and fast talking to protect their charges from any inconvenience (not unlike the vitterum of fourteenth-century Britain; see Chapter 1). In fact, a guide approaching a site with a group that's arrived in a limousine is equal to any other. For a conscientious guide, the unmet expectations of the group can be deflating.

When called upon to give a limousine tour, guides would do well to inquire if any special arrangements or appointments have been made at scheduled stops. Often a simple telephone call indicating an arrival time will make a difference to the visitor. Even if special arrangements cannot be made or a wait is necessary, calling ahead may make a difference in service. If no prior arrangements have been made, the guide might suggest that the visitor or the booking agent make them.

Although "Responsibilities to Travelers" is discussed more fully in Chapter 13, "Professional Ethics and Etiquette," it is appropriate to note a few points here. First, all clients, whatever their social standing or net worth, are Very Important People in any business. The fact that one group or individual has more money to spend should make no difference to the guide; all deserve courtesy and care. Second, guides must always consider their professional responsibility and accountability among their associates. Guides who routinely make discourteous or unreasonable demands on colleagues—drivers, front desk clerks, and others—for the sake of providing better service for their charges will quickly learn that their colleagues will be less and less willing to do favors for them.

Another challenge in limousine sightseeing is the sheer intensity of one-to-one contact over an extended period of time with a relative stranger. Paradoxically, a guide quickly learns that being trailed and surrounded by forty strangers affords a distance and space that is lost with such close contact. For example, on a typical tour the guide allows breaks for restrooms, shopping, browsing, or resting. When a guide announces to a group that they are on their own, they disperse. Although a few passengers will then approach him or her to ask questions, they are always aware that they are one of many who make demands on the guide's time and usually move on. If they do not, the guide can easily excuse himself. Such is not the case with one or two people on a limousine tour. Since those people have personally hired the guide at an often hefty price, the guide never feels as free to excuse himself. Even when a limousine guide does excuse himself to retreat to the restroom, the passenger's response is often, "Great idea!" denying the guide his respite. One guide commented that her passengers continued to ask questions throughout the entire stop in the ladies' room!

TYPES OF TOURS

Aside from differences in modes of transportation, the many kinds of tours available within the industry require different approaches and procedures. Some of the unique features of different tours are covered below.

Familiarization Tours

The National Tour Association defines familiarization (FAM) tours as "promotional programs designed to inform clients of the available services and facilities in the area by offering firsthand experience of the area on a group tour." FAM tours can be conducted by public-sector organizations (including convention and visitors bureaus, regional promotional offices, government travel bureaus, or cities) or privately run organizations (such as travel agencies, tour operators, attractions, or airlines). Also, companies that are relocating will sometimes treat their employees to familiarization tours. In such cases the emphasis is on everyday amenities rather than tourist attractions and facilities. (FAM tours are also discussed in Chapter 3.)

Participants of industry FAM tours range in number from one to forty-four and include travel writers, travel industry personnel who buy or sell travel, and tour guides and managers who require training in the points of interest a region has to offer. Since familiarization tours involve training or showcasing a region, they are usually conducted by more experienced guides who are comfortable with all aspects of the business and are not intimidated by the questions or the scrutiny of other travel professionals.

Since FAM tours are sales tools, the guide is a salesperson. By design, the guiding of FAM tours includes specifically selected sites and information, and a guide who accepts a FAM tour must be particularly mindful of his or her role. For example, if ABC Hotels International sponsors a FAM tour, they will expect that the guide will point out their own hotels and not others, and will refrain from mentioning anything even slightly unfavorable about the company or its service. Of course, since FAM tours are educational and industry-related, participants will often ask about other hotels, and guides would be expected to respond accurately (but dispassionately) to questions about competition. Conversely, if the FAM tour is sponsored by a city or by a convention and visitors bureau, the guide would be expected to present a broad menu of hotels and restaurants, deliberately avoiding any favoritism.

In the past FAM tours were believed to be free vacations for travel agents. More recently, increased competition and higher standards within the industry have initiated a trend toward more professional, educational FAM tours. Most agents and tour operators regard FAM tours as working trips and invaluable research tools. It is vital that guides tune in to their colleagues' needs to fully understand what it is that they do and the kinds of attractions or accommodations that they and their clients will actually use so that the tour will offer an efficient use of their time.

Incentive Tours

In recent years, incentive tours have become a large, lucrative market in the travel business. According to the Society of Incentive Travel Executives (SITE), over 3 million Americans take incentive trips each year, and sponsoring companies spend an average of nearly $1,700 per award winner (SITE 1991). Guides who thrive on being the center of attention often have difficulty with incentive tours, in which the clients are always center stage. Unlike most tours in which guides are in charge, guides for incentive tours take complete direction from the incentive house's trip directors or other company representatives. The nature of the guide's work varies greatly in incentive travel. Since the focus of incentive travel is to reward the participants, the emphasis shifts from sightseeing to parties, special events, and unstructured activities. Often, guides will be asked to be as inconspicuous as possible, merely making themselves available to provide information and assistance for participants.

According to the USA Hosts marketing director Don McPhail, "Incentive travel programs are expected to be perfect. The travelers expect it. The sponsoring company's top executives expect it. And the company's incentive travel organizer *demands* it." He continues, "No other travel segment is more sensitive to foul-ups than incentive programs."

Since every incentive tour is unique, there are few standard procedures for guides. The important rules of thumb are that guides should be prepared to take direction from trip directors, to make many changes in plans, and to be scrutinized more intensely than usual.

Meeting and Convention Tours

Meeting and convention tours fall into two categories: pre- and postmeeting tours, which run one day to one week or more, and brief tours, which are scheduled around meetings and are three to eight hours in length. These tours are provided as options for the attendees and their guests. Like incentive tours, tours for meetings and conventions are closely monitored by destination management companies and tour operators, and guides operate under stricter supervision and more detailed instruction than on a sightseeing tour. The key is for guides to be prepared to take instruction from on-site supervisors.

Step-on Tours

The phrase "step-on tours" refers to those tours for which a guide conducts only a small portion of a larger tour. In most cases, these tours are conducted by a tour manager or tour leader, who remains with the group throughout the tour. Guides join a tour and provide commentary only during their stay in a particular place. Since "step-on" tours are typically brief, they are usually expected to be general overviews of a place. Although basic itineraries are normally provided, guides who join a tour in progress generally take direction from the tour manager, who is more attuned to the specific interests and needs of the group.

Public Tours

As discussed here, public tours are tours that are open to the public. Unlike the tours noted above, public tours often attract individuals who do not know each other or have a specific affinity with each other. One of the challenges of guiding public tours is creating a cohesive environment among often diverse individuals.

Public tours are sold and conducted in a variety of ways. Several national companies now operate brief (ranging from three hours to all day) tours in popular tourist areas. Some of the best-known are Grey Line Tours, which operate in most major cities in North America, and Old Town Trolley Tours, which operate in eight cities in the United States. Both of these companies hire driver-guides, whose duties include driving, providing commentary, and collecting money. Both companies provide their own training, and in both cases driver-guides must conform to the route and itinerary provided by the company. In some organizations, guides are expected to follow, word-for-word, scripted tour commentaries. On longer public tours, guides generally have more freedom—and more responsibility—in creating commentary.

Many entrepreneurial guides offer tours directly to the public by advertising in local publications and through local convention and visitor's bureaus. Often such tours are among the most interesting available, as they can be specialized or based upon the guide's own expertise. In recent years such tours have become quite popular, not only with visitors but with locals as well. New York, Chicago, Seattle, San Francisco, and Washington, D.C., have many interesting personal tours available. (Some examples of these are noted in Chapter 2, "Profiles of Today's Tour Guides.")

LEADING EXTENDED EXCURSIONS

In recent years it has become far more common for guides of many regions to lead extended excursions,[3] venturing into a domain that traditionally has been associated with the tour manager. The many reasons include lower tour costs,

---

[3]An extended tour is one in which the guide travels with the group for distances of more than approximately 60 miles from the start of the tour, or for longer than two days.

smoother operation of tours, and the preferences of both guides and tour opera-tors to have one qualified person conduct an entire tour. Further, as noted ear-lier, guides who attempt to remain in the profession know that increasing their areas of expertise increases their marketability.

In every city, state, and province there are examples of this trend. A Boston guide might conduct fall foliage tours throughout New England. A New Orleans guide might conduct tours of the Cajun country. San Francisco guides often conduct tours throughout the Bay Area and along the California coast.

Most guides who lead extended excursions find that their working days are longer, and often tour operators consider them to be on duty at all times. In addition, longer tours require that guides work more closely with drivers and tour vendors and be more involved with visitors' personal concerns, such as any physical limitations, illnesses or medication requirements, or personal habits or preferences. In addition, on extended excursions guides and tour managers are often responsible for every aspect of the passenger's trip, including arrivals and departures, meals, accommodations, and all sightseeing. More administrative tasks are required, including bookkeeping, handling money, and telephoning vendors for confirmations and changes. Although many companies try to have vendors submit bills or accept checks whenever possible, guides still must carry a considerable amount of money for tipping, group incidentals, emergencies, and their own expenses. However, many guides find extended excursions ex-tremely rewarding, as they get to know passengers in a way not possible during brief encounters.

Working with Hotels

Guides who conduct tours that run longer than one day are usually responsible for checking groups in and out of hotels. Although procedures vary widely, most hotels have efficient procedures for checking-in groups. In most cases, they prefer to work with the tour manager or guide, who will communicate with each group member individually. The standard procedure for check-ins is as follows:

When the group arrives at a hotel, it is usually best for the guide to instruct the group to remain on the coach while he or she checks the group in. This allows the hotel and guide to conduct a more orderly check-in and enables the guide to accomplish all related tasks. At the registration desk, the guide should share any room changes or special requests, and the front desk clerk will give the guide a rooming list and packet of keys. The guide should review and revise the list as necessary, making sure that the bell staff also has an up-to-date copy. Before returning to the coach, the guide should find out how to get to the rooms and what facilities are available in the hotel, including the location and times of service for the hotel's dining room as well as suggestions for nearby restaurants. If the group is to get wake-up calls, the guide should indicate that time to the front desk at check-in.

Some hotels prefer having a staff person, usually someone from the sales and marketing staff, greet a group personally and inform them of the hotel's facilities while the guide is checking them in.

Before distributing keys to the group, the guide should convey all important information, especially the next meeting time. Some guides give the group their room numbers; others prefer to tell the group they can be reached through the hotel operator, to avoid the possibility of passengers appearing at their door.

At some point prior to the morning the group departs from the hotel, the bell staff will want to know the time of departure and when they should pick up the group's baggage. Some bell staffs will establish the time, based on the group's and their own schedules. The amount of time the bell staff needs to pick up and load luggage varies from thirty minutes to one hour.

Prior to check-out, guests should be instructed to pay for their incidental charges. These include telephone calls, room service charges, pay movies, laundry services, or any other charges they have incurred during their stay. It is often wise to advise guests to settle their accounts the night before check-out, or prior to breakfast, as hotel desks are often quite busy during morning check-outs.

At least one hour prior to departure, the guide should request a final bill. Often hotels will not release a final bill until all tour participants have settled their individual accounts, with the understanding that the tour operator is responsible for any unpaid charges that guests incur. Usually, if there are any outstanding accounts, the hotel will provide the guide with the room numbers and charges, and it is sometimes necessary for the guide to locate guests and remind them to settle their accounts. Once this is done, the guide can pay for or sign the hotel bill, depending upon the arrangements that were made with the tour operator.

In general, those who lead extended tours find that they must become more involved with the personal requests and needs of group members. Instead of merely expecting the interpretation of a region's history and background, visitors look to guides to help take care of them and to provide information about all aspects of their stay.

SUMMARY

No two tours are the same. Guides are asked to conduct many kinds of tours for a wide variety of people. For guides to be more effective and marketable, it is wise for them to learn about the many types of tours that are available. The information provided here will broaden a guide's understanding of the various tours and tour procedures.

11   *Travelers with Special Needs*

"I know I look handicapped, and I guess I do things that make me look that way. But I'm no different inside . . . and that's the hard part. I wish people could see me—the person in the chair—and not just the chair."

—Anonymous

Anyone who has worked with travelers for any length of time encounters people with special needs.[1] Recent years have witnessed an overwhelming increase in the percentage of travelers with disabilities and these numbers are likely to rise. One reason for this is the increase in the average ages of both the general population and the traveling population. As aging increases the likelihood of illnesses or accidents that impose limitations, there are more people living with disabilities. Another reason is the recent, worldwide progress in making sites accessible to the handicapped, especially evident in cities throughout North America. Many believe that the United Nations Decade of Disabled Persons (1983 through 1992) was a time of many successes for disabled persons. The best-known of these achievements, the Americans with Disabilities Act (ADA) of 1990, was enacted "to establish a clear and comprehensive prohibition of discrimination on the basis of disability." (Public Law 101-336.) The ADA has been likened to the Civil Rights Act of 1964 for the attention it has drawn to discrimination of disabled people and for its tremendous tangible and symbolic implications.

While the world is gradually opening up to the disabled—with flattened curbs, ramps, braille signs, and additional educational and support organizations and programs—many would argue that the progress has been far too slow and that much still needs to be done.

---

[1]The terminology regarding those with physical or mental disabilities is extremely controversial and changeable: some favor "handicapped," others prefer "disabled," still others choose the more upbeat (and most current) "physically or mentally challenged" or "people with special needs." Two experts in the field termed the latter two terms "silly euphemisms" and "too vague to mean anything." After reviewing much of the recent literature, speaking to many disabled people, and consulting with organizations and experts in the field, I have entitled the chapter "Travelers with Special Needs," since it applies to all of the disabilities covered in the chapter. When referring to persons with disabilities, I have used "disabled" most frequently, and the other terms less so.

The Earl of Snowdon, president for England of the International Year of Disabled People, writes

"Accessibility," of course, has been one of the watchwords of our endeavours. We want as many people as possible to be able to go where they want and do what they want without stumbling over barriers, great or small, that serve to shut them out from the occasions of normal life. But not all the barriers are physical ones. Architectural modifications are frequently so easy to make that we may be tempted to think that that is all there is to it. In reality, it is the mental and emotional barriers that so often keep people from recognizing their mutual humanity (Weiss 1983).

Indeed, disabled people find that emotional barriers are the most common and most formidable. Even the most well-intentioned people can inadvertently make people with disabilities feel unwelcome or uncomfortable because of their own misconceptions or discomfort. And often, the failings of the able-bodied are errors of omission rather than of commission. Snowden continues:

Whenever the able-bodied avert their eyes from the wheelchair-bound, or speak about the blind as though they lacked hearing, too, or assume that deaf means "dumb" in the colloquial sense, then there is a barrier that will keep the able-bodied and the handicapped from relating to one another in the normal modes of everyday life. This is detrimental to both, for they are equally cut off from potentially enriching social, intellectual and emotional relationships because of differences in physical capability (Weiss 1983).

Figure 11.1
Deborah Androus conducts a tour in American Sign Language before a braille plaque honoring Helen Keller. (*Photo by Grant Doyle.*)

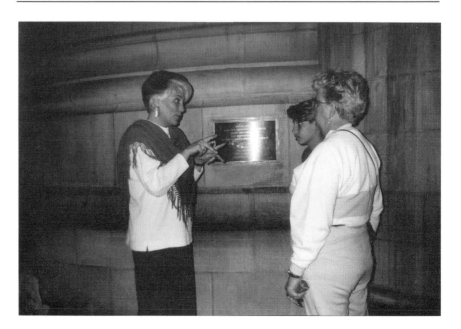

Although the percentage is usually small, most guides will encounter some individuals with disabilities on tours. It is vital for both the guide and the traveler that guides have a basic understanding of common disabilities, and of the ways in which they can make their tours more accessible, enjoyable, and enlightening for disabled people. The advantage in developing such an understanding is that the steps one takes to make a tour more comfortable for disabled travelers will usually benefit all others on the tour.

Guides who work with disabled visitors invariably come to regard their experiences with them as delightful rather than somber or problematic. People who have become acclimated to living with disabilities have been forced to face many issues and difficulties that others may only encounter in their later years. For this reason, most of them—both adults and children—are remarkably tolerant, patient, appreciative, and good-natured, and are generally more interested in the quality of an experience than the quantity of sites they see. Many guides note that they hear far fewer complaints about the aspects of tours that others regularly complain about, such as meals, accommodations, and waiting in lines.

One guide remarked that, after a few days of traveling with a group of disabled children, "I had to remind myself who was considered handicapped. Their enthusiasm and willingness to put up with some of the situations we encountered was unbelievable."

In large part, it is the guide, not the disabled traveler, who must learn to make the most adjustments during tours. Guides who have not spent much time with people with disabilities must understand several fundamental points:

- Dramatic outpourings of sympathy, however well-intentioned, are not appropriate. Disabled people who travel have likely been developing their mobility for some time and are accustomed to being resourceful in various situations. Encountering people who extend sorrowful glances or avert their eyes because they do not know what to say or do is disheartening. Instead, guides must adopt a stance of empathy. In attempting to put themselves in the disabled person's place, guides will quickly realize that disabled people, like anyone else, feel most comfortable around those who approach them naturally and offer cheerful assistance when it is needed.

- It is important to familiarize oneself with terminology and appropriate language. As noted, terminology about disabilities varies considerably throughout the world and even among people with the same disability. There are, however, some relatively common expressions that most disabled people find derogatory or offensive, for example, "bound to a wheelchair," "a victim of," "afflicted with," "suffering from," and "cripple." Many also suggest using the terms "disabled people" or "blind persons" instead of "the disabled" or "the blind," as reminders that they are primarily people rather than primarily disabled.

- One resource for working with disabled people highlights the qualities essential in working with all people, "The Three C's: communication, courtesy, and common sense" (Barry 1981). As mentioned earlier, sins of omission rather than commission are more common when working with disabled people. A guide should not hesitate to ask a disabled person questions in order to get a clear idea of how he or she can make the tour most comfortable. Most disabled people will readily and honestly acknowledge if and how they would like to be helped. Once this occurs, the guide can feel clear about and confident in an approach, knowing he or she has a better understanding of the person's needs and wishes. Courtesy must be an essential ingredient in all aspects of the service world. Disabled people, like all people, deserve to travel in dignity and comfort, and guides play a vital role in assuring their good treatment. Common sense goes a long way in working with people with special needs. When in doubt about what to do, guides can ask or use their best judgment based on what they have observed and the way they themselves would prefer to be treated.

- Finally, knowledge about common disabilities is essential, and learning as much as one can about them offers the guide the greatest chance for a mutually rewarding tour. All disabilities are different, and there are many levels of severity and ways to assist that may never spontaneously occur to a guide. Below is a list of general guidelines that apply to all people with disabilities. A discussion of specific disabilities then follows, including ways to recognize them and strategies for enhancing tours for people with those disabilities.

GENERAL GUIDELINES FOR WORKING WITH DISABLED PEOPLE

- It is vitally important that the tour operator and the guide in particular understand and accept that a slower pace than usual will be necessary. While one group might visit four sites in three hours, a group of disabled travelers may not (and probably does not wish to). Such tasks as loading and unloading wheelchairs from motorcoaches, moving or carrying people, and finding and using some handicapped entrances require much additional time. Most people with disabilities have accepted this and are comfortable with it. It is often the guide who has difficulty lowering his or her expectations about the number of things a group will accomplish. Efforts to hurry people will only frustrate both the group and the guide, and possibly offend the former.

- Guides should begin the tour without any expectations about a group or individual's level of ability and with a malleable attitude about a day's accomplishments. Each disabled person is different and has unique strengths and deficiencies.

- Guides should be aware of all entrances and accesses to any buildings included on a tour. Many buildings designated as "accessible" have, in fact, only limited accessibility. Although a building may have an access ramp at its entrance, for example, it may not have an elevator, meaning that all floors but the first are inaccessible. It is also important to remember that "accessible" does not mean easy or convenient. One major metropolitan subway system that boasts handicapped access requires that disabled visitors navigate long, dark, poorly marked, and isolated corridors to find elevators, requiring much extra time and effort. Complicated, labyrinthine methods of navigation are not uncommon, as many structures were built long before handicapped access was required. Assisting travelers with accessibility is one of the guide's responsibilities, and often requires that he or she call or visit a site prior to a tour in order to save time and prevent frustration later.

- It is important for the guide to be aware of any special services that will enhance the tour and make it more comfortable. Many places, such as airports, museums, and public buildings, offer special sightseeing or staff assistance for people with disabilities.

- When traveling with a group that has only one or two disabled people, the guide must be considerate of the abilities and the pace of the entire group, and particularly those of the disabled travelers. One way in which a guide can serve both well is to offer free time at certain places, allowing people to browse at their own pace. Guides should inform a disabled person ahead of time if there is a particularly challenging obstacle or terrain upcoming. In some cases, the disabled person might choose to stay behind and the guide can suggest that he or she explore something closer to the motorcoach. Most travelers will be willing to move at a slower pace to accommodate someone who requires it, though many disabled people prefer not to keep a group waiting. Others are choosing to join one of the widely available tours designed specifically for disabled people. (These are discussed at the end of the chapter; companies providing these tours are listed in Appendix A, "Professional Resources and Associations.")

- Guides and others in the service sector should be aware of the liability they face in dealing with the public. Most states have "Good Samaritan" laws that legally protect them from liability in cases where they are acting in good faith to assist a person in need. There are differences in the way this law is administered and interpreted, however. Rather than be prepared to "play doctor" to people in need, guides should understand a few immediate, simple actions they can and should take when an emergency occurs. (First aid is discussed in Appendix D; liability is discussed in Chapter 12, "The Business of Guiding.")

UNDERSTANDING COMMON DISABILITIES

Hearing Impairments

Difficulty in hearing is perhaps the most common disability that guides encounter. It is estimated that more than 30 million people in the United States alone have some degree of hearing loss, and about 25 percent of people over 65 are hard of hearing. Hearing impairments fall into four major categories, usually designated as mild, moderate, severe, and profound. Mild hearing losses might be indicated by an inability to hear light or high-pitched sounds; profound hearing loss means the complete inability to hear.

Ideally, a guide will be told prior to the start of the tour if there will be a hearing-impaired participant. But such is often not the case, and those who have difficulty hearing often prefer not to make it known. Some are simply unaware of the degree of their loss; others may feel embarrassed by it. Because of this, guides must do what they can to attune themselves to any signs that a visitor may be hearing impaired. Tour members with hearing problems

- Consistently move to the front of the group and study the guide's face resolutely (for lip reading).
- Ask that information be repeated.
- Ask questions that have already been answered.
- Do not follow directions as given.

Enhancing Tours for the Hearing Impaired   Because many people with a hearing impairment are uncomfortable admitting it, guides should make every attempt to make the tour understandable without patronizing or drawing attention to them. The following suggestions will greatly help those tourists who are hard of hearing. These suggestions apply to all groups, however, and especially to elderly groups.

- Always speak clearly and distinctly.
- Never speak to the group while walking or when one's back is turned.
- Practice speaking "diaphragmatically" (by using the diaphragm muscles), which creates a lower, more resonant voice. This technique is particularly important for guides with quiet or high-pitched voices. (This is discussed in Chapter 8, "Presentation and Speaking Skills.")
- Always stand in an easily-seen, well-lighted area. This may mean taking advantage of nearby steps or walls so that the guide is elevated above the group.
- Make sure light is not coming from behind the guide, as it will create a silhouette, making lip reading very difficult.
- As often as possible throughout the tour, face the person or persons who have trouble hearing.
- Repeat or somehow restate all important information given to the group, such as meeting times, dress recommendations, and changes in the itinerary. This can be done with the group as a whole, or individually, as a group departs. ("Do you have any questions, Mr. Jones? O.K. We'll see you at six o'clock.")

Working with Sign Language Interpreters   Occasionally a guide will be asked to give tours with an interpreter present for a deaf audience or individual. In recent years, many guides are themselves learning sign language so they can provide this service. Guiding in sign language or with an interpreter is extremely rewarding for guides and for those who communicate in this way. There are, however, important factors to keep in mind in order to make the experience comfortable and educational.

- Always maintain eye contact with the group rather than the interpreter.
- Although it is often unnecessary to speak slowly for a skilled interpreter, it is essential to maintain a slower pace and to speak more concisely for the benefit

Figure 11.2

Motorcoach drivers play a vital role in assisting passengers with special needs. (*Photo by Deborah Androus.*)

of the audience. Pause between every few sentences so that the group has time not only to "hear" the commentary, but to process it, to look away from the interpreter, and actually see the area or object being discussed. Neglecting to do this can be extremely frustrating for deaf travelers. Many guides need to be continually reminded of it at first, since it differs greatly from a typical tour, in which the guide and passengers can look at scenery while they talk and listen.

- Provide an atmosphere of openness and leave plenty of time for questions. Although there are no differences in the intelligence levels of deaf and hearing people, deaf people are often more limited by the pace at which they can acquire information. Much information that hearing people learn incidentally and take for granted as common knowledge may not be obvious to a deaf person. Examples include many aspects of contemporary culture, such as music and musicians or television shows and their personalities.

- Early in the tour, ask the interpreter and the audience whether your language, pace, and content are appropriate.
- Try to highlight the visual elements of a place for maximum enjoyment. On the other hand, if there is an important aspect about a place that involves hearing, do not hesitate to include it. For example, if a certain landmark is known for the echoes it creates, and people are participating in the phenomenon, a deaf person would certainly enjoy the story: "Hearing people like to stand at that wall and shout, as those people are doing."
- Guides should speak just as they would speak to the group, and not ask the interpreter to alter or omit anything that is said. This is a courtesy not only to the interpreter, but to the audience as well.

Visual Impairments

As with hearing impairments, there are visual impairments of varying degrees of severity. Those considered to be visually impaired are those who, even with correction (eyeglasses or contact lenses) have a substantial lack of vision, and those with severe, uncorrectable vision problems generally have personal or mechanical assistance (or both). A blind person might travel with a sighted person who serves as a guide, or will use a cane or dog guide.

Whatever assistance is needed, it is vital that the guide is familiar and comfortable with all options and understands their meaning and importance. All assistance devices are absolutely indispensable to the user, and should not be considered nuisances or something that might be forfeited for the sake of convenience. In fact, their importance warrants that they be considered part of the disabled person's personal body space. Therefore, a guide should never put aside another person's cane without their express direction or acknowledgment, nor should a guide tap or lean on a person's wheelchair. It is a good idea for a guide to ask disabled people (even if a caretaker is present) to let him or her know if there is anything that can be done to assist them.

Enhancing Tours for Visually Impaired Visitors   The following factors may help to enhance tours for the visually impaired:

- Talk directly to the person, not the caregiver. Even though mutual eye contact cannot be made with blind people, they are attuned to those who speak to them.
- Remember to speak at a normal volume, and avoid the annoying but common tendency to raise one's voice when talking to any disabled person.
- Whatever the person's mobility device, offer assistance; then, respect the person's decision. If a blind person prefers to use his or her guide dog, the guide should honor that and understand that guide dogs are expertly trained to lead. If the person prefers to have the guide lend assistance, he or she will generally take the guide's arm above the elbow. The guide should walk at a normal pace,

pointing out any steps, unusual terrain, or other obstacles. It is helpful to be as specific as possible, noting, for example, exactly how many feet in front of them the next step is.

- As often as possible, include sensory experiences involving senses other than sight, such as concerts or lectures.

- As noted above with deaf persons, however, guides should not hesitate to use visual verbs like "see" or "look" or to mention sights that are particularly meaningful or striking. In fact, blind people appreciate visual descriptions of their surroundings. Clear, colorful descriptions are invaluable. Again, the more that other senses are brought into the experience, the better: "You can feel the breeze coming from our left, or north. On our right is a deep, reddish canyon. . . . In front of us is a very still, clear lake and there are a few fishermen in boats. Looks like one of them just caught a big bass. The commotion you hear is some young boys trying to net it. Do you smell the honeysuckle? There's a wall of it just beside us. Let's move closer. . . ."

- Include touchable items or natural elements whenever possible on a tour. This may mean contacting a museum ahead of time to ask if there are touchable artifacts that could be made available to your group. Also, depending on the level of impairment, the traveler may be able to view certain well-lit items at a very close distance. If the guide discovers this, he or she should make an effort to take advantage of this opportunity. For example, a museum may have items they would allow a visitor to hold and view under light.

About Seeing Eye Dogs As mentioned above, guide dogs are expertly trained to orient and lead their owners, and the tour guide need not assist a guide dog. Guide dogs should not be treated as pets, and both guides and the tour group should resist talking to, petting, or distracting them in any way.

About Visually Impaired People Traveling Alone Prior to the start of the tour, the guide should mentally review the itinerary. Are all places on the tour accessible? Are there places on the tour that would be particularly meaningful to this visitor? For example, are there important objects that can be touched? Is extra assistance required or available at any of the stops?

It is wise to review the itinerary with the visitor and ask if he or she is interested in all aspects of the tour and if assistance will be necessary at any point along the way. Normally, disabled people who travel alone are extremely independent and both willing to and capable of caring for themselves. If they indicate that they are comfortable with all aspects of the tour, the guide should honor their assessment. Drawing further attention to the disability or fussing over the person, however well-intentioned, will not be appreciated.

Mobility Impairments

Common mobility impairments can be the result of accidents, paralysis, strokes, or diseases such as multiple sclerosis, muscular dystrophy, arthritis, and cerebral palsy. Although each of these impairments have entirely different causes, symptoms, and ramifications, all may require that a person use a cane, walker, or wheelchair for mobility. The severity of mobility impairments is wide-ranging, from simply slower movement to quadraplegia.

Enhancing Tours for Mobility Impaired People   As with other disabilities, it is advisable for guides to offer assistance directly to the person (not a caregiver, if present), accept the person's response, and allow for extra time throughout a tour. In addition, the following guidelines can enhance a tour:

- As much as possible, the guide should be mindful of the disabled person's comfort level, be prepared to alter plans if the person seems tired, and allow the person ample opportunity to forgo a visit to any site or to drop out of the tour.
- Deborah Androus, a Washington, D.C., guide who works frequently with physically challenged travelers, suggests, "When people actually can't go into a building or site, offer to take a photograph with their camera, or pick up a brochure or an inexpensive handbook."

About Wheelchairs   Although wheelchairs are common, few people take the time to truly appreciate the perspective of a person in a wheelchair. These simple facts about wheelchairs may be helpful to bear in mind:

- When seated in a wheelchair a person's height is diminished by approximately one-third and their width is doubled.
- Standard wheelchairs are about 25 inches wide, although some are wider and some are narrower. Generally, people in wheelchairs need doorways at least thirty-two inches wide and a space of at least five feet square to turn around.
- Both reach and the distance one can see are usually less than that of someone standing in the same place.
- Although it is courteous to offer assistance, wheelchair users may not want it, and it would be discourteous to insist.

Learning Disabilities

Learning disabilities, along with hearing impairments, have been called "silent disabilities," as they are often not easily (or ever) detected. Although there are many discrepancies in the definition and severity of learning disabilities, Public Law 94-142 offers a definition that is widely accepted:

"Specific learning disability" means a disorder in one or more of the basic psychological processes involved in understanding or in using language, spoken or written, which may manifest itself in an imperfect ability to listen, think, speak, read, write, spell, or to do mathematical calculations. The term includes such conditions as perceptual handicaps, brain injury, minimal brain dysfunction, dyslexia, and developmental aphasia. The term does not include children who have learning problems which are primarily the result of visual, hearing, or motor handicaps, of mental retardation, of emotional disturbance, or environmental, cultural, or economic disadvantage.

According to Jan Majewski, the number of learning-disabled children is estimated at between 1 and 35 percent. No estimates exist for the adult population (Majewski 1987). Signs of learning-disabled individuals include hyperactivity, hypoactivity, inattention, lack of coordination, perceptual disorders, and memory disorders.

Enhancing Tours for Learning-disabled Visitors

Since learning disabilities pose a wide range of problems and are often difficult to perceive, it is challenging for guides to appropriately adjust their interpretations. Therefore, those who work regularly with people with learning disabilities recommend that guides (1) attempt to learn more about learning disabilities, which will enhance the guide's ability to recognize them and enable the guide to give special attention when it is appropriate, and (2) adopt general practices that make interpretations clearer and easier to follow.

The following are general guidelines for enhancing tours for those with learning disabilities.

- Before the tour begins, give a clear overview of it, describing what the group will see, where they will go, approximately how long it will take, and what they will learn. (The public speaker's golden rule of "Tell them what you're going to tell them, then tell them, then tell them what you told them" is sound advice for learning-disabled groups.)
- For children with hyperactivity, hypoactivity, or attention disorders, it is wise to be clear about what behavior is expected of them, including specific rules of conduct.
- Repeat important or difficult concepts and regularly ask the group if they have any questions.
- Involve a variety of senses and learning methods. Since there are many variations in learning disabilities, using a variety of approaches increases the chances of reaching everyone.

Mental Retardation

Mental retardation is a condition that develops in infancy or childhood and is characterized by consistent, slower-than-average development and unusual difficulties with learning and social adjustment. Between 1 and 3 percent of the population is mentally retarded, and of those nearly 90 percent are considered mildly retarded. Mildly retarded people can live independently and be employed competitively. Although moderately retarded individuals develop social, academic, and work-related skills more slowly, they are also able to work and live on their own and often lead productive lives. Moderately retarded people may also live in supervised group homes. Severely and profoundly retarded people usually live under constant supervision, rarely have academic skills or hold competitive jobs, and often have emotional or physical disabilities.

It is important to note that most mentally retarded people function productively and independently. Often guides are unaware of their disabilities. Therefore, many of the guidelines for working with the learning disabled apply here as well.

When severely and profoundly retarded adults travel it is almost always with one or more caregivers, such as when institutions sponsor trips for groups of retarded individuals. It is wise for guides to work closely with caregivers and teachers. If possible, the guide should attempt to talk to the caregiver privately beforehand and get as much information as possible about the physical and mental abilities and the interests of the group. It is important to remember, however, that when working with a caregiver and anyone with a disability, the guide should direct conversations and questions to the disabled person, not the caretaker.

It is especially important for guides to offer a slower-paced tour free of crowds and stressful situations. These people will respond immediately and sometimes emotionally to stress or to problems that occur within the group.

Mental Illness

As with every disability mentioned, there are mental illnesses of varying degrees of severity. Unlike the classic image of mentally ill people as dangerous, they are more often extremely reserved and vulnerable. Often their illness has caused them to lose confidence socially and exhibit inappropriate behavior.

With a very small group it is easier for the guide to attempt to draw out individuals and encourage them to participate. With larger groups, however, it is usually unwise to single someone out, unless he or she seeks to participate.

Dealing with mental illness in public situations can be difficult. Although most mental illnesses are temporary and may abate over time and through counseling or drug therapy, such illnesses usually develop and are healed over a relatively long period of time. It is not possible, however, for a guide to evaluate or ameliorate such a complicated situation. Rather, his or her goal must be to provide interpretation and to treat people with courtesy and dignity.

Cerebral Palsy

Cerebral palsy (CP) is loss of muscular control resulting from a brain disorder suffered before or at birth or during infancy. Cerebral palsy is usually easy to recognize. Characteristics include involuntary or stiff movement of limbs and difficulty with coordination, balance, and speech. As with other disabilities, these symptoms occur in a multitude of combinations and with varying degrees of severity. Although many people mistakenly regard those with cerebral palsy as mentally retarded, those with CP have the same range of intelligence as is found in the general population.

The following are guidelines for working with people with cerebral palsy.

- Communicate directly with the person and offer assistance. If the offer is declined, respect the person's wish.
- Explain any aspects of the tour that might require difficulties. If the tour requires the group to use stairs, give the group the option of taking an elevator, and indicate its location.
- Conduct tours at a slightly slower pace, with occasional breaks.

Disabling Medical Conditions

Several common medical conditions are either disabling or carry the potential of disabling or endangering the visitor. One such condition is multiple sclerosis (MS). Many people have multiple scleroris for years without visible symptoms. In more advanced stages, however, the symptoms of multiple sclerosis are often similar to those of cerebral palsy: balance and coordination problems, stiff or involuntary movements of limbs, and problems with speech. These individuals will often use wheelchairs. It is wise for guides to follow the advice for those with cerebral palsy. In addition, it is helpful to remember that extreme fatigue is often prevalent among those with MS, so it is courteous for the guide to offer the passenger the option of leaving the tour whenever he or she wishes.

Heart Disease Heart disease is quite common, and for many is not disabling. Even so, there are certain precautions that doctors recommend. Although it is helpful if the guide is made aware of such conditions at the start of a tour, many people prefer to keep this information to themselves. In general, guides should take these precautions in anticipation of potential heart problems:

- Encourage participants to share concerns they may have about any scheduled tour activities. Give participants the opportunity to share this privately, either by passing out confidential health forms or by making a point to talk individually with each member early in the tour.
- Before embarking on a particularly long or rigorous walk or climb, the guide should warn the group of its severity. (It is preferable that the guide share plans for this type of activity a day ahead, so that participants have the option of making other arrangements for that time.) Guides should also indicate possible resting and/or waiting points, in case the walk turns out to be more difficult than someone expected.

Diabetes Diabetes is relatively common among senior citizens and less common in the general population. While diabetes is not generally a disabling disease (most of those with the disease lead relatively normal lives), the danger exists of a diabetic having extremely high or low blood sugar. In such relatively rare cases, emergency action is necessary (refer to Appendix D, "Basic Safety and First Aid"). It is much easier and less stressful for guides to take precautions to avoid those dangerous situations.

- Attempt to establish a consistent meal schedule.
- Let the group know when food will be available.
- Advise participants a day ahead of time about plans for particularly rigorous activities.
- When especially concerned about a participant, guides should carry a few pieces of candy or a sugary drink (in case of insulin shock).

WORKING WITH CAREGIVERS

A disabled visitor's caregivers can improve the tour for all involved. Usually they are compassionate, trained experts, willing and eager to work with the guide to make the tour as comfortable and successful as possible.

Caregivers are usually quite knowledgeable about the condition, medical history, and personal needs of their charges. When caregivers accompany travelers, guides should allow them to give all primary care and merely make clear that they are willing to help in any way. Guides should always defer to a caregiver's assessment of the traveler's condition and abilities. If alone with a caregiver, guides should feel free to ask him or her any questions they feel are important to better understand the situation. When the disabled person is present, however, questions should always be directed to him or her, not the caregiver.

NEW OPPORTUNITIES FOR DISABLED TRAVELERS

In recent years, more tour companies have sponsored tours specifically for those with handicaps. The many advantages for disabled people are obvious, among them comradery; traveling with people prepared to proceed at a slower pace; and greater chances of having "handicapped" motorcoaches, hotel rooms, and other amenities. Some of these companies feature unique, specialty tours that compare with the highest quality tours in the industry. (Appendix C, "Resources," lists several of these tour operators.)

As one would expect, the success of these tours has created a small but growing market for guides who specialize in tours for disabled travelers. Experience working with disabled groups and skills such as sign language make these guides more employable.

SUMMARY

For a variety of reasons, the 1990s and the decades beyond promise to provide increased travel opportunities for people with disabilities. This requires that many guides learn or polish their skills in working with people with special needs. The following are some of the most important points for guides to remember.

- Treat all travelers with dignity and respect.
- Always offer assistance, and respect the response.
- Always attempt to communicate as clearly as possible, to increase the chances that everyone (even those with hidden disabilities) can understand.
- Commit to learning more about disabilities and ways to enhance tours for those with disabilities.
- Be observant for any cues of a disability.

12   *The Business of Guiding*

"Madam, this is a cottage industry, and you're looking at the cottage."
—John Francis Marion,
Philadelphia tour guide and author

IS GUIDING A VIABLE BUSINESS?

A popular Washington, D.C., seminar for prospective guides advertises, "Wanted: D.C. Tour Guides. In peak season, an experienced freelance tour guide can make over $1,000 a week and there are never enough guides to be found. . . . Find out how to . . . cash in on D.C.'s largest industry." Over the years, hundreds of would-be guides, eager to make $50,000 per year, have flocked to the seminar.

Can tour guides make over $1,000 per week? Absolutely. Can tour guides earn $50,000 per year? Perhaps, if they combine it with tour managing and work extremely hard, or if they have another source of income. The operative words in the advertisement are, of course, "in peak season." In Washington, D.C., peak season for freelance tour guides is approximately mid-March through early June, with a much lighter season in September and October. At $1,000 per week (working fourteen-hour days, an average of six days a week), for the fourteen weeks of peak season, one could theoretically earn $14,000. However, during the "off-season" (the remainder of the year), an experienced guide could realistically expect only several thousand additional dollars from guiding in Washington, D.C.

Most other major cities in North America offer similar situations. New York City guides can earn slightly more during a longer tourism season, which surges during the spring, fall, and winter holidays. Boston's peak seasons are summer and fall, and guides there earn less than those in Washington, D.C. San Francisco, which is extremely popular for both sightseeing and conventions, has its peak season from April through November, with September and October being the heaviest months. There, guides earn $11 to $15 per hour, with a premium paid for those who are certified through the local guild. In Denver, where the busiest months are during summer and winter, guides earn $8 to $12 per hour.

The possibility of earning more than $1,000 per week in an enjoyable career that has few specific educational requirements is appealing to many people. However, it is misleading to specify such income without mentioning that few people are able or willing, over a long period of time, to live the kind of life required for that kind of income. In Washington, D.C., or New York City, for example, where guides can earn more than $200 per day, a typical working day might begin at 7:00 A.M. and end at 11:00 P.M. On some tours, guides share all three of the day's meals as well as an evening sightseeing tour with groups. Working those hours over an entire peak season is extremely demanding—both physically and mentally—and precludes a normal home or social life. For this reason, it is often said that guiding is a way of life rather than merely a job. Even those guides who can sustain such a rigorous schedule over a season often find themselves "burned-out" at its end. Tour companies are well aware of this and are often wary of rehiring guides who accept more work than they can comfortably sustain.

Setting aside the prospect of earning $50,000 per year, can a person make a reasonable living—or survive—as a tour guide? Such is a reasonable question, and worldwide there are a wide range of answers. Certainly few people, if any, have ever established fortunes from freelance guiding. Traditionally, guides have been part-time, second-income earners in a household. In recent years, however, a growing number of individuals are committing themselves to guiding as a career. Those who have sustained themselves through guiding for more than a few years have worked extremely hard and have established other related (or unrelated) roles or businesses; many examples are reviewed later in this chapter.

Four major reasons, all of which are interrelated, have contributed to the slow evolution of guiding as a viable profession:

1. *Seasonality.* Few regions of the world have a flourishing travel business year-round. Even many regions that do have favorable weather and attractions throughout the year fall prey to slow seasons when few people travel. Since guiding does not provide steady employment, guides who do not have another source of income must find work for the remainder of the year. The result of this is that most guides must move on to other careers with more reliable incomes. Those who continue to work as guides over a period of years tend not to be the sole source of income in their households—for example, retirees or others who want or need only a part-time income—and those who manage to combine guiding with other freelance work, such as writing, teaching, or tour managing.

2. *Supply and demand.* Despite the tickler for the Washington, D.C., seminar noted above, there are an abundance of guides in most cities, even during peak seasons. Moreover, during off-seasons there are many more guides than there are jobs for them, so that only the most experienced or well-connected guides can find work guiding. Moreover, guiding has long been a desirable occupation for women who are comfortable financially and looking for an interesting part-time job. Often they care little about how much they earn, and some are even willing to volunteer. Due to this deluge of guides, many of whom are willing to

work for low pay, wages remain low. Certainly, the field of guiding remains a "buyer's market" in most areas throughout most of the year.

3. *Lack of professional standards and proper training for guides.* Some tour operators and travelers—even those who believe that guides are the most important component of a tour—contend that most guides simply do not deserve higher wages. It is true that many guides are not well-trained and some feel an aversion to committing time or money to professional resources and educational programs, polishing their skills as communicators and interpreters, and learning more about the travel industry and its markets. Many guides argue that the meager opportunities for income and advancement do not justify such investments. On the other hand, many tour operators are unaware of how much effort most guides put into their continuing education and their planning for most tours. Traditionally, tour operators have paid guides flat rates, with no additional compensation for experience or education. A growing number of tour operators now have graduated pay scales and increased benefits for guides who have participated in training and educational programs. This practice is inspiring many more guides to seek training and operate in a more professional manner. Still, in areas where the benefits of guiding remain substandard, the quality, professionalism, and ethics of guides will likely correspond to those levels.

4. *Tradition.* Traditions tend to die slowly. Although most tour operators will agree that "the guide makes or breaks a tour," the professional quality and standing of guiding remains relatively low for the reasons cited above. Guiding is not unlike many other seasonal occupations in this way. In addition, the notion that people have that guiding is merely a "glamour" job, full of leisure and fun, further justifies low pay.

Whether a guide works for the National Park Service or a tour operator, he or she is selling both knowledge and service. Although many guides regard their method of work as an anomaly, it is not unlike that of many consultants, writers, and other freelance workers. Indeed, the turn toward a service and information economy and the rise in freelance and self-employed workers are, in fact, hallmarks of the late-twentieth century and trends that are here to stay.

It is vital for prospective guides to realize that the hours they will devote to their work fall into three categories: (1) research, education, and training; (2) marketing, scheduling, and bookkeeping; and (3) conducting tours. Although all of these activities are time-consuming, it is only when guides are actually conducting a tour that they are paid. Some companies offer compensation for "briefing" (reviewing the tour's itinerary beforehand) and "debriefing" (reviewing and settling accounts and paperwork after the tour), but many do not.

All business people must use their time wisely so that their income adequately reflects the time their work requires. Attorneys and consultants regard their time with clients and working directly on client work as "billable" and the remainder of administrative and research time as "nonbillable" and are well aware of the number of billable hours they need to make a living. In fact, their hourly fees reflect their education and experience as well as some aspects of nonbillable work. Few in the travel industry—especially tour guides—apply this distinction to their own work, and yet, most spend many hours engaged in marketing, scheduling, tour briefing and debriefing, bookkeeping, and research for tours. The tasks required by research, while necessary, can be extremely time-consuming, and include reading, attending lectures, taking courses, touring, and other preparation. Without coordinating all of these tasks, the guide has no business at all, and yet none of these items are typically billable. Although few would argue that guides should be paid for the time they spend marketing, researching, and planning for tours, all guides must honestly assess the amount of time these tasks take in order to know if guiding is viable for them.

One recently retired man in a training course for guides noted, "You have to love this—and have other income. The money simply doesn't add up."

Do tour guides deserve to be paid wages equivalent to teachers or consultants? In a capitalistic society, that question is often answered by supply and demand. Certainly, many guides do not deserve any higher wages than they are presently paid, though it is equally true that talented and experienced guides deserve to earn a livable wage. Surprisingly enough, in the United States few tour operators and other employers of guides pay guides on a graduated scale. For example, a guide with ten years' experience can earn exactly the same wages as a guide in training. In Washington, D.C., for example, a multilingual guide with a master's degree in architectural history and fifteen years' guiding experience will often earn the same wage as a novice guide with no language proficiency, specialized experience, or professional training. The situation is common in many areas throughout the United States and Canada, offering little incentive for talented people to remain in the field. For many years, veteran guides have asked tour operators to reconsider this policy, but few offer higher pay or incentives for more experienced guides. Such policies reflect the low regard the industry and society place upon guides, despite the cliché, "the tour guide makes or breaks the tour."

Without doubt, a new awareness is called for on the part of guides, tour operators, and others within the field. Presently in our society guiding wages do not begin to reflect the amount of time and expertise required. This can only mean that wages must increase to reflect a guide's true worth or that freelance guiding will remain a dalliance for those who have other means of income or a part-time venture for those in other fields.

Toward a Brighter Future

Fortunately, changes are at hand in the industry as a whole and the guiding profession in particular. The travel industry is growing dramatically, offering more year-round work and fewer seasonal positions, more opportunities in a wider array of places, and more educational opportunities for those interested in making travel a career.

Workstyles are also changing rapidly. Since fewer households can survive on one income, the wages of the "secondary" income earners have become more important. And yet, more and more secondary income earners are choosing freelance and part-time work in order to devote more time to family and personal concerns. Thus, part-time and freelance work are growing trends, making it more respectable and viable for people to build careers based on seasonal work.

Finally, guides overall are becoming more unified, focused, and committed to higher standards for training and professionalism. Moreover, guides are gaining more respect and attention from the industry and the traveling public.

Many believe that, as a consequence of all of these factors, agencies and travelers are more appreciative of guides. Some companies, aware of the importance of guides to their business, are offering their best guides higher salaries, year-round work, and other incentives. Although this movement is a slow one, it is clearly tangible. (Current and future trends are discussed in greater detail in the Epilogue, "The Future.")

Still, it is important for guides to understand at the outset the present limitations of guiding. Individuals who are sole supporters of a household, or who need reliable, year-round income, or who cannot be available for evenings or weekends should be realistic about the income potential of guiding. Those for whom guiding works well generally have other sources of household income.

ORGANIZING A GUIDING BUSINESS

"No, I don't have a tour business, I'm a tour guide."

While this might be an accurate legal distinction for many guides to make, it represents a frame of mind that guides would do well to dispel. A large number of tour guides are freelancers, and freelance workers basically operate small businesses.

As suggested earlier, guiding is not only a business but a lifestyle. Most guides regard their work as an act of passion and a reflection of their interests, so the travel and research necessary for the guide is often activity that the guide would perform as avocation. Still, it is often necessary for a guide to plan for and even schedule all aspects of his or her work.

Setting Up

Guiding is a low-overhead business. It could be said that the only necessary items of equipment are a telephone, an answering machine, a calendar, and a filing cabinet. Although having an office exclusively devoted to one's guiding work is ideal (and necessary for tax deduction), it is not essential.

Archives   Whether freelancers or not, most guides can boast impressive libraries and filing systems that include voluminous collections of maps, clippings, notes, brochures, and information about every aspect of their region. Many of these collections began with a few local art museum brochures or newspaper clippings that seemed too engaging to throw away. Over the course of months and years the files became fatter and more interesting, and the contents of the files took on a broader dimension, gradually including information on anything that might be helpful in understanding and sharing the region (which, for guides, seems to be almost everything they read).

Filing systems are often idiosyncratic, and the best system is the one that works well for the individual who uses it. The essential requirement of a filing system is that it allows for easy storage of and access to one's information.

As an example, any guide might find these categories of files useful: national history that impacts upon the region; regional history (perhaps further divided into subcategories, such as eras, neighborhoods, or stages of history); art museums (or separate files for each); local sculpture; architectural styles; local architects (including articles and literature on any architect who has influenced the area); regional flora and fauna; various neighborhoods; local personalities; themes ("ghost stories" or "Christmas events"); eras (Civil War, Gold Rush); and local hotels and restaurants. Aside from these topics, guides should keep files on their booked tours, including itineraries and other specific information; tour operators or job leads; and local guides, with telephone numbers and specialties. And, like other businesspersons, guides need files on courses and classes; relevant legal and tax information; and any other information that helps them better conduct their business.

Many guides eventually amass archives that rival those of any historian or academician. In light of the vast amount of research guiding requires, it is no wonder that some guides eventually write guidebooks or history books.

Calendars   A tour guide's calendar is the lifeline to his or her work and organization. A calendar is a highly personal document and there are hundreds of excellent choices on the market. Some guides prefer pocket calendars that they can carry with them at all times. Other guides are equally ardent about using desk calendars they keep at home, next to the telephone; to risk its loss would be unthinkable. Some guides keep two, one at home and a portable duplicate for ready reference. (If this is done, it is critical to remember to keep both updated.) Janice Holliday, a San Francisco guide and tour manager, also maintains a year-at-a-glance wall calendar. Being able to see how many tours she guides in a season and over a year, she says, "helps me monitor my energy level."

Sizes and styles of calendars vary dramatically. In recent years, the basic calendar has evolved into a personal reference system. Some guides carry what amounts to a miniature reference library, including facts and figures about their region; telephone numbers of tour operators, bus companies, hotels, restaurants, and attractions; small maps of the bus or subway system; and any other relevant information.

If there is a cardinal calendar rule for guides, however, it would be to use only one calendar for both business and personal life. For those who work standard business hours of 9 A.M. to 5 P.M., Monday through Friday, it is logical to keep a desk or pocket calendar for business at the office and a social calendar at home. For the tour guide, however, this practice can be deadly, as many tours run into evenings and weekends.

Considering the advance bookings (often several months ahead) and sometimes large numbers of cancellations, requiring changes to a calendar, spiral calendars that allow the removal and addition of pages are often preferable to bound calendars. For example, Daytimers, Inc., offers separate bound calendar inserts each month, which many guides like. At the end of each month, the schedule is transferred onto the new calendar. For some, recopying one's calendar each month might seem like an unnecessary waste of time. But for others the exercise is invaluable. In reviewing and recopying the new calendar, the schedule becomes easier to remember. And having a new calendar each month avoids the mess that can result when dates or tours are changed and canceled.

It is also invaluable for guides to have systems that include monthly calendars at least six months ahead. This gives guides the ability to review their schedules quickly and accept or refuse bookings easily. Regardless of the kind of calendar he or she chooses, it is wise for a guide to review it on a regular basis and to reconfirm dates and tours with companies as they approach. (Specific recommendations for calendars are listed in the Resources section.)

ACQUIRING WORK

The kinds of guiding work available are vast and varied. Although most people associate guiding with the travel industry, there are, as noted in Chapter 2, many government agencies, corporations, and other organizations that employ guides on a full- or part-time basis for a wide variety of guiding tasks. The National Park Service hires rangers who give tours and interpretations of natural and historic sites. Many manufacturing plants—factories, wineries, breweries, and printing presses—conduct tours to educate the public or promote their industry or business. Some colleges and universities hire guides to conduct tours of their campuses for prospective students and their families. Historic homes, museums, and gardens hire guides. An individual organization hires guides based on its own set of criteria and through its own system, which are best understood by contacting the organization directly. In many cases, guides have duties other than conducting tours. For example, a university guide might also work on the public relations or admissions staff as an information resource person for the university. Park rangers might also help to design printed interpretive material.

Within the travel industry, however, guiding work is often procured on a freelance basis. Although many tour operators would prefer to hire and maintain their best guides on a full-time basis, few are able to do so because of the limited amount of work they can offer throughout the year.

As with all freelance work, one of the greatest challenges for guides is achieving a balance between marketing and acquiring a desirable amount of work, while carrying out that work. In an increasingly desirable, demanding, and competitive industry, the challenge requires that guides be increasingly well-informed, creative, diligent, and patient.

Marketing—designing a product and convincing people that they want to buy it—is an essential element of any business, and in all businesses the tenets of marketing are the same. Guides, like all businesspersons, must find their niche by assessing what people need and deciding how they can fulfill it.

Elaine Curl, owner of The Convention Store, a Washington, D.C., transportation services company, offers marketing seminars for guides. "Your job is to help people get what they want," she says. Curl recommends that guides ask themselves a number of questions, including, "How much money do I need/want to earn? How many hours/days per month must I work in order to earn that amount?" She also recommends examining the types of jobs in the guiding industry and finding out which companies are hiring for those positions.

Research

The first step in acquiring any work is getting as much information as possible about the local industry, such as salary ranges, the short- and long-term prospects for business, and who's hiring. Good resources for information are local, regional, and national associations, tour operators, travel and tourism training organizations, and guides with experience in the field.

An excellent way to meet guides and tour operators and to participate in educational programs for guides is to join a local or national association for guides. (For information, see Appendix A, "Professional Resources and Associations.") Many guides find that associations are their most valuable resource, especially when starting out in the business. The educational programs, networking, marketing, and support are usually well worth the membership fees.

Although tour operators and destination management companies are the largest employers of guides, there are many others. Motorcoach companies often hire guides directly. Many of these plan extended excursions and also hire guides as tour managers. Hotel concierges are excellent contacts for tour guides, as they often receive requests to provide private tours. It is wise for guides to contact convention and visitors bureaus and local chambers of commerce, as they often hire guides directly to take visitors or potential businesspeople around the region. Corporations and professional associations also hire guides for a number of reasons. Although most hire a local ground operator or destination management company to provide sightseeing for their meetings and conventions, some have staff members who plan meetings and conventions and hire guides directly. Others will offer guided tours as a courtesy to visiting clients. The latter concept is a largely untapped market for guides. Indeed, it is worthwhile for guides to investigate the possibilities for this on a local basis. Many corporations that do not already offer guided tours might welcome this relatively inexpensive way of leaving a lasting impression on clients. One Washington, D.C., CEO regularly hires a guide to give tours for the families of visiting clients while he and his clients conduct business.

Elaine Curl suggests that guides approach real estate agencies, particularly top-selling agents and those who work with out-of-town clients. Agents who offer new residents guided tours of the area are offering an invaluable service and courtesy. In the competitive and lucrative business of real estate, many agents see this as a wise investment in securing clients.

Personal contacts make excellent contacts for guides. Out-of-town relatives and friends of friends provide continual resources for work. Unfortunately, since sightseeing is considered a pleasurable, leisurely activity that all hosts should offer to their guests, relatives and friends will often expect such a service without thinking of paying for it.

Many guides enjoy the combination of working with their own clients as well as with tour operators. When guides venture into the realm of acquiring and servicing clients on their own, they actually become tour operators themselves. This role is fraught with many liabilities and responsibilities. It is important to keep in mind the strict code of conduct among guides and tour operators on this issue: guides who are working for tour operators or destination management companies should *never* pass out their own business cards or solicit their own business while working with a company's clients. Instead, if a company's client requests information about subsequent tours, the guide should give the client the tour operator's number. (This is discussed in greater detail in Chapter 13, "Professional Ethics and Etiquette.")

Finally, the way in which many enterprising guides gain work is simply by putting together their own tours and advertising them. Often such tours are specialized and directed toward local people as well as visitors. In recent years these have become much more popular, particularly throughout North America. (Some examples of these are noted in Chapter 2.) Offering private tours to individuals, families, and very small groups appears to be a largely untapped market for guides. Often tour operators are not interested in very small groups (since profits tend to be more modest), and they will refer such groups to guides who will do them. As independent guides have lower overhead than do large tour operators, such business can be ideal for guides.

All tourism forecasts indicate that families and foreign and domestic independent travelers (FITs and DITs) are growing segments of the traveling population. These markets can be easily reached through advertising, word of mouth, hotel concierges, and industry contacts. Again, in designing and offering one's own tours (as with some of the other options noted above), the guide ventures from operating as merely a freelance worker to a business owner, along with all the responsibilities, liabilities, and expenses that arrangement might entail. Some aspects of this are covered later in this chapter (see "Financial Matters" and "Legal Considerations").

Once a guide has studied the market, explored the many options available, and pinpointed those goals that seem most appealing and attainable, he or she must establish a game plan for acquiring work.

Creating a Plan

First, in order for guides to function in the business world, it is essential that they perceive themselves as businesspeople and understand that they maintain their business identities at all times, since they can meet a potential client at any time. Clients come in many disguises, as there are many aspects to the guiding profession.

There are usually elements of guiding life with which a guide feels most comfortable or for which there is a greater need locally, and these are the best places to begin. For example, if a guide has a particular interest in or knowledge about a specific museum, building, or neighborhood, he or she might request that his first tours concentrate on those areas. Another comfortable way for guides to begin is by doing "meet and greet" or "advance" work. "Meet and greet" refers to meeting an association, corporate, or incentive group, welcoming them, and facilitating their ground transportation and/or hotel check-in; "advancing" involves going to restaurants or attractions before a group arrives to ensure that all is in order, then greeting the group and facilitating their event. Although meet and greet and advance work sometimes pays less than guiding, many guides find it ideal for becoming accustomed to working with groups.

Often there are areas about which prospective guides feel apprehensive. As with any field, the early years are an especially good time to immerse and educate oneself in the areas with which one feels he or she needs help. If the prospect of speaking in public seems overwhelming, an organization like Toastmasters, available in virtually every community, can be invaluable. To broaden knowledge about a region's historical background, local historical societies and courses in community colleges are excellent. If interviewing and approaching business contacts are difficult, many communities sponsor courses and assistance with career counseling. Again, associations are an ideal resource for novice guides, for they offer assistance and support for virtually any issue guides encounter.

As with many fields, prospective guides face the frustrating "catch-22" of needing experience to gain employment. Often the easiest way to gain experience and contacts is to volunteer. Many organizations, especially museums, offer excellent training and benefits for their volunteer docents. In return for the training given, museums usually ask for a commitment from the docent of approximately two to four days per month for a period of one year. For novice guides, these programs can be extremely helpful in learning about a particular subject, learning to speak before groups, organizing material, working with different age groups, retaining information, and making valuable contacts. And most museum training programs are ongoing. Many guides find their volunteer work and training so rewarding that they continue with it throughout their guiding careers. Certainly, tour operators are more apt to hire guides who have participated in training and conducted tours.

Finally, many companies offer and even encourage novice guides to accompany an experienced guide conducting an actual tour. Few experiences are more valuable, as he or she can see how the guide interprets a region while handling all the details of the work. In some cases, companies encourage the observing guide to act as an assistant and even take a turn giving commentary. Some controversy among guides exists on this issue because few companies offer extra compensation to guides who provide this tutelage, and some companies provide no notice that an observer will be joining the tour. Most guides are eager to help an aspiring guide and even find it personally rewarding. Others feel that, in a competitive, freelance climate in which guides are not securely employed, they are, in essence, being asked to train their rivals. To be asked to do this at all offends some guides; others merely feel that they should be asked ahead of time, that they be given the option of not having a learner aboard, and that, if they agree, they be compensated for it. Many guides feel that if they were paid at the top of a graduated pay scale, helping to train other guides would fall naturally into their job description. Industry-wide, however, the flat-rate fee is now the standard.

Approaching Companies

Finding work with tour operators is not unlike finding a job in most other companies. Of course, the best circumstance is to have the employer call and offer a job. Perhaps the next best circumstance is to have a personal recommendation from a person the employer knows well and values highly. And considerable related experience with good references greatly enhances the prospective guide's chances of employment.

Timing is important in approaching companies. It is wise to learn a particular company's busiest season, their booking season, and their hiring season. For tour operators, these are often three distinct times of year. Obviously, the best time to approach a company is during or just before their hiring season. This is often the least busy period, when managers and employers have the most time to spend with potential employees. Another good time to contact or renew contact with a company is during the busy season, when they are most likely to need a guide at short notice. Helping a company out at such a time and providing excellent work is a good way to engender the company's favor.

When approaching tour companies, it is usually standard to make an initial inquiry by telephone. It is a good idea to know the name of the personnel manager and to ask to speak to him or her. One disadvantage of a telephone call is that the caller cannot know whether he or she has chosen a good time to call. In any case, it is wise to keep this conversation short, simply stating one's name and reason for calling. Depending on the workstyle, schedule, or the number of inquiries he or she receives, the personnel manager may conduct a brief telephone interview to see if any potential exists, or may simply request that the guide send a résumé or schedule an interview.

Résumés, Business Cards, and Stationery

Résumés and stationery are rarely the sole reason for landing employment, but they do serve as powerful image tools, and they can make the difference in gaining an interview. Although many of the qualities employers seek in a guide cannot be gleaned from a résumé, many kinds of employment and experiences lend themselves to success in guiding. For example, teaching and travel experiences are wise inclusions, as well as any work or volunteer positions that involve direct contact with people. Any special relevant skills or designations should be noted, such as foreign language ability or CPR certification. And, as with all résumés, such items as personal information (address, telephone number), education, and employment background are standard.

The Interview

For tour operators, an interview is the decisive key to employing a guide. Indeed, since tour operators stake their reputations on the personalities and abilities of guides, and since guides often spend more time with their client than tour operators do, many tour operators conduct especially rigorous interviews. One tour operator put it this way: "Every time I do an interview, I literally pretend I'm an apprehensive, but experienced visitor to this place and I'm meeting this guide for the first time, just like my clients do. What kind of person would I want to find? I'd certainly want them to be on time. I'd want them to be warm and friendly and considerate, while at the same time exude the feeling of complete confidence—that everything is just going to be wonderful." During interviews, employers will ask how the guide would handle the kinds of glitches that often arise on tours. In these cases, they are looking not only for common sense responses, but for the guide's composure in simulating a response. Other important factors are a clean and pleasant appearance and evidence of organization and professionalism. And, says one tour operator, "a sense of humor is paramount."

The following are other suggestions for a successful interview:

- Study the company ahead of time and come to the interview with as clear an idea as possible of what they do, the kinds of clients they have, and what their goals are. Comment on some aspect of the business that impresses or interests you.
- Get plenty of rest before the interview so that you look and feel at your best.
- Make a point to be upbeat, focused, and as natural as possible.
- Be prepared to ask some good questions about the nature of the company's business and your possible role in it. Questions such as "What does the work involve?" would probably be unwise, as it is so general and basic. A logical question would be "How much work could I reasonably expect in the first year?"
- Respect the interviewer's time and the fact that he or she may have a busy schedule to manage.
- Thank the interviewer for his or her time and follow up within the next forty-eight hours with a note of thanks.

SUSTAINING AND EXPANDING BUSINESS

In guiding there is no one to hide behind. Generally, if a guide conducts good tours, he will garner good reviews, and the tour operator will want to continue hiring him. Many companies survey tour participants, asking them to evaluate their guide's attitude, professionalism, organization, and other qualities. It is not uncommon for tour participants to write letters of praise (or complaint) to companies, and for travel agents, incentive companies, or association representatives to request (or refuse to hire) the same guide on subsequent visits. Positive feedback is essential for guides, and ensures the offer of assignments in the future.

Considering employers' heavy reliance on passenger feedback, guides who do have the unfortunate experience of an unsuccessful tour or a negative encounter or relationship with a passenger should attempt to ameliorate any problems during a tour, document all problems, and explain any incidents about which the company might later inquire. In this way, the guide has an opportunity to air his point of view and show that he made a good-faith effort to satisfy the client. In such situations, most employers understand that occasional snafus occur and appreciate the guide's efforts and honesty.

Related Work

As guiding is highly seasonal and erratic, finding or creating related work can mean the difference between staying in the guiding business or leaving it. For many guides, the seasonality is a welcomed aspect of guiding work, as it provides dimension in their interpretation and variety in their lives. Further, many guides feel that they could not sustain, throughout a year, the intensity and stamina required in leading groups.

Tour Managing Perhaps the most common related role for tour guides is that of tour manager. This is often a logical progression for guides as their knowledge and their love of the work increases. However, since tour managers travel longer distances and for longer periods of time (often up to two months or more), the option of tour managing is not appealing for some guides, particularly parents of young children. But for many other guides, the peak seasons for guiding and tour managing in their region occur at different times, allowing them to schedule work over a longer period throughout the year. It is not uncommon for guides to work in their own regions in the spring, for example, and to work during the summer and winter as tour managers.

As tour managing is highly desirable, it tends to be even more competitive than guiding. Moreover, the largest tour operators who hire tour managers are not likely to be located in cities or towns where guides live. This means that guides who wish to become tour managers must often work hard at getting their first jobs. Since they are competing with tour managers on a national scale, a guide's experience and references are an extremely important element in making a transition or attempting to cross over to tour managing. Some guides also find they must make the investment of traveling to the city where the tour operator is located in order to land their first assignment.

Teaching For all its similarities to teaching, guiding lends itself easily to education in many forms. Many guides find themselves teaching in one of two areas: content areas and guide training. Guiding requires much study in a variety of subject areas, and many guides eventually become expert in certain content areas. For example, the study of an area's history usually prompts many guides to read everything available about it and take courses on many aspects of it. It is not uncommon for guides to teach courses on local history or geography or for local teachers and professors of these subjects to become part-time guides.

The other teaching opportunity that is opening up more and more is in the training of guides. As tourism increases to virtually all parts of the world, more and more communities and sites feel that their guides need professional training. Many experienced guides can add variety to their work and supplement their incomes by giving seminars and courses through associations, community colleges, and other venues.

Writing Many guides supplement their incomes by writing about what they do or what they know. Some of the most thorough and highly regarded guidebooks have been written by guides, and two of the best examples are about Philadelphia. John Francis Marion, one of the best-known guides in that city, has written several successful books, including *Walking Tours of Historic Philadelphia, Famous and Curious Cemeteries,* and *Philadelphia Medica.* His books and nearly legendary walking tours are as popular with locals as with visitors. Julie P. Curson, one of Philadelphia's first appointed professional guides, has written *A Guide's Guide to Philadelphia,* now in its fifth edition. Well-known New York City guides Val Ginter and Kate Simon have written *Manhattan Trivia: The Ultimate Challenge* and *New York: Places and Pleasures,* respectively. Washington, D.C., guide Jeanne Fogle has recently written *Two Hundred Years: Stories of the Nation's Capitol.* And some guides have written about their colorful experiences, as did Baxter and Corinne Geeting in *Confessions of a Tour Leader: A Romp through the Joys and Mishaps of the Guided Tour.*

Other Work   The variety of ways in which guides have eked out livings are truly without limit. One of the most enterprising examples of making the most of guiding is Jeanne Fogle, who founded A Tour de Force, a company based in Washington, D.C. Specializing in walking tours and publications, Fogle offers tours, lectures, publications, and even greeting cards that she produces with her brother, artist Edward Fogle.

Figure 12.1
As an outgrowth of their research and experiences, many guides eventually write regional guidebooks or books about their work. (*Photo by Vern Wayne Pond.*)

Other related ways in which guides can augment their incomes are by driver-guiding or polishing their skills in new subject areas, regions, or languages.

Aside from closely related occupations, many guides combine completely different, yet complementary work. Clearly, workstyles are changing significantly in the 1990s. Part-time and flex-time work is, in general, far more widely accepted as more people design their working lives to better suit their family life and their personal goals. Comedians, artists, photographers, historians, professors, musicians, and workers of all kinds have combined guiding with other work.

FINANCIAL MATTERS

As professional guiding is still in an early stage of its evolution, there are few guidelines, official policies, and commonly accepted methods of conducting business. Wages and methods of payment for guiding vary so widely that to attempt to generalize about them is almost futile.

Salaries and Wages

Any discussion of guide earnings must include a discussion of both tour managing and tour guiding, as each has been influenced by the other. Traditionally, tour guides and tour managers have operated under entirely different pay philosophies. As these roles increasingly overlap, there are more similarities in the pay scales. In most cases, guides have been paid hourly rates, depending upon the standard set within the organization or region. Tour managers, who travel with groups on extended excursions, are often paid low daily wages (ranging from $30 to $100 for twenty-four-hour duty), with the understanding that they would earn the better part of their wages from gratuities from tour participants. Most large tour operators overtly encourage the participants to tip their tour managers and even offer guidelines for tipping. Standard recommended gratuities for tour managers are usually $1.50 to $2.50 per person per day. Using the average, $2.00, this means that if a guide conducted a ten-day tour with thirty-five people aboard, he or she could theoretically expect to receive $70 per day, or $700 in gratuities, plus the daily company-paid wage. If the company paid $70 per day, this means that the tour manager would earn, in salary and tips, $1,400 for the ten-day tour. In addition, most companies provide a per diem or meal allowance. Many companies also offer optional events on longer tours, and tour managers often receive commission on their sales. As one might guess, a tour manager's actual income can vary widely. A dynamic, enterprising tour manager who conducts a nearly flawless tour and offers many popular options for passengers could earn well above the average, while a less effective or enterprising tour manager might earn far less. (Many tour managers and guides also receive money through "kickbacks" from businesses that their groups patronize, a controversial practice discussed in Chapter 13, "Professional Ethics and Etiquette.")

Tour guides, on the other hand, commonly receive higher hourly or daily wages, with the understanding that they do not necessarily receive tips from their passengers. In fact, many companies, (particularly incentive and destination management companies), specifically tell clients that all gratuities are included in their tour price and that they are not to tip their guides. The guides are also told not to accept tips if offered.

Other companies adopt a more cavalier posture toward tipping. Most pay guides higher wages than tour managers, wages they feel are appropriate to the work. While they do not recommend that their clients tip guides, they allow it and regard tips as a guide's bonus. (Guides who receive tips must remember that gratuities are part of income and must be declared as taxable income.)

The amount of money guides earn through gratuities varies widely, depending upon a tour's nature and location, the age and background of the group members, and the company's posture toward tipping. Senior citizens are far more likely to tip than are student groups. "Step-on" guides, or guides who are briefly joining a long tour, often receive small gratuities from individuals or one gratuity ($10 to $50 per day) from the tour operator who packaged the tour. Groups who spend more than a day with a guide they particularly enjoy are likely to tip individually or collectively. In summary, while tour managers receive a sizable amount of their income through tips, tour guides generally receive higher hourly or daily rates and a lower percentage of their income in tips. Tour guides are best advised not to anticipate tips when planning their budgets. Moreover, tipping is an idiosyncratic issue: some people never tip, and tipping is more commonplace in some cultures than others. Attaching quality evaluation to tipping is misguided and unproductive.

In some areas (Washington, D.C., for example) it is common for companies to pay both novice and experienced guides identical wages, allowing no additional compensation for experience. Some companies feel that experienced, more competent guides are rewarded by receiving more work than their less experienced colleagues. Many guides feel, however, that such a practice leads to lower morale and little incentive for remaining in the business or loyal to a company. Fortunately, this practice is changing slowly as more companies recognize the value of providing incentives to experienced guides.

Tax Time

The issues surrounding taxes—paying them, keeping records for them, and filing forms—sparks fear and dread among most people. Many people worry that they are not being shrewd enough in calculating taxes (that is, that they are needlessly paying too much in taxes) or that they may be audited (and found to be underpaying). J. Michael Burke, a certified public accountant who works with many guides, explains that one's conscience should always be clear. "Tax evasion is criminal," he says. "Tax avoidance is good business."

Planning for and paying taxes from freelance guiding leads to the question of whether guides are independent contractors or employees, a question that is perplexing and somewhat controversial. Most guides and interpreters who work for federal, state, or local governments, for historic sites or private homes, or in many other arenas are clearly employees. They are hired full- or part-time by an institution that establishes their hours, instructs them as to how to conduct their work, sometimes requires a uniform, and often provides benefits, which may include health insurance, sick leave, vacation time, workmen's compensation, and liability insurance. These companies also withhold taxes from guide's salaries and contribute to their social security.

The distinction is not so clear-cut among freelance guides and tour operators. Many guides and tour operators consider guides to be independent contractors. Certainly freelance guides would seem to be independent contractors in many ways, since they often work for many companies, are responsible for marketing their services individually to each company that hires them, and often negotiate their wages. And, like other independent contractors, they may accept or refuse work from a company depending upon their availability. Many guides are, in fact, clearly independent contractors.

However, in the few cases in which the Internal Revenue Service has responded to this issue in the United States, they have designated guides part-time employees. The IRS defines employees in this way:

Under common law rules, every individual who performs services subject to the will and control of an employer, as to both **what** *and* **how** *it must be done, is an employee. It does not matter that the employer allows the employee discretion and freedom of action, so long as the employer has the* **legal right** *to control both the method and the result of the services [emphasis in original].*

Two usual characteristics of an employer-employee relationship are that the employer has the right to discharge the employee and the employer supplies tools and a place to work.

If you have an employer-employee relationship, it makes no difference how it is described. It does not matter if the employee is called an employee, or a partner, co-adventurer, agent, or independent contractor. It does not matter how the payments are measured, how they are made, or what they are called. Nor does it matter whether the individual is employed full time or part time.

In the case of freelance guides working for tour operators, the tour operator usually designates exactly when and where the guide reports for work, what the guide does while he or she is working, and when the job is completed. In many cases, the employer establishes the dress code or furnishes a uniform and engages a supervisor who gives instructions on-site and sees that the guide operates within company regulations.

Although many tour operators and guides prefer that guides be regarded as independent contractors (and some companies even have guides sign contracts indicating this), the IRS has ruled differently on at least two occasions, forcing several large companies to pay taxes retroactively on guides. For this reason, many of the largest tour operators and destination management companies (USA Hosts, for example) consider tour guides employees and, therefore, withhold taxes from their paychecks and contribute to their social security. By law, they must also contribute toward unemployment compensation and, in some states, a workmen's compensation fund.

As guides and guide associations continue to sort through the often confusing and ambiguous regulations and attempt to more clearly define and protect themselves, many issues will be resolved. It is beyond the scope of this text to provide answers to these unresolved issues, but merely to highlight them as they now exist. It is wise to consult an accountant or tax advisor for a clear understanding of how to handle tax matters. Appendix A, "Professional Resources and Associations," lists publications available free from the IRS and accountants with expertise in preparing tax forms for guides.

Accounting can be a confusing issue for many guides, especially those who work for many companies. Some companies withhold taxes and some regard guides as independent contractors. Technically, a company that withholds taxes considers its guides employees. This means that the guide may not be eligible for some of the business deductions available to self-employed persons (many are noted below).

As noted above, some guides are clearly independent contractors. As self-employed persons, these guides must pay estimated taxes quarterly and pay all of their own social security in the form of self-employment taxes. They are, however, entitled to the many deductions businesses have. Some of the allowable deductions for independent contractor guides include:

- *A home office.* In recent years the requirements for qualifying for a home office deduction have become more stringent. One question the IRS asks is: is it an *exclusive* and *regular* place of business and the principal place of business. A salaried employee would have difficulty writing off the expense of a home office, because it is simply not a principal place of business. And "exclusive use" means just that. If there is a sewing machine, a closet with stored clothing, an ironing board, or recreational items, the IRS will disallow this office as a deduction.

- *Telephone.* Any relevant long-distance telephone calls and any fees for monthly service for a telephone designated only for business use can be deducted. The IRS will not allow a deduction for monthly services on the primary telephone in a residence.

- *Answering machines.* Answering machines, so vital to a guide's livelihood, are tax deductible if purchased for business.

- *Dues and subscriptions.* This category includes membership dues paid to trade or professional organizations and the subscriptions to professional, technical, and trade journals within one's field.

- *Education.* A guide can deduct expenses for education that maintains or improves skills required by law or the business or profession for maintaining pay, status, or position.

- *Licenses and regulatory fees.* When required, fees for government licenses or regulations are deductible.

- *Legal and professional fees.* These include fees paid to accountants or attorneys for counsel directly associated with one's business.

- *Transportation expenses.* The IRS regulations for deducting car expenses are complicated and it is best to consult an accountant or the IRS for specific instructions. If a car is used for business purposes, the deductible items include gas, oil, tolls, tires, repairs, licenses, insurance, depreciation, and other items. Rather than figuring actual expenses, the standard mileage rate of 26 cents per mile (the 1990 figure; this is subject to change) can also be used.

- *Travel expenses.* Travel expenses incurred to conduct business (and not reimbursed by someone else) can be deducted. In addition, a guide who travels to places for research purposes can deduct these expenses. Again, the calculations for allowable deductions in this area can be complicated.

- *Business clothing.* Only clothing that could not be considered street clothing can be deducted. The distinction the IRS usually makes is that any clothing that has an insignia on it or is specific to the work—such as a waitress' apron or a piece of clothing of unusual color—is regarded as appropriately deductible. For instance, the cost of a blazer purchased by a guide to serve specifically as a company uniform cannot be deducted unless it has a badge or insignia designating it work clothing. "The IRS is serious about this," says Cheryl Boyer, certified public accountant in Palo Alto, California. "The classic case on this one is Liberace, who was told he could not deduct his fancy costumes because he *would,* in fact, wear them on the street."

  Many guides do deduct for support hose, extra pairs of shoes, umbrellas, or the company-chosen blouse they have purchased in a color or style they would never themselves choose. "All I can say," says Boyer, "is 'remember Liberace.'"

- *Other deductions.* There are many other allowable deductions a guide can have, depending upon his or her circumstances. Again, it is important to be well-advised and to remember that tax laws and allowable deductible items change significantly over time. Morever, it is essential that receipts and records be kept for anything anyone intends to use as a deduction. The IRS is extremely rigid about documentation, and in the case of an audit, will disallow deductions if a receipt was not kept.

LEGAL CONSIDERATIONS

Some of the most common areas of legal consideration that guides and tour operators must address include matters of liability, cancellations, and contracts.

Liability

In an increasingly litigious world, liability is a growing area of concern for almost everyone. *Tour and Travel News* recently called "concern about liability" one of the major trends of the travel industry in the 1990s. Although liability is a topic that guides and many others would rather ignore, it is essential that all guides and tour operators understand their potential liability and the way in which they are—or are not—insured and protected against liability.

For what might a guide be liable? The most common and serious questions of liability occur in matters of safety. Guides regularly make decisions that could affect an individual's well being. For example, guides regularly instruct drivers on where to park and passengers on where and how far to walk. Sometimes a guide must instruct passengers to walk on cobblestone or broken pavements or in inclement weather, all of which could cause an injury. In such cases, guides have been held liable for knowingly sending a passenger toward an unsafe situation. Another common example might occur when a guide conducts a walking tour with an elderly or physically impaired person who becomes overexerted or falls during the tour.

How are guides generally covered for liability? The unfortunate answer to this question is that, in many cases, guides are *not* covered. Most large or reputable companies have liability policies that cover all guides during the periods they work for the company. On the other hand, many smaller or less reputable companies have no such policies. In many cases, guides who assume or are told they are covered by a company's liability policy are, in fact, not covered at all.

The motorcoach industry is heavily regulated in this regard, and all reputable companies have significant insurance policies that extend to passengers and guides riding in, entering, and disembarking motorcoaches. Most (but not all) states have "Good Samaritan" laws, which protect people who act in good faith to assist a person in need. Some homeowner liability policies cover individuals for liability when they are conducting business. (This is discussed in Appendix D, "Basic Safety and First Aid.")

It is important to remember, however, that anyone can sue anyone for anything, provided the incident is documented or provable and that the plaintiff can prove that the accused was at fault and that loss was incurred.

Cancellations

Cancellation is a fact of life and a bone of contention within the industry. In an already highly seasonal business, cancellations can be devastating for companies and for guides, who are often booked for work (and plan their schedules and budgets accordingly) six months and more prior to a tour.

Most companies' current policies for cancellations make guiding not feasible for a self-supporting person. To illustrate the scenario, a guide might accept a full schedule of tours several months in advance. In doing this, the guide commits herself and plans her schedule and budget with that work in mind. In the meantime, she is likely to turn down many requests for work for the same dates. It is not uncommon for companies to cancel tours a few weeks or days prior to the tour, leaving a guide without income, the possibility of booking new tours, or recourse. Such situations are devastating.

If guiding is to be a viable profession—that is, one that employs competent, committed individuals, and one that allows an individual to make a reasonable living—this practice must end. Certainly all businesses and all professionals must learn to accept inherent risks in their work. In this case, however, the burden rests too heavily on the guide.

A reasonable solution to the cancellation problem has long been utilized for other parts of the industry, and fortunately, a growing number of companies are extending it to their work with guides. When a client books a tour, a nonrefundable deposit of some amount is usually required in order to reserve a space. Portions of that deposit are then passed on to other vendors to reserve their services. A portion of this should rightfully be given to the guide as well. As the tour date nears, more money or full payment is required of the client. In the event of cancellation, the amount of money a client forfeits (and vendors keep) corresponds to the proximity of the tour date. In other words, a client might forfeit 20 percent of the tour cost three months prior to the tour, 50 percent three weeks prior to the tour, and full fare if he or she cancels the week of the tour. In turn, guides and other vendors would receive similar cancellation fees. Such a procedure is reasonable to expect in a business requiring long-range planning and reserving of others' facilities and time.

Contracts

Contracts are used sporadically for guides in the travel business. Some companies issue them for every tour as a matter of course. Others issue one each year, which outlines company policies to ensure that guides have a clear understanding of their responsibilities. Some guides themselves issue simple contracts when they accept a booking. These include such items as: a commitment that the guide is setting aside the particular dates; a reiteration of salary, per diem, transportation arrangements, and other financial matters; and a cancellation policy.

Ricardo Callejo, a San Francisco attorney with a specialization in travel law, offers these suggestions to guides:

- In preparing contracts, enforceability is the most critical issue. "If you can't collect from it," he says, "all is for naught."
- It's always easier to prevent; it's much more expensive and aggravating to cure after the fact.
- When in doubt about a party's integrity, record the telephone conversations.

"Memorialize what you say on the telephone with a letter, which might simply say, "Persuant to our conversation today . . . ,'" Callejo recommends. Sending a certified letter is an extra precaution, so that a record that the party received the letter exists. This is especially important when time is of the essence.

SUMMARY

As in other professions, guiding requires attention to many aspects of business and requires initiative, resourcefulness, and determination. Further, the growing popularity of guiding and the increase in the need for guides in the coming years assure that guides must continue to prepare themselves for the inevitable changes in the business of tourism and guiding.

13   *Professional Ethics and Etiquette*

"Ethics is our way of being human. If early man had not identified his own welfare with that of others, he could not have survived and developed."

—Ivan Hill, founder, Ethics Resource Center

Just as societies have developed accepted codes of behavior over time, professions, as they evolve, recognize or adopt certain desirable standards of behavior.[1] Every profession grapples with issues that spark controversy, such as how practitioners market themselves, how they interact with their colleagues and the public, and how they conduct themselves generally.

Traditionally, the formal recognition of ethical standards has been a predictable stage in the evolution of a field into a respected profession. Discussions about standards and the development of a code of ethics are often stimulated by pressures outside a profession, such as consumer complaints about poor or inconsistent treatment or behavior. Eventually, it is the practitioners themselves, often through professional associations, who evaluate issues and attempt to establish guidelines and standards for members of their profession. The medical professions, for example, have long adhered to high standards in education and treatment of patients. Doctors who are negligent in these areas or refuse to comply with certain standards are refused licenses or may have them revoked. Many companies and local and national associations have issued codes of ethics that their members, by virtue of membership, agree to uphold. The American Society of Travel Agents (ASTA), one of the travel industry's largest and oldest associations, originally developed a code of ethics for its members in the 1930s, revising it in 1985.

As guiding emerges as a more popular and viable career option, discussions about ethics within the profession are becoming more prevalent and more im-

---

[1] Although they have different connotations, the terms "ethics" and "etiquette" are used interchangeably in this discussion. Ethics is commonly perceived as a more philosophical term and pertains to the general nature of morals, while etiquette refers to socially correct behavior; both concepts are concerned with what is commonly held as "right" or "proper" behavior. It is not the intention of this chapter to dictate proper behavior for guides, but rather to raise questions and explore possible answers to issues of concern to the travel industry and the guiding profession.

portant. One of the earliest and most comprehensive of codes of ethics for guides was produced by the Guild of Professional Tour Guides of Washington, D.C. (see Fig. 13.1). The issues raised and standards prescribed by that document are applicable to many guides, particularly freelance guides.

DEFINING ETHICS

Just what is ethical behavior? And how does an individual, profession, or society determine standards of behavior that are suitable for and agreeable to all? Albert Schweitzer, theologian, philosopher, and Nobel Peace Prize recipient, offered this view: "In a general sense," he said, "ethics is the name we give to our concern for good behavior. We feel an obligation to consider not only our own

Figure 13.1

Code of ethics and standards. (*Source: The Guild of Professional Tour Guides of Washington, D.C.*)

1. A professional guide provides skilled presentation of knowledge, interprets and highlights surroundings, and informs and maintains objectivity and enthusiasm in an engaging manner.

2. A professional guide is prepared for each tour when the itinerary is furnished in advance. A professional guide assumes responsibility for reporting on time, and for meeting appointments and all schedules within the guide's control. A professional guide is sensitive to the interests and values of the tour group and does not share his/her personal views on controversial subjects such as sex, religion, and politics.

3. A professional guide has a wide range of knowledge of the city including its history and architecture, its cultural and political life, and the local folklore. A professional guide keeps current on new exhibits, seasonal events, and other changes throughout the city. A professional guide does not knowingly give out misinformation.

4. A professional guide knows and follows the policies of the company for whom the guide is working at the time. A professional guide does not accept or solicit a job from a client met through a company hired by that client without the consent of the company. Personal business cards will not be given to any tour participants met through the company booking. Business-related communication with the client will be through the company only.

5. A professional guide is knowledgeable about the best routes for all tours. This includes familiarity with the traffic laws as well as the idiosyncrasies of Washington driving. A professional guide informs the driver of the route in a calm, polite and timely fashion.

6. A professional guide dresses appropriately for the type of tour being conducted.

7. A professional guide accepts each tour as a serious commitment and cancels only when absolutely necessary and provides as much advance notice as possible.

8. A professional guide does not solicit tips.

9. A professional guide does not initiate patronization of souvenir shops and other places that practice "kickback" payments to the guide and/or drivers; or abuse complimentary meal privilege offered by food establishments.

10. A professional guide cooperates with other tour groups and maintains ethical and professional conduct at all times, cultivating a positive relationship with all colleagues.

personal well-being but also that of others and of society as a whole" (Hill 1991).

L. Kohlberg identified three distinct stages of development by which human beings arrive at sound standards of ethics, or what he called moral maturity. In the first stage, children come to understand that an act is wrong if they are punished for it. The second stage is characterized by a desire to maintain positive relationships with others. In this stage, people measure their own conduct against that of others to determine proper behavior. In the final and most desirable stage of moral maturity, one arrives at his or her own ethical standards based on virtue and a sense of what is good for the world. Kohlberg and others feel, unfortunately, that most people remain in the second stage of ethical development (Kohlberg 1976).

In *The Power of Ethical Management,* Blanchard and Peale (1988) suggest asking these three questions when evaluating whether or not behavior is ethical: (1) Is it legal? (2) Is it balanced? and (3) How will it make me feel about myself?

One's sense of ethics can also be viewed as a recognition of responsibilities in relationships. For guides, who wear many hats and interact with a wide variety of people, there are many people to whom they are to some degree responsible: their employers; their colleagues and their industry; their profession; travelers; their sites, cities, or regions; their society; their country; and, of course, themselves. The relationships guides have with some of these entities and the guide's responsibilities to them are discussed below.

RELATIONSHIPS WITH FELLOW GUIDES

One of the hallmarks of professionalism is excellent relationships with one's own colleagues. Most people will attempt to treat their employers and charges well, but those who foster mutually beneficial relationships with their peers are not as common and become highly respected.

As freelance guides are competitors with other guides, many guides are reluctant to share information that could benefit other guides. In fact, those who are generous with information and helpful tips reap both personal and professional rewards. Colleagues quickly identify those who are team players and those who are not. Maintaining a positive reputation among one's colleagues should be a goal of every professional.

Some of the steps that guides can take to foster symbiotic professional relationships are discussed below.

- Treat others as you would wish to be treated. Often guides work together on larger programs, and those who conduct themselves in a cheerful and cooperative manner quickly earn reputations as guides who are ideal to work with, and are usually requested to work more frequently than those who are not. Also, refrain from "office" gossip and chronic complaining.

- When taking visitors to crowded places, guides should be mindful of other guides and groups who are waiting to see a site. In especially busy seasons, this may mean spending less time than usual in certain places.

- Make a habit of sharing information that could be helpful to colleagues. This might mean informing guides of new policies or interesting information by writing articles for the association newsletter, volunteering to speak to the association about a topic in which one is well-versed, or simply sharing news with other guides. In any case, such gestures will earn respect and gratitude.

- Become active in association activities that benefit the profession. Although much of this work is done on a volunteer basis, it is extremely important. Most guides find that these contributions provide them with many industry contacts, increased visibility and business, and intrinsic personal rewards.

RELATIONSHIPS WITH MOTORCOACH OPERATORS

Positive relationships with motorcoach operators are vital to a guide's success. Drivers and guides are essentially teammates. In many cases, the tour guide is ultimately in charge (that is, the tour operator has hired the motorcoach company) and it is up to him or her to instruct the driver on timing and routing. Regardless of who is in charge, however, it is wise for guides and drivers to continually consult with each other during a tour. Those guides who respect drivers and nurture good working relationships with them will quickly be known among other drivers. Travelers also look for and appreciate cooperative professional relationships between their guides and drivers.

The following are suggestions for creating positive relationships with drivers.

- Allow plenty of time prior to a tour (on the evening prior or morning before each tour day) to meet with the driver so that he or she is clear about the itinerary, timing, meal stops, and routing.

- At the start of a tour, always take a few moments to introduce the driver by his preferred name or nickname and mention the importance of his role.

- Even if the guide is in charge of the tour, the driver will appreciate being consulted for his advice and suggestions.

- Whenever possible or appropriate, invite the driver to dine with the group and participate in other events.

- If a problem with a driver does arise, attempt to discuss it and resolve it with him or her before or instead of reporting it to the tour operator or motorcoach company.

- Avoid gossip about other drivers or guides, as such talk travels quickly and can haunt one later.

- At the end of a successful tour day or a particularly challenging drive, thank the driver in front of the group for a job well done.

Figure 13.4
Drivers are vital to the success of any motorcoach tour. As much as possible guides should acknowledge them and include them in the tour. (*Photo by Deborah Androus.*)

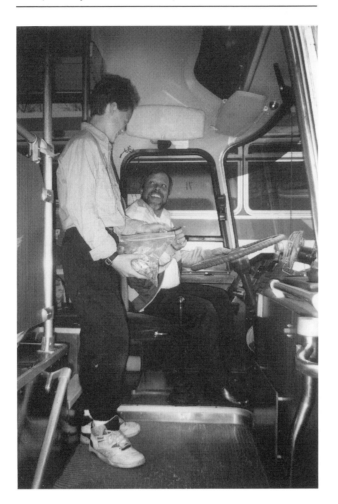

RELATIONSHIPS WITH OTHER COLLEAGUES

In the relatively young and rapidly growing travel industry, it is vital that colleagues work together. A guide's colleagues include, in addition to other guides, others within the travel industry such as travel agents, visitor information personnel, hotel and restaurant employees, and all who work at the many sites and attractions that travelers visit. Those who take extra steps toward fostering cooperation with people in these positions will be able to perform their duties more efficiently and secure more satisfied customers, profit from more rewarding work, and acquire more repeat business.

The following are guidelines for fostering better relationships with industry colleagues.

- Attempt to learn more about other aspects of the industry. By understanding the demands of a hotel front desk clerk or airline ticket agent, for example, guides work much more empathetically, cooperatively, and effectively with them.
- Always acknowledge a colleague's excellent service by noting it to the individual, the individual's supervisor, or the travelers who have benefited from it.
- If a problem does arise, attempt to discuss it privately, out of earshot of clients. Since the travelers will expect the guide to work on their behalf, having all parties present may be uncomfortable. A private conversation between the guide and the colleague can help to foster a spirit of cooperation rather than confrontation. Often, the colleague will feel more comfortable explaining the full story (an overbooked hotel or flight or rooms not yet cleaned, for example) that he or she would rather not express to the traveler. This also allows the guide and colleague to work together toward a solution (such as having a later check-in) without the travelers even being aware of a problem.
- Avoid gossip about other guides or colleagues.

Relationships with Companies   Like all employees, guides have responsibilities to their employers. This means that they understand and abide by company policies and standards and that they be courteous and loyal. As guides represent their companies, often to the extent that they spend more time with clients than company managers do, they have an obligation to represent the company favorably. This may mean that, in lieu of having a company manager on-site, the guide must answer for the company or even defend its policies or actions. If a guide cannot speak well of the company, he should seek employment elsewhere, with companies he would feel proud to represent.

One of the unusual aspects of freelance guiding is that guides often work for competing companies and are privy to trade secrets, such as client contacts, marketing techniques, or special services that each company might regard as confidential. Guides should never share such information with personnel from or other guides working for competing companies, nor initiate conversation with clients about other companies.

These factors can enhance a guide's relationship with employers:

- Always appear neat and clean, with proper uniform and badge when applicable.
- Maintain a businesslike and socially acceptable demeanor, excluding foul language and excessive drinking. Many companies prohibit drinking before or during any tour, even when dining with a group.
- Never share a company's trade secrets or internal problems with clients or with employees of another company.
- Guides must attempt to follow an itinerary and complete everything on it to the best of their abilities. When this becomes difficult because of weather, queues,

mishaps on the tour, or poor initial planning, the guide must contact the employer immediately.

- Never solicit work for oneself or another company through a company's client. Since guides work so closely with clients and often develop close relationships with them, clients often ask if they could contact the guide directly. When asked for a business card, the proper response is for the guide to provide the business card of the company that hired him or her (many companies will provide them). Even if a company does not provide business cards, the guide should provide the address and telephone number of the company to anyone on the tour who is interested, mentioning that he or she can be reached through that company.

This topic is a complicated and controversial one with some gray areas. Very often, personal relationships develop between guides and travelers, especially on extended excursions. After traveling together for a few days, it often happens that a guide has many things in common with someone in the group. When a group leader or teacher returns year after year and requests the same tour guide, a personal relationship often forms. In fact, tour managers who travel with groups for two weeks or more often form friendships and exchange personal addresses, and many tour operators expect this. The distinction the guide must make is that of conducting business with his employer's clients. Soliciting a company's clients is never appropriate. This is an issue of great concern and importance to many tour operators.

RESPONSIBILITIES TO TRAVELERS

Guides are entrusted to conduct interesting and accurate interpretations of regions. Once a tour begins, the guide is working for the traveler, but is also always working for an employer. Sometimes these two roles seem somewhat contradictory. For example, a guide's actual itinerary may not reflect the material the passengers have received. In the final planning stages, it may have been necessary to exchange one hotel, attraction, or site with another. Frequently the guide will become aware of these changes prior to the tour and can easily explain the situation to a usually understanding group. Sometimes a simple oversight was made in writing the two itineraries and the travelers and guide only become aware of the discrepancy after the tour begins. In this case, the guide must contact the company immediately to convey the misunderstanding. When slight discrepancies occur, companies will usually agree that the guide attempt to fulfill the traveler's itinerary if possible.

Sometimes the only possible outcome is that travelers cannot see something they were led to believe they could see, and it is the guide's duty to explain that to the group. This can be stressful for the conscientious guide. Normally such situations are understandable and it is easy to explain the company's position. Guides must remember that while they are working for a company they must attempt to ameliorate situations on their behalf. If they feel that travelers have valid complaints, they should note it in their paperwork and calmly recommend that travelers contact the company after the tour to voice their concerns. If a company repeatedly puts travelers and guides in such situations, and their mistakes become increasingly difficult to explain or defend, the guide should consider seeking work with other companies.

The following are guidelines for treatment of travelers:

- Guides must treat all tour members with equal time, attention, and dignity. Every customer is a "Very Important Person," deserving of equal respect, regardless of his or her social standing or the amount of money that he or she is spending.

- Guides should attempt to give as accurate and interesting interpretations as possible and commit themselves to learning more. This includes learning as much as possible about the visitors themselves, for this enhances the effectiveness of one's interpretations and promotes goodwill.

- Guides should make every effort to be as objective and diplomatic as possible. The bromide about avoiding discussions about sex, politics, and religion also applies to guides, as they can never be sure of the affiliations, beliefs, or points of view of all their passengers.

   In giving a tour of Washington to a group of contributors to the Republican Party, one guide took the opportunity to voice her own political views, which were quite dissimilar to her guests'. After the tour, several participants were angry and requested a refund. One member of the tour said, "I wanted a tour of Washington, D.C., and I certainly don't believe I should ever pay money to be insulted." When the guide was asked why so many people were offended, she responded, "Well, I guess they didn't appreciate my comments about our president," and added, "If you wanted a Republican tour guide, you should have hired one. If you hire me, you get my tour."

   The truth is that guiding is not a forum for espousing one's political beliefs. The role of the guide as host requires diplomacy and respect. Guides do not need to compromise their beliefs and adopt the points of view of their travelers. The best solution is simply to avoid controversial issues. If a guide disagrees so strongly with the beliefs of a group that he cannot conduct a tour without mentioning those differences, he should decline the assignment.

- Guides must make every effort to keep their travelers comfortable and safe and to be informed about basic first-aid procedures.

- Guides should never regard a region's customs with disdain or refer to them as strange or weird because they are simply different from their own.

- Guides should never solicit tips. Asking for tips is demeaning to all concerned—the tour company, the travelers, the guides themselves, and to the professional reputation of all guides.

RESPONSIBILITIES TO LOCAL REGIONS AND TO SOCIETY

Ethical tourism has become a popular subject in recent years. In spite of all its potential cultural and economic benefits, tourism can be extremely damaging to host communities. Throughout the world examples abound of the insensitivity some travelers have shown for local populations, particularly in developing countries. Many regions of the world are being exploited to the extent that foreign corporations and their employees are benefiting and the local people reap nothing but an intrusion on their lives and a drain on their natural resources.

Fortunately, there are several watchdog organizations that document unethical tourism practices and, some say, have inspired some corporations, tourism organizations, and government agencies to act more responsibly. The Ecumenical Coalition on Third World Tourism (ECTWT), one of the oldest of these organizations, sponsors international conferences and publishes pamphlets, a newsletter, and a quarterly magazine called *Contours* (from "concern for tourism"). The ECTWT's "Code of Ethics for Tourists" (Fig. 13.2) has been distributed worldwide. The Center for Responsible Tourism also monitors unethical tourism practices, hosts conferences, and produces literature.

If a greater need for more responsible tourism practices exists, one could also say that guides can play a powerful role in promoting more socially responsible behavior among visitors. Indeed, many travelers look to their guides for much more than interpretation, seeking guidance in interacting with a new region and its people.

Figure 13.2

A code of ethics for tourists. (*Source: Issued by the Ecumenical Coalition on Third World Tourism.*)

1. Travel in a spirit of humility and with a genuine desire to learn more about the people of your host country. Be sensitively aware of the feelings of other people, thus preventing what might be offensive behavior on your part. This applies very much to photography.

2. Cultivate the habit of listening and observing, rather than merely hearing and seeing.

3. Realize that the people in the country you visit often have time concepts and thought patterns different from your own. This does not make them inferior, only different.

4. Instead of looking for that "beach paradise," discover the enrichment of seeing a different way of life, through other eyes.

5. Acquaint yourself with local customs. What is courteous in one country may be quite the opposite in another—people will be happy to help you.

6. Instead of the Western practice of "knowing all the answers," cultivate the habit of asking questions.

7. Remember that you are only one of thousands of tourists visiting this country and do not expect special privileges.

8. If you really want your experience to be a "home away from home," it is foolish to waste money on traveling.

9. When you are shopping, remember that that "bargain" you obtained was possible only because of the low wages paid to the maker.

10. Do not make promises to people in your host country unless you can carry them through.

11. Spend time reflecting on your daily experience in an attempt to deepen your understanding. It has been said that "what enriches you may rob and violate others."

Figure 13.3
Allowing visitors private time at particularly evocative sites is often the most courteous and effective interpretive strategy. (*Courtesy of the Washington, D.C., Convention and Visitors Association, Washington, D.C.*)

The following are suggestions for guides who wish to project attitudes of responsible, ethical tourism:

- Whenever possible, encourage visitors to venture beyond their hotel's boundaries and meet local people. Certainly, guides must be wise and realistic about this. If an area is unsafe at night, for example, it is best to explain this to visitors and offer alternatives, such as walking in a group in another area or taking a taxi to a nearby location.
- Explain local customs to visitors when they differ from those to which the group may be accustomed. For example, when traveling through the Pennsylvania Dutch region, guides should request that visitors refrain from photographing the faces of Amish people. This is offensive to the Amish, as they believe that any "graven images" are forbidden in the eyes of God.
- Remind visitors of a region's commitment to a clean and safe environment. If recycling options are convenient, let visitors know how they can participate in them. In parks and recreation areas, instruct visitors of all regulations. For example, in national parks visitors are not permitted to pick flowers or plants.
- Exercise caution and respect for local people when passing through areas where poverty, crime, or recent environmental damage are obvious.
- Always travel with dignity and respect and remind visitors to do the same, par-

ticularly at sacred places, private homes, and sites with valuable artifacts. Guides should provide interpretation at least a few yards away from a gravesite, for example, leaving the site free so that all visitors (or family members) can visit quietly (see Fig. 13.3). Owners of private homes appreciate when a guide expresses the importance of not touching or leaning on valuable items.

SUMMARY

Those who choose the guiding field choose a field of service. To some, serving others and conceding that "the customer is always right" is somewhat demeaning, and service is synonymous with servitude. In fact, in an era dominated by service industries, service expert Karl Albrecht says, "If you're not serving the customer, you'd better be serving someone who is" (Stozier).

Guiding is a noble profession, one that many come to regard as a privilege. Those who are most successful and most highly respected are those who are not only willing to serve others but are, in fact, proud to serve. Virtually any aspect of life involves both serving others and relying on those who serve us, which is why the best guests make the best hosts.

Epilogue

"The 1990's will be an extraordinary time. You possess a front-row seat to the most challenging yet most exciting decade in the history of civilization."
— John Naisbitt and Patricia Aburdene, *Megatrends 2000*

Speculating about the future has long been a popular dalliance. In recent years, predicting and discussing the future has become a subject of increased sophistication and importance. Some people believe that futurists actually play a role in creating the future, as popular predictions become self-fulfilling prophecies. Telecommunications and other forms of technology have accelerated the rate of change, and assimilating futurists' forecasts is considered to be a powerful tool for planning in business.

Of course, predicting the future is an inexact science. "Making long-range projections is a very uncertain business," says Dr. David L. Edgell, director of the Office of Policy and Planning for the United States Travel and Tourism Administration. "Tomorrow is unknown to us, and the more tomorrows we put together, the more likely it is that events will take an unexpected turn" (Edgell 1990). Throughout history, doomsdayers and optimists abound, and the layperson is bewildered about who or what to believe. Indeed, no one really knows what the future will bring.

Nevertheless, there are certain perceivable and inevitable trends that emerge over time. Futurists rely heavily on demographic trends, for example, since they are measurable and revealing. "Demography is a solid base for speculating," says Joseph Coates, author of *What Futurists Believe,* "since most of the people who should concern you [in the travel industry] for the next twenty or thirty years are now alive" (Coates 1989). Moreover, experience has shown that those who use demographic information to plan ahead are better prepared to meet challenges and opportunities. It benefits everyone to pay heed to forecasts of the future.

THE 1990s

Most futurists agree that the remainder of the 1990s promises to be dynamic. Few are more optimistic (and have as impressive a track record) as John Naisbitt and Patricia Aburdene. Naisbitt's widely regarded *Megatrends* (1982), predicted such trends as a growing information-based society and a high-tech, high-touch society. In 1989, Naisbitt and Aburdene published *Megatrends 2000,* in which they offered predictions for ten new trends, and the following preview of the 1990s:

We stand at the dawn of a new era. Before us is the most important decade in the history of civilization, a period of stunning technological innovation, unprecedented economic opportunity, surprising political reform, and great cultural rebirth. It will be a decade like none that has come before. . . .

In the early 1990s, such predictions as "surprising political reform" and "stunning technological innovation" are accurate to a degree that few others might have predicted. They continue:

We have already fallen under its dominion. The year 2000 is operating like a powerful magnet on humanity, reaching down into the 1990's and intensifying the decade. It is amplifying our emotions, accelerating change, heightening awareness, and compelling us to reexamine ourselves, our values and our institutions.

GENERAL TRENDS IN SOCIETY

Futurists agree that there are some major trends that have been developing and will continue to evolve over the next decade and beyond. The following are general trends that will most likely have an impact on the guiding profession in the United States:

- *An aging population.* This is one of the most certain and most dramatic of current trends. The United States in particular is an aging society, and the average aging American is, according to Coates, accruing a lot of money and leisure time. "That aging American is educated, informed and interventionist. He is concentrating on physical, personal, financial, social and economic security, comfort and convenience. All of that is backed with a knowledge that those objectives can be achieved and that it may be necessary to push hard on the system to get them" (Coates 1989). The population is not only aging, but that aging population is healthier, more mobile, and more active. This has obvious ramifications for guides. Since senior citizens are more likely to travel in groups than are other age groups, the market for group travel should continue to grow. Moreover, many more tours will cater to a market eager for more active, adventure-oriented experiences.
- *A labor shortage.* So dramatic will the drop in the skilled labor force be that many government officials and business leaders cite it as one of the most critical issues of the next decade. The implication for the travel industry, as in many industries, is that there will be a much smaller pool of workers from which to choose. This means that businesses will need to work hard to attract the best workers by offering higher pay, good benefits, and other incentives. Workers

themselves may face less competition and more attractive employment options. An unfortunate result of the shrinking labor force may be that standards among the work force will decline, particularly in lower-paying fields, as companies may be forced to settle for less-qualified individuals. On the other hand, one benefit of this may be that employers may offer more training programs to attract and keep qualified people.

The two latter trends will have another effect on the travel industry. As the younger labor force shrinks and the population ages and yet remains more active, more companies will seek older workers. Guiding is an ideal second career for many retirees, as their life experiences enrich travelers' lives.

- *Changes in workstyle.* At the same time the skilled labor force is declining, more and more people are opting for less restrictive work schedules. Such trends as early retirement, flex-time, and part-time are becoming increasingly common, as people are choosing to spend more time with their families or on other interests. One writer speculates that "downward mobility could be to the '90's what the insatiable lust for material wealth was to the '80's" (Kaylin 1990).

  As more people continue to choose "alternative workstyles," such peripheral careers as guiding are becoming more popular and desirable. Many who now work as guides have one or more other part-time careers.

- *Demand for more vacation time in the American workplace.* Americans have traditionally had one of the lowest levels of vacation time in the industrialized world. While two weeks of vacation time per year is standard in the United States, four to six weeks per year is common throughout Europe. More recently, Americans and others with insufficient or scant free time are demanding more, with many even willing to sacrifice pay to secure more time. For the travel industry, the obvious implication of this trend is that Americans will have more leisure time and, therefore, more time to travel.

- *Growth in the use and capabilities of technological tools.* High technology has an impact on virtually every industry and individual. Most people in North America have traveled outside their states or provinces, and many have traveled internationally. Almost all have televisions and video cassette recorders, making information about other places and cultures continually available to them. Consequently, they are often much better informed about the world than previous generations have been and, in some cases, they are more sophisticated travelers. These conditions pose greater challenges for guides, who often need to give more than the basic information about a place when conducting tours for repeat visitors or visitors with a specific interest. It is not uncommon for a guide to be asked to conduct a tour with an emphasis on one of a wide variety of topics, such as architecture, art, photography, or a particular era of history.

  Another way that technology is now affecting the tour industry is by actually replacing guides with cassette recordings or videos in cars or motorcoaches, and with "computer concierge," a hotel lobby computer terminal that prints out specific travel information.

- *Increase in multicultural societies.* As individuals of different cultures interact, learn more about each other, and even adopt the other's customs, guides and other travel industry professionals must respond by being more informed about other people and places. Ethnic neighborhoods that were once previously overlooked on tours are now being celebrated by guides and travelers. Multicultural training is becoming increasingly available to help workers enhance their relationships with the wide range of cultures they encounter.

- *A desire for "authentic" experiences.* Basic sightseeing is now merely one of many travel options. Having experienced many regions and countries in a cursory way, today's travelers are opting for deeper, more personal ways of understanding another region or culture. For example, travelers might learn to make sourdough bread in San Francisco, or learn Cajun dancing in the Louisiana Bayou. As noted earlier, travelers are also seeking more active, adventure-oriented tours. Montana's popular tour company, Off the Beaten Path, for example, offers personalized itineraries for family fishing or mountaineering vacations. And, finally, many travelers are more concerned than ever about having experiences that celebrate and spring from (rather than exploit or place demands on) local populations.

    For guides, these tendencies toward more intense experiences can present many new opportunities. Guides in any part of the world, aware of people or customs that exemplify their region, can introduce them into their tours, making the experience more memorable and marketable.

TRENDS WITHIN THE TRAVEL INDUSTRY

- *Growth of travel in general.* By many measures, travel and tourism is the world's largest industry, and many predict that by the year 2000 tourism will be the largest industry in North America. As more people develop a better understanding of the world, and technology makes it increasingly easy for people to travel, more people than ever will venture around the world.

- *Growth of travel to North America.* Since World War II, Americans and others have traveled widely throughout Europe and the Far East. In recent years, North America's popularity as a destination has been increasing. Considering the powerful economic impact of inbound travel, the United States, Canada, and Mexico are aggressively promoting themselves as travel destinations abroad in an attempt to attract more visitors.

    Many feel the positive results of these promotional efforts are occurring so quickly that the local populations—Americans in particular—are not yet prepared for the consequences. For example, there is a scarcity of well-trained guides in many locations. Certainly this trend presents many opportunities for guides and others in the industry in North America.

- *Growth in travel among those previously unable.* As economies around the world are growing, and developing countries are becoming more prosperous, people from many different countries are traveling more than ever. For example, in recent years, more people are traveling from Eastern Europe, Spain, and the Far East.

- *Growth of interest in rural and previously undiscovered areas.* As mentioned elsewhere, travelers are searching for unique, unspoiled areas. Many of the new trends in tourism (adventure travel, ecotourism, and responsible tourism) cater to the traveler's desire to meet but not exploit local people and attractions.
- *Travelers staying longer in fewer destinations.* The once-popular ten-country, two-week tours are not as enticing as more in-depth journeys. Travelers today are less interested in reciting the number of places they have been than in raising the quality of their travel experiences.
- *Travelers taking more but shorter trips.* Although this may seem a contradiction of the previous trend, it is not. While people once vacationed for one week in the summer, they are more inclined to divide their vacation time so that they can have several four-day weekends throughout the year. Many airlines and hotels are responding to this trend by offering short packages to popular destinations.
- *Growing demand for professionalism among practitioners in the travel industry.* As the travel industry grows and becomes more important to local and national economies, the demands for higher standards among practitioners—from consumers and industry insiders alike—are becoming more palpable. In recent years, travel industry associations have responded by offering more educational and certification programs.

TRENDS WITHIN THE GUIDING PROFESSION

- *Growth in the exposure and popularity of guiding.* As a recent survey indicated, being a tour guide is considered by many to be a "fantasy job." As the competition and standards for guiding are increasing, guiding seems to be growing in popularity.
- *Growth of guide guilds and associations.* The growing number of guides and the increased number of travelers in many regions have motivated the establishment of several organizations for guides. Local, regional, and national associations can provide guides with career information and support, reports on education and certification, networking opportunities, health insurance, and other benefits.
- *Greater emphasis being placed on education.* Education is probably the most important tool in planning for the future. Many see education as the most important step for guides (or any professionals) to take in developing their careers. As a result, there are far more training and educational opportunities for guides than ever before. Already many tour operators and travel agents are responding by choosing guides who have participated in educational programs over those who have not.
- *Increased interest in certification.* Although the certification program for guides is fairly new, many guides are working toward it, and many other travel professionals and travel organizations are recognizing the value of it.
- *More communication and contact between "guides" and "interpreters."* Although these positions share many similarities, they have long had separate legacies. Guides are traditionally associated with the travel industry and the private sector and have not, until recently, had academic programs or professional liter-

ature available to them. Interpreters are commonly associated with public-sector organizations, such as museums or the National Park Service, and have long had resources and educational programs in interpretation available to them. As interpreters align themselves more with the travel industry and guides become more active in academic programs and interpretation philosophy and literature, the two groups will surely overlap more.

- *A growing tendency toward specialization.* As mentioned previously, many consumers are seeking more than a passing view of a place, and will look for guides who can provide more specialized tours. For example, an architect or architectural buff might want an architectural tour. A visitor to Tucson, Arizona, might want a guide who specializes in the local bird or desert life. As travelers arrive from all parts of the world, bilingual and multilingual guides are increasingly in demand. Though guides who develop specialties are more marketable, they must also learn to function as resourceful facilitators of information, offering travelers guidance in getting what they want.

UTILIZING THE STUDY OF THE FUTURE

Change and new trends are one person's joy and another's nemesis. While some fear new trends and dislike the challenges required in having to learn new skills or seek different markets, others regard such changes as opportunities to broaden their skills and make their work more interesting. Certainly the latter view is the most advantageous approach to take in a rapidly changing world.

Even those trends that seem to threaten prospects for guides may be veiled opportunities for growth. For example, some guides feel threatened by travel videos. In fact, a few agencies have already begun to use them in some regions in lieu of hiring a more costly guide. If such videos are, in fact, destined to become a significant trend, experienced guides are excellent candidates to write and produce them. Travel cassettes or videos could be an interesting and lucrative venture for guides.

It is also important to remember that competition often inspires people to work harder and grow professionally and personally. Competition can also inspire creativity. In an effort to surpass competitors, people often find new, unique tactics to distinguish themselves and their work.

Finally, something that is perceived as potential competition often turns out not to be. Although the usefulness and popularity of travel videos and cassettes should be acknowledged, they will never be able to replace the personal advantages that a traveler can gain from a guide.

SUMMARY

For anyone who wishes to thrive personally and professionally, it is vital to attempt to understand new trends and flow with changes rather than fight them.

Again, *Megatrends 2000* (Naisbitt and Aburdene 1989) offers a jubilant perspective of the coming years:

The meaning of that great symbol, the millennium, depends entirely on how it is interpreted. It can mark the end of time or the beginning of the new. We believe the decision has already been made to embrace its positive side. Within the hearts and minds of humanity there has been a commitment to life, to the utopian quest for peace and prosperity for all, which today we can clearly visualize. The 1990's will be an extraordinary time.

Appendices

Appendix A
Professional Resources
and Associations

GOVERNMENT AGENCIES

Every state and province has a tourism agency; in most cases, these agencies focus on marketing, research, and development, and can be a good resource for travel information. Regional convention and visitors bureaus (known as quasi-government agencies in that they receive funding both from government and the private sector) promote their regions and funnel visitor inquiries to their members.

> United States Travel and Tourism Administration (USTTA), U.S. Department of Commerce, 14th and Constitution Avenues, Washington, D.C. (202) 377-4028.
>
> National Park Service (NPS), U.S. Dept. of the Interior, P.O. Box 37127, Washington, D.C. 20013-7127. (202)
>
> Promotes travel to the United States, conducts research, and produces publications on tourism. Also sponsors the International Tourism Conference, held annually in Washington, D.C., in February.
>
> Tourism Canada, 235 Queen Street, Ottawa, Ontario, Canada K1A OH6. Supervising agency for tourism throughout Canada.

PROFESSIONAL ASSOCIATIONS

International

> Heritage Interpretation International, P.O. Box 6116, Station "C," Edmonton, Alberta, Canada T5B 4K5.
>
> Association of interpreters from more than thirty countries; holds triennial World Congress.
>
> International Association of Tour Managers, 397 Walworth Road, London, SE17. 01-703-9154/5.
>
> Offers a Job Bank, insurance programs, and publications, and sponsors an annual congress.
>
> World Federation of Tourist Guide Lecturers Associations, World Head-

quarters, Vienna Chamber of Commerce, Stubenring 8–10, A-1010 Vienna, Austria.
Offers a newsletter and hosts a biannual convention. 0222/51 450, ext. 243.

United States

Association of Escort Interpreters (AEI), P.O. Box 53105, Washington, D.C. 20009. (202)
Association for escort interpreters who work for the U.S. Department of State.
Offers newsletter and insurance programs.
National Association of Interpretation, P.O. Box 1892, Fort Collins, Colorado 80522. (303) 491-6434.
Offers Dial-a-Job; publications, including a bimonthly magazine, *Legacy;* an annual convention; and regional programs.
Professional Guides Association of America (PGAA), 2416 South Eads Street, Arlington, Virginia 22202. (703) 892–5757.
Offers insurance programs, a newsletter, a guide certification program, and an annual convention.

Canada

Canadian Tour Guide Association of British Columbia, Suite 108, 250 18th Street, West Vancouver, BC, Canada V7V 3V5. (604) 926-0235. Offers a newsletter, regular meetings and educational programs for guides throughout British Columbia.

RELATED ASSOCIATIONS

American Association for State and Local History, 172 Second Avenue North, Nashville, Tennessee 37201.
Offers information and training through annual meetings, seminars, workshops, and a large selection of publications.
National Association for the Preservation and Perpetuation of Storytelling, P.O. Box 309, Jonesborough, Tennessee 37659. (615) 753-2171.
A national organization devoted to encouraging the practice, use, and application of storytelling in contemporary America. Offers a year-round, ongoing program of activities and projects to preserve and perpetuate the art of storytelling. Conducts annual National Storytelling Institute, including workshops on presentation and storytelling techniques for all levels. Annual dues $25.
National Trust for Historic Preservation, 1785 Massachusetts Ave. N.W., Washington, D.C. 20036. (202) 673-4296.

Member organization dedicated to preserving valuable landmarks. Offers a regional newsletter; a monthly national magazine, *Historic Preservation;* free admission to National Trust–owned sites; numerous publications; and an annual convention.

TRAVEL AND TOURISM ASSOCIATIONS AND ORGANIZATIONS

Center for Responsible Tourism, 2 Kensington Road, San Anselmo, California 94960. (415) 843-5506.
Member organization which conducts research, offers publications, and holds seminars relating to responsible travel.
Ecotourism Society, 801 Devon Place, Alexandria, Virginia 22314. (703) 549-8979; fax (703) 549-2920.
Offers publications, a newsletter, seminars, and is planning to publish a journal.
Ecumenical Coalition of Third World Tourism, P.O. Box 9-25, Bangkhen, Bangkok 10900, Thailand.
Conducts research, holds conferences, and produces *Contours,* a quarterly newsletter.
Travel Industry of America (TIA), Two Lafayette Centre, 1133 21st Street N.W., Washington, D.C. 20036. (202) 293-1433.
Holds annual Pow-Wow (symposium/marketing show for tour operators); co-sponsors annual tourism conference.
Travel and Tourism Research Association (TTRA), P.O. Box 8066, Foothill Station, Salt Lake City, Utah 84108.
Publishes a quarterly scholarly journal, *Annals of Tourism Research;* sponsors an annual convention; oversees active regional chapters.
U.S. Travel Data Center (an affiliate of the TIA).
Conducts travel research and analysis for the travel industry. Offers numerous annual publications. Contact information same as TIA's.

Canada

Alberta Tourism Education Council, 1700 Standard Life Centre, 10405 Jasper Avenue, Edmonton, Alberta, Canada T5J 3N4. (403) 422-0781.
Conducts research and training and certification programs for the Alberta region; currently working with the Canadian government to implement certification for Canadian tourism personnel, including guides.

RELATED BUSINESS ASSOCIATIONS

The American Home Business Association, 397 Post Road, Darien, Connecticut 06820. 1 (800) 433-6361.

The National Association for the Self-Employed (NASE), P.O. Box 612067, Dallas, Texas 75261. 1 (800) 232-6273.

TOOLS OF THE TRADE

Magellan's: Essentials for the International Traveler, Box 5485, Santa Barbara, California 93150-5485. 1 (800) 962-4943. Mail order company offering many items relevant to guiding, such as alarm clocks, travel organizers, tote bags, first-aid kits, maps, games, and books. Catalog available.

PUBLICATIONS AND RESEARCH OPPORTUNITIES

American Automobile Association (AAA) (offices located throughout the United States).
Unlimited free maps and guidebooks available with annual membership fee; also sells travel-related literature and supplies.
Congressional Research Service, Library of Congress, Washington, D.C. 20540.
Provides extensive research on virtually any region or subject. This is a free service, but is accessible only through one's member of Congress.
Intercultural Press, Inc., P.O. Box 700, Yarmouth, Massachusetts 04096. (207) 846-5168; fax (207) 846-5181.
Publishes a variety of books on cross-cultural issues and travel.
National Parks and Conservation Association, 1015 31st Street N.W., Washington, D.C. 20007. 1 (800) 628-7275.
Offers an extensive selection of books, field guides, videos, maps, and games about U.S. national parks.

PROFESSIONAL RESOURCES

Public Speaking

American Society for Training and Development (ASTD), 1630 Duke Street, Alexandria, Virginia 22314. (703) 683-8100.
Offers seminars and publications on training and presentation skills; has active regional chapter program.
Toastmasters International, World Headquarters, 2200 North Grand Avenue, Santa Ana, California 92711. (714) 542-6793.
Offers monthly *Toastmasters* magazine, and regular meetings and educational materials for training in public speaking.

Interpretation

The Interpretation Publication Center. For a publication list and information
about seminars on interpretation, contact: John Veverka & Associates,
P.O. Box 26095, Lansing, Michigan 48909. (517) 394-5355.
Offers seminars and a wide range of publications—books, technical reports,
and videos—for interpreters and guides.

Cross-Cultural Understanding and Training

David M. Kennedy Center for International Studies, Brigham Young University, 280 Harold R. Clark Building, Provo, Utah 84602. (801) 378-6528.
Offers numerous excellent publications on cross-cultural understanding;
popular "Culturegrams" provide in-depth cultural overviews of more than
100 countries.
National Council for International Visitors (NCIV), 1420 K Street N.W.,
Suite 800, Washington, D.C. 20005-2401. (202) 842-1414.
National agency representing 100 community affiliates (Councils for International Visitors, or CIVs) and 49 national organizations that host and
serve international visitors and foreign students. Offers volunteer opportunities for guides or prospective guides to receive training and work with
international visitors.
International Society for Intercultural Education, Training, and Research
(SIETAR International), Georgetown University, 733 15th Street, Suite
900, Washington, D.C. 20005. (202) 737-5000.
 Organization of educators, researchers, and practitioners of cross-cultural
study and training. Offers an extensive number of publications and seminars.

The Business of Guiding

Sheryl Boyer, Accountant. Offers a tax planning/accounting book designed
especially for guides/tour managers for a small fee. 2390 Williams, Palo
Alto, CA 44306. (415) 856-3131.
J. Michael Burke, Burke and Associates, #3 Bethesda Metro Center, Suite
750, Bethesda, Maryland 20814. (301) 961-4880.
Offers accounting, financial planning, and tax assistance.
Day-Timers, Inc., One Day-Timer Plaza, Allentown, Pennsylvania 18195-
1551. (215) 395-5884. Produces calendars and travel and organizational
supplies.
Internal Revenue Service (IRS), Forms Distribution Center, P.O. Box 25866,
Richmond, Virginia 23289. 1 (800) 829-3676. Provides many free publi-
cations on all aspects of tax preparation.

Small Business Administration. 1 (800) 827-5722. Offers many publications and local seminars.

Disabilities

National Federation of the Blind, 1800 Johnson Street, Baltimore, Maryland, 21230. (301) 659-9314.
Offers publications and resources relating to working with the blind.
National Information Center on Deafness, Gallaudet University, 800 Florida Avenue N.E., Washington, D.C. 20002. (202) 651-5109.
For information about working with deaf travelers, learning American Sign Language, or other related inquiries.
Smithsonian Institution, Office of Elementary and Secondary Education, Arts and Industries Building, Room 1163, Washington, D.C. 20560. (202) 357-1697.
Produces a book and accompanying video, *Part of Your General Public is Disabled;* both are available for purchase and the video is available for rental.
Society for the Advancement of Travel for the Handicapped (SATH), 347 5th Avenue, Suite 610, New York, NY 10016. (212) 447-7284.
Offers support services, books, and other publications relating to travel for the handicapped; send SASE for information.
USTTA (see contact information above, under "Government Agencies").
Offers a pamphlet, "The United States Welcomes Handicapped Visitors," which outlines resources and travel services available to people with disabilities.

First Aid

For First Aid and CPR Instruction:
Contact a local chapter of the American Red Cross or the American Heart Association (Heart Savers Program).
For First Aid Kits:
Contact AAA, the American Red Cross, or any pharmacy.

Appendix B:
Educational Programs

The educational requirements and opportunities for guides, interpreters, and docents vary widely throughout the world. In many European and Asian countries, three or more years of post-secondary education are required for guides. In North America, however, college-level courses for most careers in travel and tourism have only recently become available, with a surge in such curricula throughout the United States during the 1980s. The 1992 edition of *Peterson's Four Year Colleges* (Peterson's Guides, Inc.: Princeton, N.J.) listed forty-four colleges and universities that offer undergraduate degrees in travel and tourism. These and other universities in the United States and Canada also offer masters and doctoral degrees in travel and tourism, though only a few offer specific courses on guiding.

It is important to note, however, that tourism and travel departments and degrees are not the only path toward guide training. Courses in interpretation, hospitality services, and guide training often fall within the jurisdiction of other departments, such as Parks and Recreation, Hotel and Restaurant Management, Geography, or Museum Studies. Because of the growth of the travel industry, many of these departments have added tourism courses to their curricula.

In addition, due to the lack of guide training in academic institutions, many companies and private organizations train the guides they hire. Fine examples of this exist throughout North America in museums, historic sites and homes, factories, and major tourist destinations such as Colonial Williamsburg. Many of these organizations require their guides and docents to take their own ongoing training programs, which are as extensive as many college and university programs.

As the industry evolves, more communication and cooperation is unfolding among these once separate fields. This, in turn, is providing greater educational opportunities for guides. For example, academic programs in interpretation that have had a continued public-sector emphasis now regularly include courses in travel and tourism. Students in many fields, such as history, architecture, and foreign languages, are combining their established coursework with courses in tourism.

The following is an overview of options for those who want formal training for guiding.

PRIVATE-SECTOR GUIDES TRAINING

For an updated listing of the colleges, universities, and proprietary schools that offer programs and courses specifically for guides and tour managers, contact the Professional Guides Association of America (PGAA), 2416 South Eads Street, Arlington, Virginia 22202-2532. (703) 892-5757.

Colleges and Universities

Chico State University, Department of Travel and Tourism, Chico, California 95929-0400.
Offers a course on tour guiding and management.
Metro State College, Department of Hospitality, Meeting and Travel Administration, 1006 11th Street, Box 60, Denver, Colorado 80204. (303) 556-3152.
Offers courses on guiding and tour management, and sponsors a multicourse certificate program for the Silver Badge of Tour Management of the International Association of Tour Managers (IATM).
Miami Dade Community College, North Campus, 11380 N.W. 27th Avenue, Miami, Florida 33167. (305) 347-1093.
Offers a certificate program in tour guiding.
Northern Virginia Community College, Annandale Campus, Travel and Tourism Department, 8333 Little River Turnpike, Annandale, Virginia 22003. (703) 323-3457.
Offers a certificate program in tour guiding and management.
West Los Angeles College, Department of Travel, 4800 Freshman Drive, Culver City, California 90230. (213) 836-7110.
Offers courses in tour management and guiding.

Proprietary Schools

International Guide Academy, 3003 Arapahoe Street, Suite 101, Denver, Colorado 80205. (303) 296-5572.
Contact Lynette Hinings Marshall, owner.
International Tour Manager Institute (ITMI), 625 Market Street, San Francisco, California 94105. (415) 957-9489.
Offers training programs in San Francisco and other cities for tour guides and tour managers.
Pacific Rim Institute of Tourism, P.O. Box 12101, 930-555 West Hastings Street, Vancouver, British Columbia, Canada V6B 4N6. (604) 682-8000; fax (604) 688-2554.
Provides programs and certification for many sectors of travel and tourism. Supported by Canada's Ministry of Tourism.

TRAVEL AND TOURISM

A growing number of travel and tourism departments now offer courses in guiding. For a listing of colleges, universities, and other organizations that offer accredited travel and tourism programs, consult the *Directory of Tourism Education Programs: A Guide to Programs in Aviation, Hospitality, and Tourism* (available in library reference sections), or contact the Council on Hotel, Restaurant, and Institutional Education, Inc. (CHRIE), 1200 17th Street N.W., 7th Floor, Washington, D.C. 20036. (202) 331-5990.

INTERPRETATION

Courses in interpretation can be found in colleges and universities within many departments, including Parks and Recreation, Museum Studies, and Geography. The National Association for Interpretation (NAI) publishes a comprehensive listing of colleges and universities in the United States and Canada that offer interpretation, entitled *Interpretation: A Resource and Curricula Guide for the United States and Canada,* edited by Gail A. Vander Stoep (cost: $10.00) Contact the NAI, P.O. Box 1892, Fort Collins, Colorado 80522. (303) 491-6434.

The National Recreation and Park Association (NRPA) provides a listing of accredited academic programs in parks and recreation. Contact the NRPA at 3101 Park Center Drive, Alexandria, Virginia 22302. (703) 820-4940.

RELATED FIELDS

For information about academic programs in related fields such as museum studies, geography, or hospitality services, refer to *Peterson's Four Year Colleges,* (Princeton, New Jersey: Peterson's Guides, Inc.), which is updated annually.

Appendix C
Recommended Topics of Study

Because guides are found in virtually every region of the world and specialize in a wide variety of subject areas, it is difficult to establish a curriculum that is appropriate for all guides.

Topics of study for guides could be categorized in two ways; the first is those subjects that are relevant to all guides anywhere (such as the contents of this text). This category includes, but is not limited to, the following topics:

- travel and tourism
- interpretation
- educational theory and practice
- public speaking skills
- social skills
- cross-cultural understanding and communication
- business and marketing aspects of guiding
- safety and first aid

The second category of curriculum for guides must include those topics that are specific to the guide's region or subject area, such as its history, as well as geography, architecture, and art history.

More and more, guides are called upon to specialize in a wide variety of areas, such as a particular historical figure or building; or an era, such as the eighteenth-century; or a subject, such as geology, native people, modern art, or literary figures. These guides require in-depth study in those areas. The region in which a guide works often dictates the kinds of specializations that guides might consider. Thus, guides being trained in various parts of the world engage in a wide range of subject areas and guides and trainers of guides are the best judges of their own needs.

It could be said that any guide, as a representative of a place, should be culturally literate (see Chapter 6). Travelers expect to be able to ask a guide questions about many aspects of the region. The following is a general list of suggested topics for guides in any region of the United States.

History
Prehistory
World History
    Early Civilization
    History of the New World: native peoples; Alaskan land bridge; Columbus;
    first English Settlers;
American History: the Revolution; the War of 1812; the Civil War, the
Reconstruction, World Wars I and II; the Depression; modern history; the
presidents; and so forth.

Geography
Geology
    Underlying formations, history, and so forth
    Relationship to architecture, building materials, and lifestyle
Climate
    Seasonal features
    Rainfall, snowfall, and annual temperature ranges
    Climatic influences from north, south, east, and west
        Broad view of climatic influences
Physical Features
    Rivers, streams, estuaries, caves, soil
    Local flora and fauna

Industry and Commerce
Shipping and trading
Overview of industries
USA's role in world economics
Stock exchange
Banks and banking
Taxation
Employment and unemployment

Transportation
Passenger carriers within a region
    Airlines
    Trains
    Buses
    Tour services
Best modes of transportation for various destinations

Culture
Literature
    Writers

Past and current representative literature: places, culture, the "American spirit"
Theater and drama
Dance
Art: crafts, folklore, fine art
Music

Architecture
All basic styles

Religion
Role in society
History
Sects and cults
Religion today

Government
History and development
The Constitution
Laws and lawmaking
The court system
The Presidency

Appendix D
Basic Safety and First Aid

Guides are regularly placed in a position of responsibility for many travelers. At some point, situations are bound to occur that require immediate action, and it behooves all guides to be aware of basic emergency procedures that could mean the difference between life and death.

Ideally, all tour guides, or anyone who works extensively with the public, should have a basic knowledge of common first-aid procedures. Many organizations, including the American Red Cross and the American Heart Association, regularly offer local courses in first aid and CPR. Many companies and jurisdictions are now requiring basic courses in first aid.

First aid is merely emergency care given before professional medical care is available. The most important goal of first-aid training for guides is to prepare the guide faced with a medical emergency to remain calm and keep the victim and other passengers reassured and out of further danger; to make quick, appropriate decisions; and to keep the victim protected and stabilized until emergency medical services arrive.

The increase in lawsuits in recent years has instilled in the general public a fear of getting involved in medical emergencies. Guides and others in the service sector should be aware of the liabilities they face in working with the public and handling emergencies. Although laws regarding medical attention vary from state to state, most states have "Good Samaritan" laws, which extend legal protection to those who act to assist in good faith and are not guilty of gross negligence or willful misconduct. It is wise to remember, however, that "gross negligence" and "willful misconduct" can be widely interpreted. In addition, the type of rescuer covered and the scope of the law's protection also varies from state to state. For example, in some states doctors, nurses, or emergency medical technicians, as trained medical professionals, are not protected by Good Samaritan laws. Some legal professionals suggest that this may indicate that it is unwise for a guide to receive advanced emergency medical instruction other than CPR courses. Because of this, it is vital that guides know and understand the laws that prevail in their jurisdictions.

According to the American Red Cross, "Legally, a victim must give consent to an offer to help before a person trained in first aid begins to help him or her" (Braslow 1987). However, the law assumes that an unconscious person would give consent, and consent is implied for someone who is badly injured or so ill that he or she cannot respond. In addition, the Red Cross states that "you should also make a reasonable attempt to get consent from the parent or guardian of a victim who is a minor or who is mentally or emotionally disturbed. If a parent or guardian is not available, you may give first aid without consent."

Rather than attempt to play doctor to people in need, guides should understand a few immediate, simple actions they can take to help or stabilize a victim until trained, medical personnel arrive.

First aid in travel is more important than ever as more—and older—people travel. Ideally, a tour guide will know ahead of time if a member of the group has a major illness, but this is not always the case. On shorter trips, such as city tours, guides are rarely told of such problems. Even with longer trips, when passengers' health problems are most likely to surface, guides are often unaware of potentially serious medical situations. Many people prefer to keep a problem to themselves to avoid embarrassment or attention. Some companies ask tour participants to complete a medical overview form, which is given to the guide at the start of the tour. In recent years, however, many companies have eliminated this practice, since being aware of a passenger's medical condition can increase the company's liability should an emergency occur.

HANDLING EMERGENCIES AND FIRST AID

This section reviews some specific, basic techniques for common emergencies. But this brief overview should not be regarded as a course in first aid. It is important for any guide to receive first aid instruction from trained medical personnel.

Again, because of liability issues and the limitations of medical knowledge, the priority in an emergency should always be to contact professional medical help as quickly as possible while protecting the victim from further harm until help arrives.

General Guidelines for Safer Tours

- Before a tour begins, encourage participants to share any concerns they may have about a tour's schedule, pace, activity level, food, or any other aspects.
- Attempt to avoid or use extreme care with any walking conditions that could present difficulty. Examples include wet surfaces, uneven terrain such as cobblestone walks or natural areas, or steps or steep terrain.
- Be mindful of exposure to extremes in temperature. For example, in extreme heat or humidity, providing liquids and frequent breaks is advisable. On motorcoaches, guides should regularly walk around to monitor the temperature, as it can differ in the front, center, and rear of the coach.
- Be especially observant of those who do have known medical conditions, such as heart disease or diabetes.

- Know the location of a hospital in any region in which the tour travels.

Handling Specific Emergencies

When Someone Falls A person may fall for a wide variety of reasons. It is important to try to ascertain the cause of the fall, as different treatments are required depending on the situation. No matter the reason for the fall, the following are basic guidelines:

- Attempt to remain calm.
- Have someone call for help.
- Do not attempt to move the victim unless he or she is in danger (such as in the middle of a street) or if a head or neck injury is suspected. If a head or neck injury is suspected, it is important to keep the victim stationary until medical professionals arrive. In that case, the guide should cover and protect the victim and ask for help in diverting people or traffic away from him or her.
- If the victim must be moved, hold him under the armpits to drag him to a safe location nearby.
- If the victim is conscious, ask her how she is feeling and what her symptoms are.
- If the victim is unconscious, position him on his back, lift his chin, and tilt his head back. This will open the victim's airway.
- Listen and look for breathing and check for pulse.
- If the victim is not breathing, either the guide or the most qualified person available should immediately begin mouth-to-mouth resuscitation. (A person who has stopped breathing could die within six minutes.)

When Someone Is Choking

- As long as the person can still cough forcefully, do not interfere. Coughing usually dislodges the blockage.
- If coughing fails to dislodge the blockage, or if the victim can no longer cough or breathe, call, or have someone call, for help.
- Begin the Heimlich maneuver: Stand behind the victim and clasp your arms around him. Find the spot in the center of the front of the body above the naval but below the rib cage. Clench one fist and pull back both hands with a quick, upward thrust. Repeat until the blockage is dislodged. The Heimlich maneuver is a simple, highly effective technique that can be performed on children, infants, and the elderly.

For Diabetic Emergencies (Coma or Insulin Shock) The most common and most dangerous emergency for diabetics is insulin shock. The victim may appear drunk or lethargic and may pass out. It is critical to get a simple sugar of any kind (juice, soda, or candy) into the diabetic's system. Then call for help.

Responsibility to Other Passengers

Although attending to the victim is the first priority, a guide must also be mindful of the other passengers. As soon as the first steps to protect the victim are taken, the guide should instruct passengers to move aside if they have not already done so. Once the victim is in the hands of medical personnel, the guide must quickly make a decision about the progress of the tour. Depending on the seriousness of the accident, the guide might offer an option for some passengers to return to the hotel. If the group was en route to a scheduled event, it is usually wise to attempt to continue the tour. In such a case, the guide should assure passengers that he or she will be closely monitoring the victim's progress and will keep them informed.

The other passengers will naturally be curious about what occurred. Often an emergency will cast a pall over the group, which the guide must respond to. A preorganized group or a group that has become well acquainted while traveling will often become preoccupied with the event. In that case it might be appropriate for the guide to incorporate some free time into the tour. On the other hand, a group of individuals traveling separately, while concerned in the moment, may expect the guide to continue with the tour.

Recording the Event

Immediately following any medical emergency the tour guide should make certain he has documented and conveyed to the tour operator everything he knows about the incident, the medical attention received, the times involved, the names of any attending physicians or EMTs, the names and addresses of hospitals or taxicab companies, and any other problems encountered. Even if a company appears not to have a policy or is not particularly concerned about paperwork or legality, the guide should express his concern and record in writing any steps he took, as well as all details relevant to the situation.

Be Prepared

A guide's basic first-aid kit might include water, gauze bandages, adhesive, rubbing alcohol or antiseptic cream, scissors, sugar cubes or candy (for diabetic emergency), and a flashlight.

Glossary

The following words are defined as they are used within the guiding field. For further information and the addresses of associations and organizations refer to Appendix A, "Professional Resources and Associations."

ABA: American Bus Association; an association for motorcoach owners and operators.

á la carte: Items on the menu that are chosen and priced individually.

AP: American Plan; a method of hotel, cruise, or resort pricing that includes three meals (breakfast, lunch, and dinner).

Amtrak: The National Railroad Passenger Corporation; the government-subsidized corporation that operates all major passenger train service in the United States.

ASTA: American Society of Travel Agents.

Back to back: Scheduling with no days off between tours.

Baggage allowance: The number of pieces of luggage allowed at no cost on a tour; for trips of five days to two weeks, it is usually two. It is normally the responsibility of the guide or tour manager to charge the passenger an additional fee for extra baggage.

Courier: A term used more often in Europe to denote a tour manager or tour escort, or one who leads a group on excursions. *See also* Tour conductor; Tour escort; Tour leader; Tour manager.

CTC: Certified Travel Consultant; a designation awarded by the Institute of Certified Travel Agents to those travel professionals with five years or more industry experience and who have completed a two-year, graduate-level travel management program.

Escort: *See* Tour escort; Tour manager.

Escort interpreter: Title used by the U.S. Department of State for individuals who accompany foreign visitors. Their duties include translation, coordination of the visitor's schedule and transportation, and providing hospitality.

FAM tours: Inexpensive or free promotional tours, often sponsored by travel bureaus, airlines, and tour operators or agencies, to sell and/or familiarize industry personnel with a destination; also known as Familiarization Tours.

Gratuity: A payment of appreciation given directly to the worker from the customer. The percentage of income a guide derives from gratuities varies greatly. Many tour operators recommend a gratuity for their passengers (generally an average of $2.00 per person per day). Other tour operators pay their guides and tour managers higher salaries and indicate to their clients that gratuities are included. For most tour managers and many guides, however, gratuities represent a substantial portion of total income.

Ground operator: A company that handles all or many travel arrangements (such as hotels, transportation, restaurants, and sightseeing) in a particular area; also called Land Operator or Tour Operator.

IATA: International Air Transport Association. Headquartered in Geneva, its function is to provide communication and stabilization for the international aviation community.

Incentive Travel: A large and growing segment of the industry that works with businesses and other organizations to provide travel as reward or incentive for sales or other company goals.

Incidentals: All costs to the passenger not covered by the tour cost, usually, telephone calls, room service charges, and so forth.

Independent tours: This type of tour is further classified into two types: domestic (DIT) and foreign (FIT). DITs and FITs are a type of customized tour designed for individuals who prefer freedom and flexibility to the structure of a guided tour.

Intermodal travel: Travel that includes two or more modes of transportation. For example, an intermodal tour might include a flight to Vancouver, British Columbia, a cruise of the Inside Passage, and a train ride to Alaska's interior.

Interpretation: (1) A communications process of revealing the meanings and relationships of natural, cultural, historical, and recreational resources. (2) The field whose practitioners make their living as interpreters.

Interpreter: One who interprets, or reveals the meanings and relationships of natural, cultural, historical, and recreational resources.

Meet and greet: The service of meeting, assisting, and orienting individuals and groups upon their arrival at a new destination.

MAP: Modified American Plan. Pricing that includes two meals, usually breakfast and dinner.

NAI: National Association for Interpretation.

Net rate: The rate given by a wholesaler to a retailer, to which the retailer adds a markup or commission (usually about 10 percent).

NTA: National Tour Association. A professional association embracing the travel and tourism industry, and includes tour operators and related vendors and educational institutions throughout North America.

NTO: National Tourist Office. A government agency designated for the promotion of travel.

Options: Extra excursions or events offered during a tour but not included in the tour price. Also known as Optional Tours.

Overbooking: A common practice among hotels and airlines of booking more than capacity to attempt to balance any cancellations that might occur.

Parallel tours: Similar tours running concurrently. Companies will often offer joint events for parallel tours and expect guides to work together on them; other companies prefer to keep parallel tours separate.

PAX: Industry abbreviation for passengers.

Per diem: "Per day" spending allowance for meals and some necessary incidentals.

PGAA: Professional Guides Association of America.

Porterage: The gratuity given to porters or baggage handlers. The amount varies from region to region, and among hotels, airports, and train stations, but is generally $1.00 per bag.

Positioning: Providing transportation and compensation for a guide to arrive at a destination for the start of a tour. For example, if a guide lives in Los Angeles and begins a tour in San Francisco, the company will usually offer transportation and a positioning fee, such as one day's pay.

Preregistration: Common for group arrivals, registration completed prior to arrival to allow quick, simple check-ins.

Rack rate: A hotel's printed, undiscounted rate.

SATH: Society for the Advancement of Travel for the Handicapped.

Seat rotation: On a motorcoach tour, the practice of reassigning seats from the front to the back of the coach on a regular basis, allowing all passengers equal access to front seats and encouraging them to socialize. This policy is adopted by many tour operators on tours of two days or more in length.

Single supplement: An additional cost added to a tour price for individuals traveling alone.

SITE: Society for Incentive Travel Executives.

Step-on guide: A guide who joins a tour to provide interpretation in a particular city or site.

TIA: Travel Industry Association of America. An association composed of members from all sectors of the travel industry, government, educational institutions, and others interested in promoting the travel industry.

Tip: *See* Gratuity.

Tour conductor: Synonym for tour manager, tour courier, or tour escort. *See* Tour manager.

Tour escort: One who accompanies a tour and attends to logistical details. Synonym for tour manager or tour leader, *see* Tour manager.

Tour guide: A widely used term for any individual who leads groups and provides commentary for them. Within the travel industry, "tour guide" usually refers to someone who gives tours of his or her own site, city, or region. Also called a city guide, sightseeing guide, or step-on guide.

Tour leader: Widely used to refer to anyone who is responsible for leading a group. Some organizations will have a representative tour leader attend to the scheduling and logistical details and hire a tour guide to provide commentary. A tour leader, however, can also act as tour guide or tour manager on the same or other tours.

Tour manager: An individual hired to accompany a group from beginning to end and manage all aspects of the tour, including meeting a group at their arrival point and coordinating all details of dining, accommodation, and sightseeing throughout the tour.

Tour operator: A company that plans, packages, and oversees prepaid tours, usually for groups, and sells these tours to travel agents, other retailers, and consumers. The term "tour operator" is sometimes used interchangeably with "tour wholesaler."

Travel agent: An individual or firm authorized to sell travel services to the general public.

TTRA: Travel and Tourism Research Association. An educational association devoted to the study and advancement of tourism. The TTRA publishes a scholarly journal, *Annals of Tourism Research.*

USTOA: United States Tour Operators Association. An association composed of the largest tour operators in the United States.

WFTGLA: World Federation of Tourist Guide Lecturers Associations. An organization of member countries, headquartered in Vienna, which seeks to promote higher standards in the guiding field.

WTO: World Tourism Organization; established in 1975 to promote and develop tourism around the world.

Bibliography

CHAPTER 1: THE TOUR GUIDE: A HISTORICAL OVERVIEW

Casson, Lionel. 1974. *Travel in the Ancient World*. London: George Allen & Unwin Ltd.
Feifer, Maxine. 1985. *Going Places: The Ways of the Tourist from Imperial Rome to the Present Day*. London: Macmillan.
Lochsburg, Winifred. 1979. *The History of Travel*. Leipzig: Edition Leipzig.
Mead, William. 1914. *The Grand Tour in the Eighteenth Century*. New York: Houghton Mifflin.
Smith, Valene L. 1961. "Needed: Geographically Trained Tourist Guides." *The Professional Geographer*, VIII:G, November.
Twain, Mark. 1980. *The Innocents Abroad*. New York: New American Library.
Wells, H. G. 1961. *The Outline of History*. New York: Doubleday.

CHAPTER 2: PROFILES OF TODAY'S TOUR GUIDES

Cherem, Gabriel Jerome. 1977. "The Professional Interpretor: Agent for an Awakening Giant." *Journal of Interpretation,* 2: 1, August.
D'Arcy Masius Benton and Balles. 1989. Poll conducted for *Time*, April 24.
Frommer, Arthur. 1990. *The New World of Travel*. New York: Prentice Hall.

CHAPTER 3: TOURISM

Coltman, Michael M. 1989. *Introduction to Travel and Tourism: An International Approach*. New York: Van Nostrand Reinhold.
Cooke, Suzanne. 1990. Discover America. Washington, D.C.: U.S. Travel Data Center.
D'Amore, Louis J. 1990. "Tourism—The World's Peace Industry." Canadian Parks/Recreation Association, March.
De Tocqueville, Alexis. 1935. *Democracy in America*. New York: New American Library, 1984.
Edgell, David L., Sr. *International Tourism Policy*. 1990. New York: Van Nostrand Reinhold.
Gee, Chuck Y., James C. Makens, and Dexter J. L. Choy. 1989. *The Travel Industry*. New York: Van Nostrand Reinhold.
Hawkins, Donald E., and Lloyd E. Hudman. 1989. *Tourism in Contemporary Society: An Introductory Text*. Englewood Cliffs, New Jersey: Prentice Hall, Inc.
Mill, Robert Christie. 1990. *Tourism: The International Business*. Englewood Cliffs, New Jersey: Prentice Hall, Inc.
United States Travel and Tourism Association. 1991. *Discover America 2000: The Implications of America's Changing Demographics and Attitudes on the U.S. Travel Industry*. Washington, D.C.: U.S. Travel Data Center.
———. 1991. *1989–90 Economic Review of Travel in America*. Washington, D.C.: U.S. Travel Data Center.

Van Harssel, Jan. 1988. *Tourism: An Exploration.* Elmsford, New York: National Publishers of the Black Hills, Inc.

CHAPTER 4: THE TRAVELER

Axtell, Roger E., ed. 1985. *Do's and Taboos Around the World.* New York: John Wiley & Sons, Inc.
Frommer, Arthur. 1990. *The New World of Travel.* New York: Prentice Hall.
Smith, Valene L. 1977. Hosts and Guests: An Anthropology of Tourism. Philadelphia: University of Pennsylvania Press.

CHAPTER 5: INTERPRETATION AND THE ROLE OF THE GUIDE

Albrecht, Karl, and Robert Zemke. 1985. *Service America!* Homewood, Illinois: Dow Jones-Irwin.
Alderson, William T., and Shirley Payne Low. 1985. *Interpretation of Historic Sites.* Second Edition. Nashville, Tennessee: American Association for State and Local History.
Blatti, Jo, ed. 1987. *Past Meets Present: Essays about Historic Interpretation and Public Audiences.* Washington, D.C.: Smithsonian Institution Press.
Carlzon, Jan. 1987. *Moments of Truth.* New York: Ballinger Publishing Company.
Cohen, Erik. 1985. The Tourist Guide: The Origins, Structure and Dynamics of a Role. In *Annals of Tourism Research.* Vol. 12, pp. 5–29. Salt Lake City: Pergamon Press, Ltd.
Covey, Stephen R. 1989. *Seven Habits of Highly Effective People.* New York: Simon & Schuster.
Grater, Russell K. 1976. *The Interpreters Handbook: Methods, Skills and Techniques.* Southwest Parks and Monuments Association.
Holloway, J. Christopher. 1981. The Guided Tour: A Sociological Approach. In *Annals of Tourism Research.* Vol. 8, No. 3, pp. 377–402. Salt Lake City: Pergamon Press, Ltd.
Machlis, G. F., ed. 1986. *Interpretive Views: Opinions on Evaluating Interpretation in the National Park Service.* Washington, D.C.: National Parks and Conservation Association.
Naisbitt, John, and Patricia Aburdene. 1985. *Re-inventing the Corporation: Transforming Your Job and Your Company for the New Information Society.* New York: Warner Books.
Shames, Germaine W., and W. Gerald Glover, eds. 1989. *World Class Service.* Yarmouth, Maine: Intercultural Press, Inc.
Sharpe, G. W., ed. 1982. *Interpreting the Environment.* Second Edition. New York: Macmillan Press.
Tilden, Freeman. 1957. *Interpreting Our Heritage.* Chapel Hill, North Carolina: University of North Carolina Press.
Wells, Marcella, and Bret Wright. 1990. *Evaluating National Park Service Interpretation: A Tool Kit.* Washington, D.C.: National Park Service.

CHAPTER 6: EDUCATION

Bloom, Allan. *The Closing of the American Mind.* 1987. New York: Simon & Schuster, Inc.
Cheney, Lynne V. 1989. *50 Hours: A Core Curriculum for College Students.* Washington, D.C.: National Endowment for the Humanities.
Cheney, Lynne V. 1990. Tyrannical Machines: A Report on Educational Practices Gone Wrong and Our Best Hopes for Setting Them Right. Washington, D.C.: National Endowment for the Humanities.
Coollins, Zipporah W., ed. 1981. *Museums, Adults and the Humanities.* Washington, D.C.: American Association of Museums.
Kidd, J. R. 1978. *How Adults Learn.* Englewood Cliffs, New Jersey: Prentice-Hall, Inc.

Knowles, Malcolm. 1984. *The Adult Learner: A Neglected Species.* Houston, Texas: Gulf Publishing Company.

Simonson, Rick, and Scott Walker, eds. 1988. *The Graywolf Annual Five: Multi Cultural Literacy.* St. Paul, Minnesota: Graywolf Press.

Tuchman, Barbara W. 1981. *Practicing History.* New York: Ballantine Books.

CHAPTER 7: LEADERSHIP AND SOCIAL SKILLS

Albrecht, Karl, and Robert Zemke. 1985. *Service America!* Homewood, Illinois: Dow Jones-Irwin.

Axtell, Roger E., ed. 1985. *Do's and Taboos Around the World.* New York: John Wiley & Sons, Inc.

Carlzon, Jan. 1987. *Moments of Truth.* New York: Ballinger Publishing Company.

Cherem, Gabriel Jerome. 1977.

Kohls, L. Robert. 1984. Values Americans Live By. Washington, D.C.: Meridian House International.

Vetter, Charles T., Jr. 1983. *Citizen Ambassadors: Guidelines for Responding to Questions Asked about America.* Provo, Utah: Brigham Young University David M. Kennedy International Center.

CHAPTER 8: PRESENTATION AND SPEAKING SKILLS

Brown, Lillian. 1989. *Your Public Best: The Complete Guide to Making Successful Public Appearances in the Meeting Room, on the Platform, and on TV.* New York: Newmarket Press.

Glass, Lillian. 1987. *Talk To Win.* New York: Putnam Publishing Group.

Hoff, Ron. 1988. *I Can See You Naked.* Kansas City, Missouri: Andrews and McNeel.

Zenker, Arnold. 1983. *Mastering the Public Spotlight.* New York: Dodd, Mead & Company.

CHAPTER 9: BRINGING A PLACE TO LIFE

Campbell, Joseph, and Bill Moyers. 1977. *The Power of Myth.* New York: Doubleday.

Cornell, Joseph. 1979. *Sharing Nature With Children.* Nevada City, California: Dawn Publications.

Garvey, Joan, and Mary Lou Widmer. 1984. *Beautiful Crescent: A History of New Orleans.* New Orleans: Garmer Press, Inc.

Gurganus, Allan. 1989. *Oldest Living Confederate Widow Tells All.* New York: Ivy Books.

Hiss, Tony. 1990. *The Experience of Place.* New York: Alfred A. Knopf, Inc.

Krockover, Gerald H., and Jeanette Havok. 1980. "Training for Docents: How to Talk to Vistors." Nashville, Tennessee: American Association for State and Local History. Technical Leaflet 125, *History News,* 35:3, March.

Maguire, Jack. 1985. *Creative Storytelling: Choosing, Inventing and Sharing Tales for Children.* New York: McGraw-Hill Book Company.

Naff, Clay. 1987. "Philadelphia's Happy Historian." *Philadelphia Inquirer Magazine,* April 5, 1987.

Tilden, Freeman. 1957. *Interpreting Our Heritage.* Chapel Hill, North Carolina: University of North Carolina Press.

Waterfall, Milde, and Sarah Grusin 1989. *Where's the ME in Museum: Going to Museums with Children.* Arlington, Virginia: Vandamere Press.

Whyte, William H. *City: Rediscovering the Center.* 1988. New York: Doubleday.

CHAPTER 10: THE NUTS AND BOLTS OF CONDUCTING TOURS

Cross, Don. 1991. *Please Follow Me: The Practical Tourist Guide's Handbook.* Salisbury, England: Wessexplore Tourist Service.

Mancini, Marc. 1990. *Conducting Tours: A Practical Guide.* Cincinnati, Ohio: South-Western Publishing Co.

Reilly, Robert T. 1982. *Handbook of Professional Tour Management.* Albany, New York: Delmar Publishers, Inc.

CHAPTER 11: TRAVELERS WITH SPECIAL NEEDS

Majewski, Janice. 1987. *Part of Your General Public Is Disabled: A Handbook for Guides in Museums, Zoos, and Historic Houses.* Washington, D.C.: Smithsonian Institution Press.

CHAPTER 12: THE BUSINESS OF GUIDING

Edwards, Paul and Sarah. 1985. *Working from Home: Everything You Need to Know About Living and Working Under the Same Roof.* Los Angeles: Jeremy P. Tarcher, Inc.
Whittlesey, Marietta. 1988. *The New Freelancer's Handbook.* New York: Simon & Schuster, Inc.

CHAPTER 13: PROFESSIONAL ETHICS AND ETIQUETTE

Hill, Ivan. 1991. *Common Sense and Everyday Ethics.* Washington, D.C.: Ethics Resource Center, Inc.

EPILOGUE

Cornish, Edward. 1990. *The 1990's and Beyond.* Bethesda, Maryland: World Future Society.
Naisbett, John, and Patricia Aburdene. 1990. *Megatrends 2000: Ten New Directions for the 1990's.* New York: William Morrow and Company, Inc.

APPENDIX B: EDUCATIONAL PROGRAMS

Vander Stoep, Gail A. 1991. *Interpretation: A Resource and Curricula Guide for the United States and Canada.* Fort Collins, Colorado: National Association for Interpretation.
Cross, Don. 1991. *Please Follow Me: The Practical Tourist Guide's Handbook.* Salisbury, England: Wessexplore Tourist Service.
Grinder, Alison L., and E. Sue. McCoy. 1985. *The Good Guide: A Sourcebook for Interpreters, Docents, and Tour Guides.* Scottsdale, Arizona: Ironwood Press.
Lewis, William J. 1989. *Interpreting for Park Visitors.* Philadelphia, Pennsylvania: Eastern National Park & Monument Association.
Mancini, Marc. 1990. *Conducting Tours: A Practical Guide.* Cincinnati, Ohio: South-Western Publishing Co.
Novak, Vera. 1989. *Step-up to Step-on Guiding.* Salt Lake City, Utah: Vera Novak.

APPENDIX C: RECOMMENDED TOPICS OF STUDY

Fadiman, Clifton. 1988. *The Lifetime Reading Plan.* New York: Harper & Row.
Zahler, Diane, and Kathy A. Zahler. 1988. *Test Your Cultural Literacy.* New York: Simon & Schuster.

APPENDIX D: BASIC SAFETY AND FIRST AID

Braslow, Allan. 1987. *American Red Cross: Adult CPR Workbook.* Washington, D.C.: The American National Red Cross.

Beshers, Martha, Karen J. Peterson, Lawrence Newell, Frank Carroll, Zora Travis Salisbury, Vikki Scott, and M. Elizabeth Buoy. 1988. *American Red Cross Standard First Aid Instructor's Manual.* Washington, D.C.: The American National Red Cross.

1988. *Reader's Digest Action Guide: What to Do in an Emergency.* Pleasantville, New York: Reader's Digest Association, Inc.

Hill, James A., and Stanley M. Zydlo, Jr. 1990. *The American Medical Association Handbook of First Aid and Emergency Care.* New York: Random House.

Index

Index

Kennedy, David M., Center for International
  Studies, 245
King, Aubrey, 34
Kohlberg, L., 225
Kohls, L. Robert, 59–62
Knowles, Malcolm, 86–7, 89

LeFleur, Henry, 133, 145–6
Language, use of, 131–5
  importance of, 148
Lateness, handling of, 118–9
Leader, as guide role, 76–8
Learning, concepts of, 89–92
  and guiding, 91–3
  facilitation of, 92–3
Learning disabilities, 194–5
Liability, and guiding, 178, 220
Licensing, and certification, 9, 19–20, 94
  of Gettysburg Battlefield Guides, 8–9
Listening, importance of, 136–7
Louisiana Certified Travel Professional (LCTP),
  40
Louisiana, tourism in, 40, 98
Louisiana Travel Promotion Association, 40

Majewski, Janice, 195
Marion, John Frances, 23, 146, 200, 213
Marketing, for guides, 206–15
Maslow, hierarchy of needs, 54
Mather, Stephen J., 9–10
McBride, Earl, 24
McCaffery, John, 144
McHugh, Jeff, 97, 112
McPhail, Don, 181
Medical conditions, working with, 197–8
"Meet and Greet," 44, 258
Meeting groups, 161–4
Meetings and conventions, tours for, 181
Megatrends 2000, 234–5, 240
Metaphor, use of, 148
Metro State College, 248
Mentor, guide as, 2
Mental illness, and conducting tours, 196
Mental retardation, and conducting tours, 195–6
Mesa Verde, 142–3
Miami Dade Community College, 248
Microphones, use of, 135–6
Mobility impairments, and conducting tours,
  193–4
Moments of Truth, 77, 108
Motorcoach operators, and guides, 172–7,
  226–7
Motorcoach tours, 171–7
Multi-lingual guiding, 122–3, 134, 329
Museum guides, description of, 30–1
  training of, 11

Naisbitt, John, 77, 134–5, 240
Nasality, of voice, 129–30
National Association for the Preservation and
  Perpetuation of Storytelling, 242
National Association for Interpretation, 16, 249
National Association of Travel Organizations, 36
National Council of International Visitors
  (NCIV), 245
National Endowment for the Humanities, 101
National Federation of the Blind, 246
National Information Center on Deafness, 246
National Park Service, Gettysburg National Mili-
  tary Park, 9
  interpretation in, 9–10, 73, 241
National Parks and Conservation Association,
  244
National Recreation and Parks Association, 249
National Tour Association (NTA), 40, 258
  and FAM tours, 180
National Tourist Office, 259
National Tourism Organizations, 39
National Tourism Policy Act, 33
Nature, interpretation of, 152–3
Nervousness, and speaking, 125
Neurolinguistic Programming (NLP), 91, 116
New Orleans, guides in, 19
New York City, walking tours in, 19–20, 21–2,
  38, 166–7
Northern Virginia Community College, 248

Offices, setting up, for guiding, 204–6, 218
Old Town Trolley Tours, 45, 182
Organization of American States, guide training
  program, 95

Pacific Asia Travel Association (PATA), 36
Pacific Rim Institute of Tourism (PRIT), 19, 95,
  248
Package tours, 43
Parallel tours, 259
Part of Your General Public is Disabled, 246
Passion, importance of, 141
Personalized/private tours, 177–80
Peterson's Four Year Colleges, 247
Pitch, of voice, 128–9
Porterage, 259
Positioning, 259
Posture, importance of, 126
Pow Wow, 243
Pre-tour planning, 158–61
Problems, on tours, 117–9, 165
Professional Guides Association of America
  (PGAA), 14, 15, 16, 41, 95–6, 242, 248
Pronunciation, importance of, 134
Public relations representative, guide as, 80–2
Public tours, 58, 182